Current Practice in Program Budgeting (PPBS)

Analysis and Case Studies
Covering
Government and Business

DAVID NOVICK, EDITOR

CRANE, RUSSAK
NEW YORK

Published in the United States by
Crane, Russak & Company Inc.,
52 Vanderbilt Avenue
New York, New York 10017

ISBN 0-8448-0153-4

Library of Congress Catalogue Card Number 72-91627

Manufactured in the United States of America

CONTENTS

Foreword

This manuscript was made ready for the publisher late in 1971. At that time, it said. "A foreword will be prepared when the publication date is set. It will attempt to bring the reader up to date, not only in terms of new or additional events, but also with respect to measures of success of the activities described in the case histories." In May of 1972 that seems to have been a very good idea. A great many things have taken place in program budgeting and, without reference to a relative order of importance, they are:

1. Publication by the state of Pennsylvania of its fiscal year 1972 program budget. This means that the new system had demonstrated its utility and survivability. Governor Shapp, the Democratic head of the state's government, had inherited program budgeting from his Republican predecessor. The governor says in his budget message: "The Program Budgeting concept in Pennsylvania responds to a need to know the effects the budget programs will have upon the problems of the Commonwealth and its citizens. Program budgeting assembles all functions and activities in relationship to the accomplishment of a specific objective. . . ." From the foregoing it is obvious that the program budgeting system is in place. Chapter 21 covers the pre-1972 development in Pennsylvania.

2. In the United Kingdom, the Department of Education and Finance has prepared its fourth budget in program terms and, in so doing, has moved out of the development stage and into operation.

3. New legislation, *Bundeshaushaltsrecht,* or budgetary statute, recently adopted in Austria makes possible, and mandatory, a program-budgeting approach. Earlier developments in Austria are the subject matter of Chapter 7.

4. The state of Hawaii continues to make very real progress in the implementation of its program budget. The Hawaiian undertaking is treated briefly in Chapter 4.

5. Approximately 20,000 school districts in this country, as well as the state education budgets, are rapidly turning to program budgeting. Frequently they call it the Educational Resources Management System, which is covered in Chapter 20. In many states and localities legislation now makes this mandatory; in others, it follows from voluntary action.

6. The French adopted the term, *Rationalisation des Choix Budgetaires* or RCB, for their program-budgeting effort. This is described in Chapter 14. By the late spring of 1972, the numbers of ministries engaged had expanded from the three to six referenced in the chapter, to fourteen, including the government-managed Air France. Also by the spring of 1972, an effort to utilize RCB as part of the recently adopted plan for decentralization of local government in France was underway.

7. Possibly more important than any of the foregoing is the less easily described further development and experimentation with the program-budgeting concept by a large number of government units and a substantial number of business organizations throughout the world.

There are a great many different names now used to describe the techniques that make up program budgeting, the planning-programming-budgeting system (or PPBS), and it is likely that many other names will be used in the future. The significance of all of this is that the techniques of program budgeting are being tried, modified, and embodied into the decision making processes of business and government. Although the pace of innovation inevitably fluctuates, the direction is clear. Program budgeting is being implemented throughout Western society and will continue to develop.

As organizations grow in size and scope, there is increasing concern about the adequacy and effectiveness of the methods used for determining resource allocations. Some of the questions that are raised are:

1. What is the present budget commitment to relevant ongoing activities?

2. What additional gains might be expected from additions to the budget commitment?

3. What kind of budget commitments would usefully underwrite activity in new problem-areas?

4. Can operationally meaningful differentation be made to the effectiveness of various approaches to the same problem?

Historically, three major efforts have been made to deal with these issues. The first was performance budgeting, which became popular in the 1930s and still continues in operation. The second was management by objective, which has not yet achieved widespread popularity but is gaining an increasing number of recruits. The third was the program budgeting or the planning, programming, budgeting system, which has had its great burst of activity since 1965.

These three approaches to the planning, programming, and budgeting problem are each quite different. Performance budgeting provides the means for choosing between alternative approaches to a predetermined problem. It does not deal with the major decisions involved in selecting the problem for which alternative methods of performance are under evaluation.

Management by objective again deals with the way of implementing decisions made by some higher authority. It differs from performance budgeting chiefly in the extent to which it is an ongoing operation and permits greater flexibility of choice as the activity progresses.

The difference between program budgeting and the other two major budgeting innovations is very significant. PPB is a decision making system. It undertakes to use the budget process for analyzing objectives and the future consequences of alternative programs available for achieving them. It is, in essence, a decision making process to determine, first, objectives, then programs to be used in achieving the objectives, and, finally, the amounts of available resources to be allocated among the various programs.

The basic philosophy can be summarized succinctly. It is that more resources are wasted doing the wrong things efficiently than can ever be wasted doing the right things inefficiently. Performance budgeting and management by objective are concerned with efficiency. Program budgeting aims at the "big choices."

David Novick

Santa Monica, California
May 29 1972

CHAPTER 1

Reasons for This Book

David Novick

PPBS, the planning-programming-budgeting system, program budgeting, and *rationalisation des choix budgetaires* are all designations widely used to identify a management decision-making system that was practically unknown as recently as 1961, and not well known even in 1965. In 1961 program budgeting or, as it was sometimes called, the program-package-budget approach, was introduced in the U.S. Department of Defense by its new chief—Secretary Robert S. McNamara. In 1965 President Johnson applied this method, which had been so successful in the Defense Department, to all executive departments and agencies of the federal government. This new system is now either in use, being readied for introduction, or being studied for possible application in the national governments of most western countries, and in many state and local governments within the United States, England, Austria, and some other countries.

Since a substantial body of information is now available (1972), selections have been brought together here, first, for those who want to learn more about this management concept for possible application in their own organizations; second, for those who would like to improve their already established practice by learning more about other establishments; and third, for teachers and students in specialized program-budgeting courses as well as in administrative management, public administration, business administration, and political science curricula.

Organization and Content of This Book

The bulk of this book is made up of twenty-one essays prepared by individuals who have played an active role in some phase of program budgeting. These are introduced by five chapters of setting and analysis, of which this is the first. Chapter 2 explains what program budgeting is and is not. Chapter 3 provides a short background and history. Chapter 4 gives a critical summary of the experience available through the year 1970, including a rich mixture of experience available from organizations not covered in the individual essays. The fifth chapter discusses standards for appraising this experience.

The case histories of the national governments of nine countries, two state

1

governments in the United States, local governments in this country and abroad, two business companies, and a number of other organizations are presented in Chapters 6 through 26. To begin with governments other than that of the United States are taken up alphabetically. They include the first steps taken in the Ministries of Agriculture and Health in Belgium, the development of program budgeting in the Ministry of Defence in Canada, the beginning efforts undertaken at the local government level in Great Britain, the efforts to persuade the federal and local governments of Austria to adopt program budgeting, and activities under way at the national level in France, Japan, Australia, New Zealand, and Great Britain.

These are followed by two cases from business. One describes program-budgeting activities at the John Hancock Mutual Life Insurance Company of Boston, Massachusetts. The other, the application of the method to General Electric Company's Research Laboratory at Schenectady, New York.

There is then a review of a unique effort to make program budgeting available to the 20,000 school districts in this country. Next the state and local government experience in the United States is represented by reports on Pennsylvania, Vermont, and New York City. The two following chapters deal with federal government recruitment, education, and training for program-budgeting experience in the United States. The last of the case chapters is an analysis of the experience in the U.S. federal government.

The brief summary of U.S. federal government experience presented in Chapter 26 touches on a large mass of material that has already been published. The Subcommittee on National Security and International Operations of the Senate Committee on Government Operations, under the leadership of Senator Henry M. Jackson, conducted hearings during the period 1967-1969 that were a "frank stock-taking of the benefits and costs of the planning-programming-budgeting system." The testimony and subsequent dialogue allowed a meaningful assessment of program-budgeting policy, management practices, personnel selection and performance, program-evaluation procedures, and individual department and agency experience. Starting in 1967, the subcommittee issued, in addition to its *Hearings,* a series of committee prints, designed to present various facets of the system. These have included essays such as "Uses and Abuses of Analysis," "Program Budgeting in Foreign Affairs: Some Reflections," and "Rescuing Policy Analysis from PPBS."

The Joint Economic Committee, through its Subcommittee on Economy in Government, held hearings in 1967, and subsequently prepared two compilations of papers on the role of PPBS. The first, issued early in 1969, was entitled "Innovations in Planning, Porgramming and Budgeting in State and Local Governments" and provided a review of program budgeting at the sub-Federal level through a series of illustrative case studies. Later in the same year, "The Analysis and Evaluation of Public Expenditures: The PPB Systems" was issued by the subcommittee. This three-volume series contained an instructive foreword by Senator Wiliam E. Proxmire, the chairman, and commentary by more than fifty specialists and experts. All of the above are available and have been the subject of a substantial amount of discussion and criticism in the current literature.[1]

Although the U.S. Department of Defense represents the largest single effort in program budgeting, it is not included here since it has already been the subject of several books, a substantial number of articles, and numerous and lengthy congressional hearings. In addition, and possible more important, there has been a strong feeling in business and the nondefense parts of governments that military problems are both different and more manageable than those of nonmilitary organizations. Therefore, there is widespread feeling that national-security experience cannot be readily translated into the requirements of other kinds of managements.

State and local government experience in the United States is developing rapidly. Included in the cases herein are the states of Pennsylvania and Vermont, Chapters 21 and 22, and the city of New York, Chapter 23. To include the large number of other striking developments, for example, Hawaii; Montgomery County, Maryland; Orange County, California; the city of Dayton, Ohio; and Sparta Township, New Jersey, would require doubling or tripling the size of this volume and defer publishing until late in the 1970s. For this reason, these are treated when appropriate to the analysis, and the reader is given references for additional information.

[1] See also *Survey of Progress in Implementing the Planning-Programming-Budgeting System in Executive Agencies,* by the comptroller general of the United States, July 1969, and *How much is Enough?,* Alain Enthoven and Paul Smith, Harper & Row, 1971, for a specialized review of U.S. Department of Defense experience.

CHAPTER 2

What Program Budgeting Is and Is Not

David Novick

During the 1960s the concept of program budgeting generated substantial interest, speculation, experimentation, and literature in business and at all levels of government throughout the western world. With the widespread introduction of this new management idea after the middle of the decade, a great variety of activities were undertaken in its name. Some of the proposals, however, bore little resemblance to it other than the use of the words *program budgeting* as part of an argument for changes in management that were not at all program budgeting or the planning-programming-budgeting system. (PPBS).[1]

What Program Budgeting Is

Program budgeting is a management system that has ten distinctive major features. These are:

1. Definition of an organization's objectives in terms as specific as possible.

2. Determination of programs, including possible alternatives, to achieve the stated objectives.

3. Identification of major issues to be resolved in the formulation of objectives and/or the development of programs.

4. An annual cycle with appropriate subdivisions for the planning, programming, and budgeting steps to ensure an ordered approach and to make appropriate amounts of time available for analysis and decision-making at all levels of management.

5. Continuous reexamination of program results in relationship to anticipated costs and outcomes to determine need for changes in stated programs and objectives as originally established.

6. Recognition of issues and other problems that require more time than is available in the annual cycle so that they can be explicitly identified and set apart from the current period for completion in two or more years, as the subject matter and availability of personnel require.

---

[1]PPBS is the more common usage in the United States and many other countries. Programme budgeting is widely used in England. In France, it is "Rationalization des Choix Budgetaires" (RCB). Program budgeting (PB) will be the preferred usage herein.

7. Analysis of programs and their alternatives in terms of probable outcomes and both direct and indirect costs.

8. Development of analytical tools necessary for measuring costs and benefits.

9. Development each year of a multi-year program and financial plan with full recognition of the fact that in many areas resource allocations in the early years (e.g., years one through five) require projections of plans and programs and their resource demands for ten or more years into the future.

10. Adaptation of existing accounting and statistical-reporting systems to provide inputs into planning and programming, as well as continuing information on resources used in and actions taken to implement programs.

The General Approach

Traditional budgeting is aimed largely at efficiency in carrying out specific tasks. It is an appropriation rather than a policy-making approach. Program budgeting sets its sights on larger purposes, the objectives of an organization. These are stated in terms of available alternatives, which in turn are appraised in cost-benefit considerations. Once the issues involved in establishing policy are illuminated, the decision-makers can better make the overall decisions. When these are placed in a context of available resources, the next steps to efficiency in operation or performance can be taken as they usually are. That is, in the terms of the traditional budget.

To carry out the major objectives of program budgeting, three general areas of administrative and operational activities are involved. These are program format, analysis, and information and reporting.

1. *Program format* concerns the organization's objectives and the programs established to meet them. Program budgeting begins with an effort to identify and define objectives and to group the organization's activities into programs that can be related to each objective. This aspect of the system is revolutionary, since it requires groupings by end product or output rather than, as in traditional budget practice, by line items of input arranged in terms of object classes, administrative organizations, or activities. The new method allows us to look at *what* is produced—output—in addition to *how* it is produced—which *inputs* we consume.

One of the strengths of program budgeting is that it cuts across organizational boundaries, drawing together the information needed by decision-makers without regard to divisions in operating authority among jurisdictions. Examining a program as a whole has its obvious advantages. Contradictions are more likely to be recognized, and a context is supplied for consideration of changes made possible only by cutting across existing agency line barriers.

The purpose of program budgeting is to identify and understand relationships and interdependencies. That is, to consider individual items in terms of related activities and the totality. For example, in planning for a local government, the program budget considers not only the customary issues of land utilization, aesthetics, and architectural design, but goes beyond them into the economic and social consequences of the physical changes in structures, streets, and neighborhoods. Once such effects are identified, decisions can be reached on whether or not the output is worthwhile, and if it is, how much of the organization's limited resources should be appropriated to it.

The program-budgeting summary document presents resources and costs categorized according to the program or end product to which they apply. This contrasts with traditional budgets that assemble costs by type of input—line item—and by organizational or object categories. The point of this restructuring of budget information is that it focuses attention on competition for resources among programs and on the effectiveness of resource use within programs. The entire process by which objectives are identified, programs are defined and quantitatively described, and the budget is recast into a program-budget format is called the format or structural phase of program budgeting.

An outstanding feature of program budgeting is an emphasis on analysis at all stages of activity. Although it is sometimes not recognized, the developments of the appropriate format or structure in and of itself requires analysis. The examination of an organization's objectives and the identifying of its programs and program elements can constitute a major contribution to improvement of management even when the more complete analytical capability contemplated in the program budget is not fully developed.

One product of the structural phase is a conversion matrix or crosswalk from the budget in program terms to the traditional line-item, organization, and object-class budget. In program budgeting, organization gives way to program, and line-item detail is aggregated into summary figures more appropriate to policy-making decisions.

For example, the wages and salaries figure for the environment program in Figure 1 is not only the sum of personnel service payments in the program elements which constitute environment-oriented activities in water, air, land, pollution, etc., but also an aggregation of pieces of the wages and salaries data in each operating department whose activities contribute to environmental control. If Figure 1 were not abbreviated, the illustration would include the contributions from other departments and supporting services such as central electronic data processing. Detail is not the purpose, however, and such activities are instead grouped into a general support program.

Program structures rarely conform to the appropriation pattern or to the organizational structure. Therefore, the program presentation of activities and resource requirement cannot be interrelated with budget data on appropriation and/or organization except by the crosswalk. As indicated earlier, the program structure provides insight into the objectives of the organization; and the

7

David Novick

allocation of budget authority to programs provides a measure of the organization's priorities. The selected agency budgets grouped by program categories in the U.S. federal budget documents are an example of the crosswalk at a very high level of aggregation.[1]

FIGURE 1   Crosswalk: Traditional Line-item Budget to New Program Budget

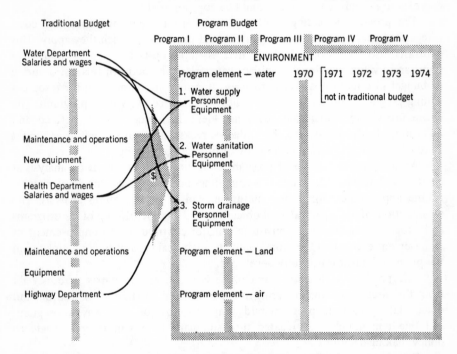

Fig. 1 reproduced from *Management: A Book of Readings* by H. Koonz and C. O'Donnell, 3rd ed. copyright 1972 by McGraw-Hill Inc. Used with permission of McGraw-Hill Book Company

The crosswalk prepared for the members of the Pennsylvania Legislature as part of their program budget for 1971-1972 may be the most useful illustration available. It is set out in terms of organizations, appropriations, Commonwealth (of Pennsylvania) major programs, and program subcategories.[2]

To aggregate the multitude of line items of the traditional budget or even the summaries of its operating departments into their program-element

---

[1] *Special Analyses,* Budget of the U.S. Government, pp. 289–317, U.S. Government Printing Office, Washington, D.C. 1971.
[2] *Commonwealth of Pennsylvania,* Program Budget Vol. 1, July 1971–June 1972, pp. 261–314. Also see pp. 67 & 68 herein.

contributions or costs, it is necessary to make allocations, and some of them may be rather arbitrary ones. The important features of the crosswalk are (1) to have the two documents balance no matter what the dimensions of the classifications, and (2) to ensure that decision-makers and reviewing entities can identify next year's traditional budget in program terms, and vice versa.

By use of the crosswalk we also are able to convert data in existing records and reports into that needed for program planning. It permits program decisions to be translated into methods already in use for directing, authorizing, controlling, recording and reporting operations. If the management methods currently being used in any of these areas are inadequate or unsatisfactory, they should be improved, whether or not the organization has a program-budgeting system. In any case, the program budget must derive its information and relationships from existing management records and practices and must rely on them for the implementation of the programs.[1]

2. The second area of the general approach is *analysis*. The program-budgeting method of decision-making subsumes a systems-analysis capability with which the resource and cost implications of program alternatives and their expected "outputs" or accomplishments may be estimated, examined, and compared. When a system-analysis capability does not exist or is inadequate, it should be created or upgraded, since analysis is the most important part of this approach to management decisions. A wide range of techniques is employed in these program analyses, including statistical analysis, modeling, gaming, simulation, operations analysis, and econometrics. Both the resource-cost side and the benefit-effectiveness side of program consequences are analyzed.

Quantification is sought wherever possible, but many matters do not readily lend themselves to quantitative measurement. In these instances, qualitative analysis is required. In every case, whether the analysis is quantitative, qualitative, or an appropriate mixture of the two, there is to be explicit identification of the problem, the alternative ways of resolving it, and an attempt to measure the cost and effectiveness of each possibility.

Program analysis is not confined to predetermined alternatives; development of new and better alternatives is part of the process. It is likely that analysis of possibilities A, B, and C will lead to the invention of alternatives D and E, which may be preferable (more cost-effective) to the original candidates. Therefore, the analysis part of program budgeting cannot be viewed merely as the application of a collection of well-defined analytical techniques to a problem. The process is much more flexible and subtle, and calls for creativity by the managers and the analysts and interaction between analysts and decision-makers during the process.

[1]For a different point of view see "The Use and Abuse of Program Structure" by Allen Schick, International Federation of Operational Research Societies, Washington, D.C., 1967.

David Novick

3. The third part of the program-budgeting system deals with *information and reporting*. The accounting and related statistical-reporting systems identify information for all activities of the organization. Neither new accounting nor new statistical-reporting systems are called for. Instead, reidentification or restructuring in the existing systems is required for utilization of information in the planning and programming parts of the new activity. When program determinations are made, the reporting requirement imposes on existing systems the need to provide continuing information (usually monthly and/or quarterly) on the use of resources and the operational steps taken in the implementation of the programs.[1]

Although the accounting and statistical reports of necessity are carried on in terms of actions in the current calendar, the reporting provision must require and provide specific identification of today's activities in terms of impact in both the balance of the current year and the future years of the multiyear plan.

Information and reporting is an important part of the total system since (a) accounting for appropriated funds is a requirement in any government or business, (b) knowing and measuring progress towards stated objectives is important, (c) analysis for the future can only be based on measurements derived from past experience, (d) much of the mystery of traditional budgeting derives from the esoteric nature of the reports, and (e) a huge mass of data is now produced by modern record-keeping practice, office machines, and the computer in the name of information and reporting. (Instructions for preparing documents and forms used to collect, store, and report information are procedures and are not included here. Any good program structure can readily be converted to the coding of any accounting, statistical, or reporting system.)

All of the ideas in program budgeting are best developed when they are adapted to the special requirements of the organization introducing the new methodology. This is even more true of the information and reporting activities, since here it is definitely a matter of adapting an ongoing accounting, statistical, or reporting system to meet the program-budgeting requirements.

A brief summary that relates the areas of operation to the major features of program budgeting and to the kinds of documents the system produces is sketched in Figure 2.

Reasons for Program Budgeting

The primary reason for program budgeting is that it provides a formal, systematic method to improve decisions concerning the allocation of resources. Obviously, these allocation problems arise because available resource supplies are limited in relation to the demands for them. This leads to a need for making

---

[1] Complete enumeration on a periodic basis is not always required. For example, sample surveys might be used.

choices among demands in terms of what to do, how much to do, and when to do it.

FIGURE 2   Sketch of Program Budgeting

MAJOR FEATURES	OPERATION AREAS	REPRESENTATIVE DOCUMENTS
Define objectives Determine programs Assign activities to programs Establish plan-program-budget cycle	Structural Aspect	Multi-year program and financial plan
Develop cost/benefit measurement methods Identify and evaluate alternatives Develop and apply criteria	Analytical Aspect	Program memoranda including alternatives Issue Analysis Special studies
Use existing reporting system Update programs	Data and Information Aspect	Accounting and statistical reports Program change proposals

---

Fig. 2 reproduced from *Management: A Book of Readings* by H. Koonz and C. O'Donnell, 3rd ed. copyright 1972 by McGraw-Hill Inc. Used with permission of McGraw-Hill Book Company.

Program budgeting is designed to open up debate on these questions and put the discussion on a new basis. It does this by requiring explicit identification of all actions—ongoing or new proposals—in terms of programs related to stated objectives. This enables the top decision-makers to act in terms of the total organization rather than on the basis of ideas limited by individuals or operating units. The orientation of this new method is to plan the future in both short-term and long-range aspects, and to make decisions on what is to be done.

A second reason for program budgeting is that planning should be carried on with adequate recognition of what costs are. When an organization's plans call for more resources than it has or is likely to have available to it, planning becomes a game not played for "keeps." An organization that is unable to carry the costs of its objectives should revise its objectives; otherwise it will be wasting some of its substance. Resource considerations introduce realism into planning.

Since as many alternative plans as possible should be examined at the planning level, resource considerations should be in highly aggregated terms. We should use "in the ball park" estimates of costs to facilitate examining a large number of possibilities in a reasonably short period of time. In program budgeting the name of the game is "alternatives" and we seek a menu of the most relevant ones.

When we have selected the most promising plans from that list, we analyze them in a less aggregative but still not completely detailed form. This is programming. Here activities are identified and feasibility is established in terms of capability, resource requirements, and timing of each one of the alternatives.

11

The selection is linked to a budgetlike process because the final budget decisions determine the allocation of resources not only for the next year but in many cases make commitments for many years into the future.

To formulate a single program requires that we make decisions on feasibility, resource demands, and timing. Even so, data used for programming are still not as detailed as next year's budget. The budget is an operating and financial document and, as such, must give great detail for inputs like personnel, supplies, and equipment, and assignment of such resources to administrative units. That kind of detail overwhelms decision-making and makes unmanageable a process designed for choosing among alternatives.

The third basic reason for program budgeting is that it provides for a basis of choosing between available and feasible alternatives, a choice that takes place at the conclusion of programming. At that point the issues involved have been illuminated. The decision-makers can exercise their judgment and experience in an appropriate and informed context, as they determine "what to do."

Given these decisions, the details of "how to do it" can then be laid out. This is the point at which performance budgeting, management by objective, work measurement, and other methods of improving efficiency take over. In program budgeting the focus at this point is on annual allotment of funds for the next step to be taken along a path that has been thoughtfully set by policy-makers at all levels. Probably more important, the direction of the path and the distance to be covered in the next year will have been established after the consideration of a number of possible futures for the entire government or business organization.

This means that program budgeting is not designed to increase efficiency in the performance of day-to-day tasks, nor is it designed to improve administrative control over the expenditure of funds. It is instead a recognition of the fact that more money is wasted by doing the wrong thing efficiently than can be wasted by doing the right thing inefficiently. In short, program budgeting aims at the decision-making process; that is, top-level determination of what to do, how much to do, and when to do it, rather than deciding on how to carry on day-to-day operations, decisions which are best made by those who are closest to the activity.

What Program Budgeting Is Not

Some systems that have been called program- budgeting systems may be useful improvements, but they do not deal with choosing objectives, developing plans through systematic analysis of costs and effectiveness, resource allocation, and the other major decision areas which are its essentials. These include:

1. Reorganization plans justified on the basis that the organization must fit the program structure.

2. New accounting or statistical systems that identify program elements.

3. Management-information systems undertaken as a substitute for major PB features.

4. Elaborate new personnel recruiting, education, or training undertaken without developing the PB organization and procedures which will utilize them effectively.

5. Extensive use of the words *program* and *program budgeting* in existing documents and procedures in lieu of developing and introducing the PB concepts and required changes.

6. Treating performance budgeting and other methods for improving administration of specific tasks as a substitute for PB treatment of major decision-making problems.

The General Disclaimer

In both government and business, responsibility for the work required to accomplish a coherent set of objectives is divided among a number of organizations. In government, for example, programs with objectives for health and education are distributed among a dozen bureaus and independent agencies as well as levels of government. The activities of each are sometimes complementary, sometimes in conflict. As a result there is no overall coordination of the resource allocations relevant to program objectives.

Since program budgeting cuts across organization and administrative lines, there are cases where this has been translated to mean that the activity is limited to the structural phase and resultant reorganization to fit the new identification or programs. This is not only an incomplete view of what is involved but also a most undesirable one.

It should be recognized that the PB management concept calls for continuous reexamination of program results and for reidentifying and restructuring programs and objectives. Normally, this would be done on an annual basis. One can readily visualize the chaos that could result in administration and operations if organizational changes were required for every change in program format.

The program budgeting system is not a re-organization plan nor does it seek or require changes in organization to fit the program structure.[1]

In the same way, the information and reporting requirement of program budgeting, with its emphasis on accounting and recurring statistics, has sometimes been translated into the need for the development of a new

[1]Change in organization may be desirable, but it is not one of the general principles of program budgeting. For a discussion of the organization implications of program budgeting see R. J. Mowitz, *The Design and Implementation of Pennsylvania's Planning, Porgramming, Budgeting System,* The Pennsylvania State University, 1970, pp. 39–41. Also, for the impact in terms of President Nixon's reorganization proposals in 1971, see Chapter 26.

accounting system or a major change in the existing one. As indicated in the preceding discussion of organization, programs can be expected to change or, at a minimum, be modified on a recurring basis. This makes it not only unnecessary but undesirable to change the accounting or the reporting systems to conform to the currently identified program structure.

The emphasis on maintaining existing accounting and reporting systems derives from the recognition of two major factors. First, temporary change is always undesirable and since programs and objectives are both subject to change, molding them to fit the format developed at any one point in time provides only limited advantage and has all the disadvantages that will be encountered when they must be changed to fit the next development of the format. The second reason is that both the operators and the decision-makers are knowledgeable about the existing system and therefore find it more comfortable to do their work in a situation in which changes have been kept to a minimum and are of a kind that are made essentially once and for all time.

Another reason for not making frequent changes is that in providing information for the inputs into the planning and programming process, and in reporting on actions taken in the execution of programs, the emphasis on detail is different from that in traditional line-item budgets. As we move through the process from the lowest level of operation and decision up through the higher levels of executive decision-making, there is a steadily increasing need to present aggregated instead of detailed information. The important new development for accounting and statistical reporting is to ensure that, as we move up the ladder and aggregate the data, the units of record do not lose integrity through the continuing introduction of judgment or "fudge factors."

Program budgeting is not a new accounting system nor does it necessarily require changes in the existing accounting and statistical reporting systems to fit the program structure.[1]

What is needed is an examination of both the accounting records and the basic records from which statistical reports are drawn to ensure that these can in fact be translated into the required inputs in planning, programming, and budgeting activities as well as in recording and reporting. This means an emphasis on units of account that are "pure." That is, units that can be carried upward in the accounting or statistical-reporting system as is and do not require the introduction of adjustments when accumulated into more aggregative units of information.

Program budgeting is not a management-information system, even though a good MIS is very useful to its operations.

---

[1] Changes in the accounting or reporting systems may be desirable and in fact may be suggested by the program-budgeting analyses, but they are not required by this management system.

Management-information systems have come into fashion recently. As a result, in many cases the development of program budgeting has been regarded as synonymous with the installation of a new computer system and the related techniques for making management data more readily available—and nothing more. Although a good MIS is always desirable and can be used to very good advantage in the working of a program-budgeting system, it lacks the planning emphasis and surely does not include the appropriate recognition of the development of programs, the analysis of alternatives, and the development of all of the related analytical activities and tools that are so important in the concept of program budgeting.

Although program budgeting, because of its emphasis on analysis, frequently calls for individuals with an analytical approach and/or training, program budgeting requirements are not met just by introducing elaborate new personnel recruiting, education, or training efforts. For the most part, what is needed is some redirection of existing personnel and the kind of education and training essential for this purpose. But the program requirements will not be met just by new personnel policies and activities.

The word *budget* in program budgeting, or the planning-programming-budgeting system, sometimes leads to the assumption that, if the title *program* is introduced into the existing budget documents, the result is in fact a program budget. Obviously, the word *program* is available for anyone to use in any manner that he sees fit.

The emphasis on program in this new system is on output, or end-product measurement, rather than on the inputs as they are emphasized in traditional budget-making. Therefore, whether the existing budget is the straight line-item type, performance-oriented, or based on organization and object class, adding the word *program* in selected places or in the title does not make it a program budget and in no way accomplishes the purpose of program budgeting.

It is especially worth noting that program budgeting is not performance budgeting. Performance budgeting developed mainly in the 1930s and has had a major impact at the state and local government levels. It has also been used extensively in business. The performance budget is a way of choosing between a series of alternative ways of "how to do" a specific task. It does not provide for evaluation of the importance of the task in terms of either the total program or individual programs designed to meet a set of goals. In short, it is a way of choosing among alternative means available for doing a task rather than a way of determining whether the task should be performed at all or, if it is to be undertaken, the amount of it that is required.

Program budgeting recognizes the need for administrative and organizational budgets as well as performance budgeting and does not contemplate that they be abandoned or relabelled. Instead, it requires that they be used in conjunction with the PB by means of the crosswalk.

15

The program budget has a time element that extends beyond the typical next-year's budget. The multiyear program and financial plan lays out not only next-year's financing but also the estimates of funding that would be required for future years on the basis of decisions already made when the final action is taken. In this sense, next-year's budget is an important first step in the operation of the multiyear program, and the five and ten year projections represent the "spend-out" implications of decisions made to date.

This does not mean making fundamental changes in existing budget practice. In the traditional line item, object-class, performance, or organization and activity budget, there is a need for detailed identification by object or activity classes which requires, as we have seen, more detail than is either necessary or possible to use as we move up to the policy level in the decision process. For this reason, the primary change is in adding program budgeting to the traditional annual-budgeting process. This permits the development of the multiyear program and financial plan at a high level of aggregation from which a "crosswalk" can be made to the traditional one-year, line-item budget by object class.

The Contrast in Brief

In short, program budgeting is characterized by an emphasis on objectives, programs, and program elements, all stated in output terms. Cost, or the line items of the traditional budget, is treated at an appropriate level of aggregation which ensures that plans and programs are developed with adequate recognition of their resource implications.

Analysis and the use of a large variety of analytical techniques are the backbone of this new system of management. PB requires explicit identification of assumptions, the development of all relevant options and alternative outcomes to the extent that time and personnel permit. PB's process of analysis forces recognition of the organization and operation line-cutting features of programs. In the same way, the analytic process forces translation of a broad goal, like better education, into operational terms like courses, students, teachers, libraries, etc., that identify both the purposes of the education process and the resources that can reasonably be made available for it. Analysis takes many forms and places substantial emphasis on the use of such tools as computers and mathematical models. However, the computer and the model are simply part of the kit of tools for analysis; they are not the decision-makers.

Program budgeting also places a new emphasis on continuous reporting of both the accounting and statistical type, including ad hoc data-collection methods when appropriate. These serve the purpose of providing the inputs into the next planning and programming cycle, as well as of measuring how the determinations on resources and program are being carried out (progress reporting).

16

New organization charts, accounting systems, personnel recruitment and training systems, management-information systems, or the generous use of the word *program* in traditional budgets are not in themselves program budgeting. They cannot promise the improvement in decision-making that is the primary goal of the program-budgeting process.

CHAPTER 3

Brief History of Program Budgeting

David Novick

Although program budgeting was not widely known before the late 1960's, it has a history of earlier application and development. This background is summarized briefly here in terms of program-budgeting-type activities in industry in the United States starting around 1920, steps taken in the U.S. government from the beginning of World War II until the introduction of program budgeting in the Department of Defense in 1961, and finally, recent developments in both the United States and a number of other countries.

U.S. Business Origins

In industry, management tools of the program-budgeting type were developed first by DuPont around the time of World War I and in General Motors at least in the early 1920s.[1] When Henry Ford II came into control at Ford Motor Company at the end of World War II and faced very serious financial problems, among his emergency actions was the hiring of several new executives from General Motors. They brought with them the General Motors management methods. According to Professor Christenson of the Harvard Business School, this transfer from General Motors to Ford extended to the point where "for a while, Ford actually used the same forms in ... its system."[2] At that time, Henry Ford II also hired a group of ex-air force officers known as the "Whiz Kids," to work on his company's management problems. One of them was Robert S. MacNamara, another was C. B. ("Tex") Thornton.

When the Chrysler Corporation was in financial difficulty in 1958, there were reports that it, too, had repeated what Ford had done earlier in terms of borrowing both manpower and management methods from General Motors (and Ford). The only publicly available document on program budgeting at Chrysler

---

[1] The only General Motors material available to the public is a series of four articles, "Tuning Up General Motors" by A.H. Swayne and Donaldson Brown, *Management and Administration*, Vol. 7, Nos. 1, 2, 3 and 4, Ronald Press, New York, 1924.

[2] Some Lessons in Business from PPBS, *Analysis for Planning Programming Budgeting*, WORC, Potomac, Md., 1968, p. 58.

David Novick

is PROBE,[1] which appeared in 1967. The acronym stands for Program Review of Budgeted Expenses. This paper refers to program budgeting, and claims for PROBE some of the same management improvements that usually are attributed to program budgeting. It cites the application of the methodology at Ford and in the U.S. federal government in its support.

Just as managerial personnel moving from one auto company to another in Detroit carried program budgeting with them, so did executives going from the automotive giants to corporations in other lines of business. As far as the writer has been able to determine, all of these companies treat their management concepts and methods as proprietary. They do not make their manuals available to outsiders or authorize publication of information on their methods. As a result, published accounts of experience in business are limited. One is Alfred P. Sloan's reference in *My Years with General Motors.* Another is the application of program budgeting to research and development at General Electric, Chapter 18 of this book. Still another is the 1968-1970 development of program budgeting for the John Hancock Mutual Life Insurance Company presented in Chapter 19.

Some of the concepts used in program budgeting have had significant application in business under such terms as strategic planning, project management, and the like. When such experience is included, a substantially larger part of the business picture can be identified as utilizing the major features of program budgeting.

Early U.S. Government Use of *Program*

Prior to 1940, the word *program* appears occasionally in U.S. federal government budget documents. For example, in his fiscal year 1939 budget message, President Roosevelt refers to a "Fiscal Program for Revenues and Receipts." On the expenditure side, the word *program* was used at that time in "General Public Works Program." In this instance, it brought together the activities of all agencies and departments for construction financed by public works authorizations. The Agricultural Adjustment Program used *program* to focus on expenditures to be made for cutting back farm production.

For FY 1940, Roosevelt's budget message included a supplemental item: New National Defense Program, $210 million. However, "program" in this instance is used to distinguish it from a category identified as "Total National Defense, etc.":

Total National Defense, etc.	$4,672 million
National Defense	$1,126 million
Interest on Public Debt	$1,050 million
Agricultural Adjustment Program	$ 694 million

[1]*Program Review of Budgeted Expenditures,* Chrysler Corporation, Detroit, Michigan, 1967.

In FY 1944 there was reference to a $100-billion Expenditure Program. FY 1945's budget message included a War Program which was further divided in terms of two major components—(1) Munitions Program and (2) Farm Program. This was followed in 1946 by reference to the "War Program" in contrast to a classification "Appropriations and Expenditures for Other Than War Activities."

These references illustrate the limited and varied uses of the word *program* in the federal budget before and immediately after World War II. Subsequently, a concept of grouping major activities developed. The groups were presented under the heading of "Function" according to "Major Programs within Each of These Functions." A summary in this form appeared first in the *Budget in Brief* in 1955.

However, as one moves from the President's budget message through the summary and into the detailed budget document in those years, *program* is used in limited context and with varied meaning. The major emphasis in the budget was on detail by object classes:

02   Supplies & Services
05   Communication Service
06   Travel Expense
07   Transportation of Things (Service)
10   Utilities
11   Rents
12   Repairs & Alterations
13   Special & Misc. Current Expense
30   Equipment
32   Structures & Parts

Although detailed information by object class still made up the great bulk of the budget documents in the 1960s, there was a shift in both the President's message and the *Budget in Brief* to the program budgeting or output-oriented use of the term *program*. The Bureau of the Budget played an important role in this change: first, as a collaborator in the developments in the Department of Defense that started in 1961; then, in 1965 when it was given the executive responsibility for the application of this new management concept in the nonmilitary agencies and offices of the U.S. government.

Since the late 1930s the Budget Bureau has had the major responsibility for the Executive Budget, but Congress—which enacts the U.S. budget by appropriation legislation—has also played a role in developing this country's budget policy and procedures. There have been actions by its own members, congressional committees, and steps such as P.L. 108, Eighty-Third Congress, 1953, authorizing the Second Hoover Commission. It is sometimes claimed that program budgeting originated in that commission's proposals.

The original Hoover Commission recommended that "the whole budgetary concept of the federal government should be refashioned by the adoption of a budget based upon functions, activities, and projects: This we designate a 'performance budget'."[1] The Second Hoover Commission recommended "the Performance (or Program) Budget" but it is clear that their emphasis was on efficiency, as in performance budgeting. The inclusion of "or Program" in parenthesis labels it as a concession to a new word, rather than a recognition of the program-budgeting concept of designing programs to meet objectives, long-range planning and systematic analysis, and the problems of resource allocation which are the substance of program budgeting.

U.S. Federal Government Program Budgeting in the 1960s

In many respects the history of program budgeting in the United States government started with President Johnson's news conference of August 25, 1965, when he said:

> This morning I have just concluded a breakfast meeting with the Cabinet and with the heads of federal agencies, and I am asking each of them to immediately begin to introduce a very new and very revolutionary system of planning and programming and budgeting throughout the vast federal government, so that through the tools of modern management the full promise of a finer life can be brought to every American at the lowest possible cost.
>
> Under this new system each Cabinet and agency head will set up a very special staff of experts who, using the most modern methods of program analysis, will define the goals of their department for the coming year. And once these goals are established this system will permit us to find the most effective and the least costly alternative to achieving American goals.
>
> This program is designed to achieve three major objectives: It will help us find new ways to do jobs faster, to do jobs better, and to do jobs less expensively. It will insure a much sounder judgment through more accurate information, pinpointing those things that we ought to do more, spotlighting those things that we ought to do less. It will make our decision-making process as up to date, I think, as our space-exploring programs.
>
> Everything that I have done in both legislation and the construction of a budget has always been guided by my own very deep concern for the American people consistent with wise management, of course, of the taxpayer's dollar.
>
> So this new system will identify our national goals with precision and will do it on a continuing basis. It will enable us to fulfill the needs of all the American people with minimum amount of waste.
>
> And because we will be able to make sounder decisions than ever before, I think the people of this nation will receive greater benefits from every tax dollar that is spent on their behalf.

[1] Commission on the Organization of the Executive Branch of the Government, *Budgeting and Accounting,* U.S. Government Printing Office, Washington, D.C., 1949, P.8.

Two months later, the Bureau of the Budget issued Bulletin No. 66-3 to the heads of Executive departments and establishments to explain planning-programming-budgeting and how it proposed to establish the new system.

Professors Bertram Gross and Michael Spring (*Annals of the American Academy of Political and Social Science*, May 1967) described President Johnson's introduction of program budgeting as "potentially the most significant management improvement in the history of American government. . . ."

Several years later, Professor Frederick Mosher wrote in *Public Administration Review* (March-April 1970):

> . . . the system known as planning-programming-budgeting (PPBS), which future historians may consider the most significant administrative innovation of the 1960s. PPBS in some form and to some degree is now installed in most federal agencies—all the large ones—in the majority of states, and in many of the largest cities and counties. It is doubtful that any definition would satisfy all students and practitioners of PPBS, but most would agree that a central feature is the objective analysis of the probable costs and effectiveness of alternative courses of action to achieve goals, independent of political considerations (in the narrow sense of "Political"), bureaucratic considerations, and personal wishes or hunches. In the words of one federal official "PPBS is simply a means to make public decision-making more rational."

With the inauguration of President Nixon in 1969, there was widespread discussion in the federal government of what to do about program budgeting or the planning-programming-budgeting system—the name developed by the U.S. Bureau of the Budget to label its post-1965 effort. The situation was described by Senator Proxmire (Wisconsin) in the Proceedings of the 91st Congress, First Session:

> It should be emphasised that the use of PPB and systematic analysis in the Government is not a partisan issue. While originally implemented pursuant to the instruction of President Johnson, .it also is supported by the new administration. As Budget Director Robert Mayo has stated, it is now quite clear that any administration needs techniques of program analysis and evaluation if it is to make effective decisions on resource allocation and affirm the objectives of planning, programming, and budgeting.
>
> The absence of partisan dispute over the use of PPB points to the recognition by responsible Government officials that we must be rational in our approach to public policy decisions. For, to use PPB to obtain information about the gains and losses to be anticipated from a decision is to demand no more than that the decision be rational. Properly designed, PPB is the most basic and logical planning tool which exists: It provides for the quantitative evaluation of the economic benefits and the economic costs of program alternatives, both now and in the future, in relation to analyses of similar programs[1]

---

[1]*Congressional Record,* Vol. 115, No. 85, Washington, D.C., May 23, 1969.

David Novick

There were no formal announcements from the Executive office of the President about continuing or abandoning PPBS. The budget as originally prepared in program terms for fiscal year 1970, as well as the one in traditional form, was presented in January 1969 by the Nixon administration.

More important, later in that year the Bureau of the Budget reissued Bulletin 68-9 as the guideline for the preparation of the FY 1970 budget. It should be noted that Bulletin 68-9 was first issued in April 1968, that is, in the last year of the Johnson administration, for the preparation of the budget for FY 1969. Since that time the Nixon administration has continued to operate largely through the procedures previously established, and that remains the practice at this time.[1] A few lines from the President's 1970 message presenting the FY 1971 budget are indicative of the position of program-budget thinking in the Nixon administration at that time.

Budget strategy. Long-range planning involves developing a resource alloca-tion strategy that specifies objectives, describes alternative approaches, and anticipates possible outcomes. The optimum budget would be one that most fully meets the objectives in each year and brings us nearest to long-range goals. Each year, projections should be revised and the best course of action again chosen. This approach emphasizes the value of comprehensive and flexible strategies.

Overall fiscal and monetary policy influence (and are influenced by) the level of employment, price trends, and conditions in financial markets. At the same time, the projected economic environment establishes the framework for specific program decisions and the likelihood of program success. For example, the kinds and levels of manpower training, income security, and housing programs must be geared to the economic environment. A compre-hensive strategy must recognize these important policy and program interrelationships.

Feasible strategies are those that balance new programs with available resources. A comprehensive strategy includes consideration of tax changes, reductions in the base of the budget, debt reduction, and the addition of new programs. This year's proposals to terminate and reduce outmoded and un-economic programs will help relax the constraint of limited resources.

Nonetheless, the funds available will be grossly inadequate to accommodate all meritorious new initiatives. Therefore, new initiatives for program increases, budget surpluses or tax reduction can be fitted into successive budgets over time only as resources permit.

This presentation is a new departure in Federal budgeting. The publication of a long-range outlook is intended to provide perspective by emphasizing the

---

[1]In late 1970, steps were taken to increase the analytical capability in the Office of Management and Budget (formerly Bureau of the Budget). As shown in Chapters 21 and 22, actions to increase and improve the capacity for analysis in most federal departments and agencies started in 1965 as part of the introduction of program budgeting.

lack of resources relative to claims and to encourage a longer-range strategy for Government actions.

It is virtually certain that the 1975 budget will not fit any projection that possibly could be made at this time. Rather, it will reflect the experience and changing needs of the intervening years.[1]

Although there is no specific reference to program budgeting, the first paragraph above is an embodiment of numbers 1, 2, and 5 of the distinctive features of program budgeting set out early in this book and the last two paragraphs, plus the third, are a close approximation of the reasons for program budgeting presented on pages 11 and 12 of Chapter 2.

President Nixon's message on the fiscal 1972 budget again stresses the need for emphasis on output, long-range planning, and the resource allocation process—the guts of program budgeting—instead of the traditional object classes or line item type of activity.

Excess in the number and detail of appropriations often diverts attention to minutiae. It also impairs the ability of agency heads to manage their agencies responsibly and economically.

The budget is our principal instrument for coordinated management of Federal programs and finances. Close cooperation between the executive and legislative branches is needed now to make the budget an efficient and effective instrument for this purpose. Therefore we must seek a more rational, orderly budget process. The people deserve one, and our Government, the largest fiscal unit in the free world, requires it.[2]

Federal budget decisions must be made with an awareness of their influence on the economy and on resource allocation in the future as well as the present.

Too often in the past, consideration of objectives and priorities focused only on Federal spending. Only immediate issues, rather than longer-term goals, were considered. And this fact was ignored: when we increase the priority of some programs, the relative priority assigned to others must be reduced. In short, the sum of the resources allocated to the various functions—such as health, education, defense—cannot exceed the total resources that we command.

. . . the allocation of each year's resources is largely a reflection of our past priorities.

As we make choices this year, we will be determining the use of our available resources and expenditures in future years.

. . . resources allocation questions . . . the Nation will answer—either explicitly or by default.[3]

---

[1] *The Budget for Fiscal Year 1971*, U.S. Government Printing Office, Washington, D.C., 1969, P. 61.

[2] *The Budget for Fiscal Year 1972*. U.S. Government Printing Office, Washington, D.C., 1970, p. 12.

[3] *Ibid.*, P. 15.

David Novick

Related History Outside the United States

After World War II there was widespread dissatisfaction with the handling of the national budget in Great Britain. There was no way of projecting long-time demands for programs, nor was there a framework in which an individual program could be considered in relationship to its competitors for public money. One result of this was that in 1946 investment programs were examined together and made part of a kind of five-year economic projection for the country as a whole. Another result was the introduction by the Ministry of Defence of five-year estimates for its proposal undertakings. The public Expenditure Survey System was developed following the report of the Plowden Committee in July 1961, which said, "Decisions involving future expenditures should always be taken in the light of public expenditure as a whole, over a period of years, and in relationship to the prospective resources."[1]

The relationship between the Public Expenditure Survey Committee, the rolling plan, output budgeting and program budgeting is well described in *Output Budgeting for the Department of Education and Science, HMSO*, London, 1970 (pp.3-5).

... Output budgeting is one way of carrying further, within a block of expenditure, the ideas implicit in the annual work of the Public Expenditure Survey Committee ("PESC").[2] By International standards the PESC survey is already a sophisticated method of examining public expenditure, at least in some respects; it looks forward for five years, deals generally with all public expenditure rather than central Government expenditure, and groups expenditure into functional blocks. The PESC forecasts are considered in conjunction with annual assessments of the economic prospect over the same period. Output budgeting can take this further in particular areas by relating expenditure to objectives, rather than simply to functions, by looking at what is being achieved, and by taking into account, where appropriate, costs other than public expenditure costs.

Output budgeting has to be considered as a system, and not just as a new way of setting out the tables of figures in respect of public expenditure. The whole system is intended to ensure that the objectives underlying the programmes are reviewed regularly, that the necessary studies are carried out to establish the effectiveness of what is being done, and that alternative policies are properly examined and costed. The nature of the system is perhaps better described by the name used in the United States, with

[1] The background of program budgeting in the United Kingdom central government is included in Chapter 11.
[2] See the Green Paper "Public Expenditure: A New Presentation," Cmnd 4017, April 1969, for an account of these surveys. (Footnote from *Output Budgeting . . .*)

Canada the only country[1] which has applied the techniques on a significant scale outside the defence field, a "planning-programming-budgeting system." The name emphasises that it links expenditure with the planning process and with the attainment of objectives. In some ways it conveys the flavour of what is useful in the technique better than "output budgeting" if the latter term is taken to imply that all outputs must be specifically forecast in advance and measured after the event.

There are three essential elements in output budgeting:

a. the allocation of expenditure to programmes which are as closely identified as is practicable with objectives. This is the programme budget which shows, for each programme, expenditure—proposed, forecast or actual—and whatever quantitative measures of output can be meaningfully constructed and used on a regular basis;

b. the systematic review of programmes on a regular basis.[2] This includes the questioning of the continued validity of the objectives as well as consideration of alternative ways of achieving them and of the progress so far made;

c. special studies, either to establish the value of alternative ways of achieving the given objectives, or to evaluate the progress made towards achieving particular objectives if this information is not available on a regular basis.

Output budgeting in its early years will naturally concentrate on the construction and discussion of programme budgets, since in many, if not all, areas of activity the measurement of final output presents formidable conceptual and practical difficulties. A programme budget constructed as part of an output budgeting system will be similar to what has hitherto been known as "functional costing"; the essential difference will be that the functions are related to objectives rather than to the institutional pattern as is the functional costing at present used in the PESC education block.[3] An output budgeting system could, however, be progressively developed as and when assessment of output was carried further and new measures of output

---

[1] In those countries a considerable amount of attention has been given to the use of PPBS in providing for the first time forward estimates of expenditure for a number of years. In this country such forward projections are already carried out; it may, however, be noted that the Ministry of Defence have found that their system of output budgeting has improved the accuracy of their forecasts. (Footnote from *Output Budgeting . . .*)

[2] The PESC system, including the "costed options," at present performs an analogous role for public expenditure as a whole. The programme reviews would do the same for a block of expenditure in greater depth. In the U.S.A. and Canada annual submissions are made to the Bureau of the Budget in Washington and the Treasury Board in Ottawa, on a programme basis, supported by programme review documents which survey the whole field and argue the case for the particular appropriations proposed. (Footnote from *Output Budgeting . . .*)

[3] The present PESC classification is considerably more "objective-oriented" than was the U.S. expenditure classification before the introduction of programme budgeting. The classification of objectives in the U.S. programme budget for education is still closely linked to types of education institutions. (Footnote from *Output Budgeting . . .*)

were devised; the extent and speed of this development would depend on the field of application.

The successful application of output budgeting and the forward-looking rolling program in Great Britain led to the adoption of those concepts in other Commonwealth countries. In New Zealand, there has been a five-year rolling program for public works since 1949 and three-year expenditure forecasts by all ministries have been called for each year since the mid-1950s. A "Five-Year Rolling Programme" was introduced in the Department of Defence in Australia in 1969.

Canada's decisions about program budgeting developed from a quite different background. Mr. MacDonald details this in his essay on pages 71-78.

Hopefully, the confusion between output budgeting, the five-year rolling plan, and program budgeting has been largely cleared up at this time. Nonetheless, there are many people who still confuse the older concept with the new idea of program budgeting now being introduced in Australia, Canada and New Zealand[1] as well as being seriously studied for application to the entire national government in Great Britain.[2]

In addition to output budgeting and the forward-looking rolling program as developed in England and other parts of the Commonwealth, budget reform has been undertaken in a great many other countries in recent years. These relate almost entirely to the introduction of long-range planning for capital outlays or efforts to increase efficiency in the handling of specific day-to-day government activities.

Long-range planning for capital outlays is not handled separately in program budgeting. Capital outlays and annual expenditures are considered together and at the same time. Each one is a cost element in every program. Separate treatment of investment tends to avoid a basic part of program budgeting—full, complete or total costing.

[1] The Presidential Commission of Inquiry into the Fiscal and Monetary Policy of South Africa in 1970 recommended that program budgeting be introduced there.
[2] The Ministry of Defence and Home Office, Scotland Yard, are already engaged in Programme Budgeting. See Chapter 11.

CHAPTER 4

Program Budgeting, 1971

David Novick

At the end of 1970 there was relatively less activity in program budgeting in the United States than in other countries as compared to the mid-1960s. Both the attitude and the approach in this country had changed markedly from that of earlier years. In the great burst of enthusiasm for program budgeting which followed President Johnson's announcement, much of the activity in this country was uninformed or misdirected.

In the United States, in 1965-1967, there was an obvious desire to jump on the bandwagon and, as quickly as possible, to take advantage of what sometimes was described as a miraculous cure-all for management's ills. As Professor Gross put it, "As with many new managerial techniques, PPB was initiated in a burst of grandiose claims of 'breakthroughs' and exaggerated applications to irrelevant situations. It has been pioneered by many technical specialists with little understanding, less interest and no experience in general management."[1]

It has long been common practice to associate the term *budget* with the books or documents presenting the financial data rather than with the policy-making and planning that lie behind the pages of numbers. [2] As a result, the format or structural part of the new methodology was given the greatest emphasis in most of the 1966-1967 efforts. In fact, in many cases it was assumed that putting a format together was the only task—and an easy one at that.

The beginnings of program budgeting outside the United States were quite different. Although there were a few false starts, in general the approach was a slow and cautious one, with attention to understanding the concept and evaluating potential difficulties in applying it. The situation in England is typical. The English Defence Ministry, in early 1963, started to explore the McNamara management innovations in the U.S. Department of Defense. A year later it decided to go forward with a similar system.

[1] B. M. Gross, "The New Systems Budgeting," *Public Administration Review*, March–April 1969.

[2] The description in Chapter 21 of the pre-1968 situation in Pennsylvania is a good illustration.

David Novick

"It [programme budgeting] has proved an effective and invaluable instrument in the Defense Policy Reviews and [it] aroused interest in the Treasury in how far such systems might usefully be applied in the civil fields."[1] This was the basis for two feasibility studies initiated in 1967. One,[2] in the Department of Education and Science, produced a formal and widely used report on program budgeting for education. (It is covered in detail in Chapter 12.) The other test was in the Home Office and concerned the police. It led to some major changes, as set out in Chapter 11.

When the Conservative party came to power in June 1970, the new government invited a small team of businessmen to carry out a study for regular review of programs and of major policy options. This was considered a natural extension of the Public Expenditure Survey System and of the new methods of planning public expenditures that had been introduced in 1965. They recommended continuing the program-budgeting efforts.

Local governments in England became interested in program budgeting following the issue of the Maud Report, *Management of Local Government*, in 1967, which presented a new interpretation of the activities of English governments outside of 10 Downing Street. In that year, the Institute of Municipal Treasurers and Accountants set up working parties to explore the possible application of program budgeting at its level of governance. Several reports were issued on its work.[3] Developments by the English "authorities"[4] are described in Chapter 13.

Much of the decline in both the rate and the volume of program budgeting activity in the United States derived from the difficulties organizations encountered in trying to identify their objectives and relate activities to them in program terms. The emphasis on objectives in program-budgeting literature led many organizations to assume that the proposal contained some kind of electronic "black box" that would develop objectives and programs for achieving them through a new brand of computer magic. In some situations, when experience demonstrated that there was no magic or easy way, and that analysis and hard work were required, the effort was abandoned. In other cases it resulted in recognition of the value of identifying objectives through program memoranda or writing issue papers or some combination of them. When this happened, the across-the-board effort was cut back to some of the program

---

[1]J. M. Bridgeman, *Planning Programming Budgeting Systems,* O & M Bulletin, London, November 1969.

[2]*Output Budgeting for the Department of Education and Science,* HMSO, London, 1970.

[3]"Preliminary Statement and Report No. 1," by IMTA Programme Budgeting Working Party, *Local Government Finance,* IMTA, London, March 1970. Subsequent reports appear in this same publication.

[4]Unit of local government in England, like city, county, or school district in the U.S.

budgeting components and the main emphasis was on analysis. The state of Vermont and the city of New York are typical of this kind of development in government. In the private sector, the John Hancock Life Insurance Company and the nonprofit Lutheran Missionary Hospitals illustrate this approach.

An exploratory feasibility-testing, piecemeal approach, like the one taken in England, now characterizes most of the program budgeting work going on in the United States. There are several examples of across-the-board efforts to apply the concept in this country. In government, they range from the large industrial state of Pennsylvania to the small township of Sparta, New Jersey, and include Montgomery County, Maryland; Orange County, California; Dade County, Florida; Dayton, Ohio; and the Education Resource Management System for local school districts. The state of Hawaii has enacted legislation on program budgeting and, from the preparatory studies and reports, appears on the way to becoming another across-the-board success when the law becomes effective next year. In business, General Motors and Ford Motor Company are outstanding examples.

Fortunately, the very real problems created by the search for objectives leads some organizations to recognize in these problems an important management activity in and of itself. In so doing, they are learning to do what Peter Drucker urged some years ago:

> It is not possible to be effective unless one first decides what one wants to accomplish. It is not possible to manage, in other words, unless one first has a goal. It is not even possible to design the structure of an organization unless one knows what it is supposed to be doing and how to measure whether it is doing it.
> In fact, it is never possible to give a final answer to the question, "What is our business?" Any answer becomes obsolete within a short period. The question has to be thought through again and again.
> But if no answer at all is forthcoming, if objectives are not clearly set, resources will be splintered and wasted. There will be no way to measure the results. If the organization has not determined what its objectives are, it cannot determine what effectiveness it has and whether it is obtaining results or not.[1]

To establish objectives requires analysis of what the organization wants to accomplish, appraising the activities now carried on, creating possible alternatives and then deciding upon a future course of action in program and program-element terms.

---

[1]Peter F. Drucker *The Age of Discontinuity: Guidelines to Our Changing Society*, pp. 190-191, Harper & Row, New York, 1968.

David Novick

Building an Analytical Capability

The primary function of program budgeting is to provide an improved method for making decisions on the major policy issues an organization faces so that it can better determine the allocation of its limited resources. It does this through the use of analysis, with particular emphasis on system analysis.

The activity required is described succinctly and well in Hawaii's second report on program budgeting for that state:

The analytic procedures characteristic of the PPB approach to problem solving can be reduced to the following steps:

1. Identify and quantify if at all possible the *real* objective, a task fraught with intellectual and practical hazards.

2. Array all of the alternatives for accomplishing the objective, not just the popular and orthodox ones.

3. Compute or estimate the true total costs and the real effectiveness of each of the alternatives.

4. Compare the changes in marginal costs and marginal benefits within and between alternatives for various levels of effectiveness taking care to reexamine the amount of the objective desired and the possibility of more efficient "mixed solutions."

5. Estimate the spill-over effects and the risks and uncertainty associated with each alternative and do "sensitivity analysis" where appropriate to answer the "what if . . . ?" kind of questions.

6. Using an appropriately designed criterion, select a particular alternative, or mix of alternatives, as the recommended solution, again taking special care to note the results of "5" above.

In general, the use of this approach provides a way of looking at problems of economic choice-making (i.e., a viewpoint and an attitude), of identifying essential items of information, and of creating a structure or framework for organizing and comparing these data in a manageable and analytically insightful way.[1]

The above statement presents an ideal that every organization should strive to achieve but rarely, if ever, attains in practice. To do good policy analysis is just a very difficult task.

Although it may come as a surprise to many people, analysis has had only limited application to the problems of government and business. In government it has been applied chiefly to Department of Defense procurement of major new equipment and to natural resources. Decisions on locating new dams and timber management in public forests are examples of the latter. In business it has been applied to activities such as investment in new plants or major equipment, warehouse location, or production scheduling, and for these usually on a one-at-a-time basis.

[1] *Progress Report in Implementing Act 185, Session Laws of Hawaii 1970,* submitted by Hiram K. Kamaka, Director, Department of Budget and Finance, December 21, 1970.

That the use of analysis in government or business is on a small scale undoubtedly comes as a shock to a society that is: (1) highly technology-oriented, (2) able to put a man on the moon, (3) willing and able to introduce the "new math" in its secondary schools, and (4) seeing computer developments that seem to offer "magic" as a substitute for reasoning. But analysis of reasonable quality outside the natural and physical fields is still a scarce commodity.

Reasons for Scarcity

The scarcity of reasonably useful analysis in the social sciences is explained primarily by the difference in phenomenology from that in the natural and physical sciences. Secondarily, it results from a combination of quite late application of quantitative techniques to social and economic problems,[1] a preoccupation with imaginary and hypothetical problems rather than with attention to observable reality, and a concern with methods that are bright and shiny rather than with those that promise better performance.[2]

This evaluation of the use of analysis in the social sciences brings two problems to the fore. The first is the lack of demand for good analysis on the part of the managers. The second is difficulty in supplying good analysis when it is requested.

Managers Do Not Seek Analytical Studies

Managers have no occasion to want the assistance of analysis unless there is a crisis which threatens their control. There is a tendency to think of the manager as Marvin Bower of McKinsey & Co. describes him, as "an artist in the broadest sense: a creative allocator of resources, an orchestrator of diverse technical disciplines . . . "[3] He rarely fits this ideal. Another essay in the same book points out what is closer to the real situation, that "most chief executives do not want a strong, independent group of directors. . . . The majority . . . looks for a rubber-stamp board."

---

[1] Although there are isolated examples of analytical studies prior to the mid-1960s (see footnote on p. 54 [Prest and Turvey]) a substantial amount of work in these fields is a recent development.

[2] The writer kicked off a major discussion of this problem in "Mathematics: Logic, Quantity and Method," *The Review of Economics and Statistics,* November 1954. Paul A. Samuelson MC'd a discussion by Professors L. R. Klein, J. S. Duesenberry, J. S. Chipman, J. Tinbergen, D. G. Champernowne, Robert Solow, Robert Dorfman, T. C. Koopmans, Samuelson himself, and the editor, Seymour Harris. That discussion continued in *The Review* for several issues and spilled over into other learned society journals. As retiring president of The American Economic Association, Wassily Leontieff probably has revived the discussion in his "Theoretical Assumptions and Nonobserved Facts," *American Economic Review,* March 1971.

[3] *Arts of Top Management,* edited by Roland Mann, McGraw-Hill, 1971.

That is, they do not want to be appraised or held accountable. This second quote comes close to the writer's own concept:

1. Managers strive to maximize their own autonomy.
2. Managers do their thing.
3. Managers tend to ignore past mistakes.
4. Managers have little tolerance for uncertainty.

They have no obvious reason to want to change the existing system, which is the one that brought them to success. In the absence of a crisis or threat to his leadership, the manager has little or no incentive for self-examination.

Difficulties in Supplying Good Analysis.

When analysis is requested, it is not easy to respond. There are difficulties in applying methodology developed in the natural and physical sciences on the basis of stable phenomena to the constantly changing and volatile activities of business, governments, and people that are the subject matter of social sciences. At present we lack both basic data and special methodology in these areas. What we have now is only a very limited start on filling these needs.

These deficiencies create serious problems for both would-be teachers and students. As a result, teaching the use of quantitative methods is relatively new even in economics, which is the granddaddy of the social-science efforts. With few courses and until very recently, few students, the supply of available analysts is small.

Out of a bibliography of ninety items which Prest and Turvey list in their excellent survey of cost-benefit analysis, only three items were cited as published prior to 1950.[1] Although the survey did not attempt to assure completeness, it is nonetheless a good index of the amount of quantitative work done in economics prior to that year. To be sure, a count for the years through 1960 would have increased the number of citations, but not significantly.

Analysis of various kinds can and should be applied at different levels of managerial decision making from (1) day-to-day operations, (2) short-run changes over the forthcoming six to eighteen months, to (3) long-range plans for determining where the organization wants to be and what it should be doing two, five, ten or more years in the future.

As we step up the ladder of managerial decisions, the problems to be solved become less clear. In day-to-day operations the questions are the relatively straightforward ones of efficiency translated into production schedules, mail-room procedures, individual work loads, and the like. Over a longer period measured in months, there is some opportunity to deal with more complicated problems of efficiency in terms of inventory control, changes in activities or

---

[1] A. R. Prest, and R. Turvey, "Cost Benefit Analysis: A Survey," *The Economic Journal* December 1965, Vol. 15, No. 300, pp. 683–735.

ways of performing them, and of emphasizing one activity over another. In short, minor shifts in emphasis and direction of a flow of activities already well in motion are analyzed. Since World War II, operations research and related mathematical and logical methods of analysis have been applied successfully to improving efficiency at these first two levels, where everyone has a fairly good idea of what "more efficient" means. It is when questions of the third level are involved that analysis becomes a most difficult task.

As a former counsellor to President Nixon put it:

> Tracing the complex and involute interconnections by which inputs produce outputs in a large social system is not the work of amateurs. It is not now done in any area of social policy save in economics, and there, most economists would insist, it is done imperfectly. It is not done elsewhere because no one really knows how to do it. It is just that most persons who have considered the matter feel it has to be done, and accordingly someone will have to learn how.[1]

Program budgeting has put more people to work trying to learn how to do analysis of social systems than any other management effort in history.

Analysts in the Case Histories

A number of approaches have been taken to deal with the difficulties arising from program budgeting's demand for analysis. None of these has provided more than a partial solution. This is not surprising in light of the problems in both demand and supply just discussed. There also are demand and supply effects arising from the timetable used in putting program budgeting into effect.

Chapter 5 discusses the demand for *instant analysis* created by the U.S. Bureau of the Budget in Bulletin 66-3 when it launched the new system in 1965. The essay was based on a study made by the authors for the Budget Bureau in 1968. Part of their conclusion was that "the dilution of the quantity of analytical professionals who had the required skills caused by the demand for *instant analysis* in all agencies almost guaranteed that the quality of analysis would suffer." Earlier, they pointed out, "there seemed to be a sufficient number of analyst's positions authorized. . . to make the PPB system work by 1968 even though the positions might not be optimally placed." In addition, they found "a scarcity of analytic skill . . . in most agencies. . . ." and that "one possible explanation for this scarcity . . . among persons selected for the analysis staffs is that many . . . transferred into PPB work from agency occupational categories such as budget analyst, program analyst or management analyst without specific reference to prior quantitative or analytic work."

This problem is also discussed by Chester Wright, director of the Management Sciences Training Center, U.S. Civil Service Commission. In

[1] D. P. Moynihan, National Goals Research Staff, *Toward Balanced Growth: Quantity with Quality*, p. 7, U.S. Government Printing Office, Washington, D.C., July 1970.

Chapter 24 he writes, "Looking for analysts inside the government . . . there already existed many so-called analytic positions. . . ." However, only a few of the government's available analysts could fill the need.

For that reason Wright addresses the question of the requirements for an analyst in program budgeting.

The job of program-budgeting analyst clearly is not easy to fill. That this is the case is set forth again and again in the case histories.

Belgium: ". . .the almost nonexistence in Belgium of analytical capability, adequate statistical information. . . ."

Canada: "Speaking subjectively, mostly for lack of evidence to the contrary, it would appear that the immediate impediment to progress in analysis is the general absence . . . of junior officers qualified to conduct analysis and senior officers who really want it conducted."

France: "The shortage of qualified analysts must be underlined. The existence of trained analysts, working at the right place, is a prerequisite of success. . . . civil servants often lack analytical capability since most of them have a humanities training which does not include the use of quantitative methods."

Ireland: ". . . difficulty of securing adequate skilled personnel to do the work involved . . . limited number of 'trained' personnel available and these persons, themselves, were 'learning by doing'."

Japan: "The nondefense areas of government have not had a long experience in systematic analysis. The number of young analysts is gradually increasing, but the number is still not large enough."

Despite continuing complaints, the situation is not at all hopeless. There are a number of cases where the development of just enough capability has made possible better decisions than would have been available in the absence of a program-budgeting effort. New York City's experience, as discussed in Chapter 23, is representative.

Developing A Program Format

Recruiting and training analysts and building an analytical capability has been the largest single problem in applying program budgeting. There have been others, too. As indicated earlier, difficulties in developing a program structure brought some of the efforts to an early end. In other cases, the activity was redirected to a piecemeal approach. However, many organizations have succeeded in building appropriate program structures. Representative cases include Belgium, which is moving into a total-government-program structure on a ministry-by-ministry basis.[1]   Another is Hawaii, which introduced a

---

[1] In other countries the status varies widely. In France, one ministry is complete, two are well advanced, and most of the others are only starting. The situation in England, Australia, New Zealand, Ireland, and Canada is much like that in France. Austria and Japan are still in the preliminary phase.

state-wide program structure at the beginning of 1972.[1] In the state of Pennsylvania an organization-wide program structure is in operation.[2] The last example is the city of Philadelphia, which has followed a step-by-step approach.

In Belgium, two ministries are complete, three are in process and two are about to start. As stated in Chapter 8, they

> attached the greatest importance to the drawing up of the first program structure for a ministry. This procedure involves several months of joint work by the institute's researchers and the chief department administrators. It is necessary to make the latter think in terms of goals, concrete objectives, and the alternative ways of attaining these, instead of legal terms and previous regulations. Drawing up of the program structure helps to make explicit the objectives that are implicitly behind the department's ongoing activities. It also leads to a regrouping of these activities in a manner that will collect and present information adequately for future political decisions.

Since the need for thinking in terms of goals, concrete objectives, and alternative ways of attaining these, rather than in terms of law and existing regulations, is too often overlooked or misunderstood, it is worth repeating here. This barrier usually stopped those who were looking for a "black box" to solve all decision problems.

The "Institute's researchers" also merit special attention. The researchers are from the "Institut Administration-Université," which is a joint venture of the government's civil service, a nonprofit school of public administration—the Institute—and the Belgian universities. It was the Institute that was asked by the government to study possible budget reforms for Belgium. It recommended program budgeting as the vehicle of change.

Hawaii's Standing Committee Report No. 401-70 provides an excellent illustration of the successful application of the structural or format part of program budgeting. Its discussion of program structure recognizes the role of analysis in the new methodology. As indicated earlier, analysis is the first step in developing the program structure and can be of great value to the organization in understanding its objectives and the extent to which its ongoing activities serve them. Failure to recognize the need for analysis in developing the format and inability to provide it were the reasons that many of the organizations trying to do program budgeting did not complete this first step.

The Hawaiian approach ties the two together in a clear-cut way. The first three sentences of the paragraph following are a succinct summary of the purpose of all program structures. This statement on analysis clearly identifies the essential requirements.

---

[1] Not included in the case-history chapters are Montgomery County, Maryland; Orange County, California; Dade County, Florida; Dayton, Ohio; and Sparta, New Jersey, which are representative of a number of other organizations with successful complete program structures.

David Novick

The State Program Structure. Under PPBS, a program structure is the arrangement and grouping of governmental programs into objective-oriented classifications so that programs with common objectives may be considered together. Each program is placed in the program structure under the objectives to which it primarily contributes and it is placed without regard to its formal organizational placement. The major purpose of the program structure is to make possible better analysis of government programs by organizing cost, program size, and effectiveness information so as to include all areas relevant to a problem. The State program structure developed by the administration, the latest of which is dated September 30, 1969, is deficient in several respects: (1) many of the "programs" identified in the program structure are actually the existing functions and budget categories of the departments rather than programs in the PPBS sense of representing a combination of resources and activities designed to achieve an objective or objectives; (2) the upper levels of the program structure are occupied by non-operational goals, thus forcing meaningful subcategories of programs off the structure (e.g., agriculture appears at the fourth level in the State program structure, and there would be no place for the program subcategories which appear in the program structure developed by the Agricultural Coordinating Committee for the agricultural development plan); (3) there are incongruities in the placement of programs at the same level in the program structure (e.g., the entire agriculture program is at the same level as three forestry programs: forest development, forest protection and maintenance, and forest research). Your Committee has determined that it is necessary to revise the program structure to overcome the deficiencies noted and that, in doing so, the administration carefully consider the following:

Determine the appropriate number of levels to be included in the program structure. To avoid cluttering the program structure, there should ordinarily be no more than four levels. At the same time, the structure should descend to at least that level (the lowest level) which displays those programs or program subelements which are the simplest units of activities, each unit producing a specific identifiable result, about which resource allocation decisions are to be made by the governor and the legislature. For example, under agriculture, milk control and meat and poultry inspection would probably be placed at the lowest level of the program structure.

Arrangement of the structure from the top down in accordance with some classification theme so that there will be meaningful grouping of programs and congruity at each level.

The development of an improved program structure should allay the concern expressed by the departments with respect to effectiveness measures. A properly designed structure will facilitate the selection of effectiveness criteria for programs at every level of the structure.

Analysis. As it is with the PPB approach generally, the crux of the new system is analysis, the systematic examination of alternative courses of action for meeting governmental objectives. The new system is designed to induce analysis, not just any kind of analysis, but analysis of a particular type. The

38

basic elements of analysis to be performed under the new system shall include the following:

A clear definition of the problem;

Identification of the governmental objectives or end results to be sought;

Selection of criteria or measures of effectiveness which will permit estimation of the progress made toward attaining the ends being sought;

Identification and description of the key features of the alternatives available to attain the ends;

Determination of the full cost implications of each alternative;

Identification of the major uncertainties involved in cost and effectiveness estimation and the quantification of those uncertainties to the extent possible;

Identification of the major assumptions made so as to spell out the degrees to which effectiveness or cost may be sensitive to these assumptions;

Identification of the major cost and benefit trade-offs among the alternatives;

Documentation of the findings to permit others to understand and evaluate what has been done.

Your Committee expects the Department of Budget and Finance to furnish additional guidance to the departments for the performance of analysis, including such matters as the appropriate interest rate at which future cost and benefit streams are to be discounted to their present value.[1]

Hawaii has developed eleven major programs to satisfy its objectives. The first of these is "to make available a graduated series of high quality, formal educational systems at various levels intended to maximize the realization of each individual's intellectual potential in terms of personal development, social effectiveness and vocational satisfaction." This is the stated objective of the Formal Education Program. Ten other major programs have been established, the last of which is "to maximize the effectiveness and efficiency with which the objectives of the state are achieved by providing executive direction, overall policy-making and general support for all programs."

The eleven major programs for Hawaii are:

I. Formal Education

II. Health

III. Economic Development

IV. Transportation Facilities and Services

V. Employment

VI. Physical Environment

VII. Public Safety

VIII. Social Problems and Standard of Living

IV. Protection of the Individual

X. Leisure Time

XI. Governmentwide Activities

[1] *Standing Committee Report No. 401-70.* State of Hawaii, 1971, pp. 6 and 7.

Each one of these is in turn broken down into five sublevels of activity or organization.

Pennsylvania's published material provides further amplification of the purpose of and steps in developing the program structure. It starts with a translation of the major goals of the state government's activities in terms of program areas. "A goal is defined as a desired state of affairs based upon current knowledge and societal values." These reflect the state's constitution, statutes, and authoritative judicial, legislative and executive decisions.

The program categories are the next breakdown and lend themselves to further subdivision into sets of programs with identifiable impacts. The third level represents major substantive activity groupings which aim at specific quantifiable impacts upon individuals or their environment.

The lowest level of classification is the program elements. These are the activities performed in terms of modules or, as the then Assistant Secretary of Defense (Comptroller) Mr. Hitch described them in his 1961 testimony in Congress, "Program packages." They are the packages of resources required to produce a specific output, or as Pennsylvania puts it—impact.

The development of program budgeting in the state of Pennsylvania is the subject of Chapter 21. The structure or format part is highlighted here:

Program Structure

In preparing the program structure instructions, PPBS terminology such as *program categories, subcategories,* and *elements* was employed. But these terms were redefined as they were to be used within the Commonwealth system. First, a distinction was made between goals and objectives. A goal was defined as a desired state of affairs based upon current knowledge and values. . . . To make the transition from questions of value to questions of fact, an objective was defined as that which can be described quantitatively in terms of units of desired impacts upon individuals or the environment to be achieved within a given time-frame and employing available resources. To illustrate, a goal would be to "maintain a system of health care that will minimize preventable deaths," while an objective would be to reduce infant mortality to a specific rate. The goal of good health would likely remain constant over time, whereas the objective, a specific optimum rate, would vary over time with changes in scientific knowledge and technology and with changes in the social and economic systems. Goals are thus expressed in words and objectives are expressed in numbers. . . .

Translating these concepts to the language of program structure resulted in eight goal-oriented major Commonwealth programs. . . .

For example, under the Commonwealth program 'Health, Physical and Mental Well Being,' a program category would be 'Maintaining a Physical Environment with Minimum Health Hazards'.

Under the Commonwealth system, the program subcategory was the critical point of conversion from values, expressed in words, to facts, as represented by numbers. The program subcategory represents the major substantive element clusters which are directly aimed at accomplishing specific quantifiable impacts upon individuals and/or the environment. . . .

Program subcategories were in turn broken down into program elements. Program elements are the basic modules of activities, that is the building blocks that, when aggregated, make up the program subcategories. An example of elements under the Air Pollution Control subcategory would include plant inspections, air monitoring, education for private industry, and so on. Each element consumes resources and has specific outputs. For example, number of inspections and number of trainees. The aggregate effect of the elements should be to accomplish the objective of reducing or slowing the increase . . . of the amount of air pollution. The elements, their mix and quantity, are the means selected through budget allocations to accomplish the objectives expressed as impacts at the subcategory level.

Since the program structure logic required that agencies classify all of their activities within a framework in which the work that they performed in terms of outputs was related to the effects of that work as measured in terms of impacts, the agencies, in effect, were being asked to demonstrate the causal relationships between what went on within government and what happened as a result of organized governmental efforts. Although all agencies had some degree of difficulty in applying the logic to prepare program structures, two types of problems are worthy of note.

One problem stems from the propensity to define goals in idealized terms and the reluctance to define achievable impacts in realistic terms. Clean air is a laudable goal for a program category, but achievable impacts, given current resources, technology, and attitudes, may at best be to retard or stop the rate at which the atmosphere is getting dirty. Since traditional program rhetoric is usually optimistic in its claims of promised results, there is often resistance to a program-structure logic that insists on stating objectives in terms of effects that can actually be measured. This resistance was greatest in those program areas where the results of governmental effort is likely to be imperceptible, or so mixed with other activities, such as an advertising program to attract new industries to a state, that the impact of the governmental effort is difficult to identify.

A second problem, particularly related to programs in the human services, is the acceptance of doctrine as establishing a relationship between outputs and impacts. For example, doctrine supplies many of the formulas for resource allocations such as teacher/pupil ratios, psychiatrist/patient ratios, and so forth. The inference is made that if professional staff levels are maintained as prescribed by professional doctrine, objectives will also be obtained. A system with a built-in capacity to examine the relationship between an element output based upon doctrine and target objectives measured in terms of impacts has an ongoing capacity for examining the efficacy of that doctrine. Especially at a time when traditional doctrine in education, social welfare, public health, and other human service programs is being questioned, the relationship between doctrine and impacts is a particularly sensitive one.

41

A consequence, therefore, of the requirement to develop program structure is conflict both within agencies and between agencies and the central fiscal office concerning the use of outputs based upon doctrine as a substitute for an impact measure. For some programs in mental health and welfare, program personnel insisted that impacts could not be identified and that outputs would have to be treated as if they were impacts. What this resistance demonstrates, is not so much reluctance to change per se within the bureaucracy, but, rather, the primitive nature of the state of knowledge concerning what can be accomplished by organized efforts through many of the human services programs which now receive vast resources while citizens are increasingly dissatisfied with the results.

Several features of the Pennsylvania approach merit further attention. The first is identifying a goal as a desired state of affairs and then translating it into objectives that can be described quantitatively in terms of units of desired impact. This move from the general to the specific is a fundamental first step in the analysis. Unfortunately, the need to do it is frequently not recognized.

Second, the concept of programs, program categories, subcategories, and program elements effectively presents the logic of moving from defined objectives into programs and operating activities in meaningful and realistic terms.

The third, and probably most significant, development in this approach was to require that goals and programs be stated in terms that permit realistic measurement of achievable impact. This took the development of the program structure out of the idealized descriptions that are too frequently used and required, instead, effective translation of plans in terms of operating activities. The work done in Pennsylvania on defining and measuring program impact is the most advanced to date. Impact is not quite the same thing as effectiveness. However, using "impact" is one way to cut through the difficulties in establishing measurements of effectiveness.

The city of Philadelphia is another illustration of a successful development of the program format. Although it is not included in the case histories herein, major steps in developing the city's program structure are highlighted below.

In a February 1967 briefing to the quarterly commissioners' meeting, the director of finance outlined the city's activities in program budgeting and emphasized that Philadelphia had decided on an evolutionary rather than a revolutionary approach. Extracts from his remarks follow:

We do not expect to install a complete Planning-Programming-Budgeting System overnight. Instead, we plan to take it step by step, and make the changes this year that are within our current capability, and lay a foundation for taking subsequent steps in future years as our capability increases. . . . [1]

[1]*PPB in the City of Philadelphia,* a case prepared for class discussion, by Graeme M. Taylor, Management Analysis Center, Inc., Boston, Massachusetts, (no date), p. 10

... there will be extensive dialogue among the departments, the Managing Director's Office, and the Finance Department during the development of each department's program structure. Many of the departmental operations will be very difficult to assign to one program and subprogram in preference to all others. In many cases, whatever decision is eventually reached will be easily challenged because very good reasons for a different assignment can be presented. However, it is our belief that our principal orientation should be toward identifying the major problem areas and developing a program structure which can serve as a vehicle for developing solutions to those problems.[1]

The best possible program structure for the City Government will be developed by your careful examination of the major program framework and determining how your agency's operations relate to the framework, and then determining your program elements accordingly. If you cannot fit a particular segment of your agency's operations into the program framework, please feel free to suggest additions to the program framework which will provide for such inclusion.

It should be kept in mind that the program elements are the most significant segments of the entire City program structure. The program element is considered to be the "building block" of the program structure.

Keep in mind that the primary purpose of the PPB System is to help agency management focus its attention on the most important functions and decisions of the agency. For this reason, it is desirable that your program element structure be relatively "clean"; that is, unburdened by unnecessary detail."[2]

The primary purpose of Planning-Programming-Budgeting is to provide for complete and thorough long-range planning to identify and develop solutions for the City's problems. Agency management will carry most of the burden of identifying and developing solutions for these problems.[3]

The program presentation in this Budget Document (the Mayor's operating budget for 1968-69) is a radical departure from previous Philadelphia operating budget presentations. All City agencies prepared their 1968 Operating Budget requests by Program Element keyed into an overall Program Structure for the City as described above.[4]

The latest report on the status of program budgeting in the city of Philadelphia is in *The Mayor's Fiscal 1971 Budget and Programs*. This presents a summary by program of the mayor's recommendations for the year July 1, 1970 to June 30, 1971. It is the third budget document which incorporates the framework of a program-budgeting system for the city.

Philadelphia has engaged in a step-by-step development in the new planning

[1]*Ibid.*, p.12.
[2]*Ibid.*, p.13.
[3]*Ibid.*, p.14.
[4]*Ibid.*, p.17.

and decision-making method, and it has not yet completed and introduced all of the components of a fully operative system. Considerable progress has been made in (1) developing an output-oriented program structure. (2) identifying budgeting and accounting systems to incorporate program-structure identification, and (3) creating a program-analysis capability.

The city's program structure consists of nine major programs, each divided into subprograms and then into program elements. Each program element is a major activity carried on by a city agency or a quasi-public agency which contributes to a major program. The operating budget requirements for all city agencies for FY 1970 were prepared by program element.

As stated by the mayor:

1. All activities of City agencies and quasi-public agencies involved in City affairs are separated into end-product oriented Program Elements and brought together in a rational overall Program Structure for the entire City. This Program Structure is keyed to the major problem areas of the City and serves as a vehicle for identifying activities currently being carried on to combat each major problem.

2. All relevant expenditures at each level of the Program Structure are identified, including capital expenditures as well as operating expenditures.

3. The exact nature of each major problem is thoroughly and comprehensively defined; conducting data-gathering research wherever necessary.

4. Long-range Program Objectives based on the problem definitions are established. These objectives are sufficiently concrete and specific so that quantitative measures can be determined which will measure progress toward achieving the objectives.

5. Current activities and all possible alternatives are analyzed to determine their productiveness in relation to the Program Objectives and in relation to their cost.

6. A long-range Program Plan to achieve the Program Objectives is developed. This Program Plan is based on the analysis of cost and productiveness, as well as the intangible factors which must always be given consideration.

7. Departmental Capital and Operating Budget requests are based on the Program Plan, and evaluated in terms of how well they implement the plan.

8. An output measurement reporting system is developed to inform City management of actual progress in carrying out the Program Plan, so that corrective action can be taken when necessary.

9. The Program Objectives and Program Plan are revised annually to keep abreast of changing conditions and new knowledge.[1]

The nine major programs[2] for Philadelphia are:

A. Community Development

B. Transportation

---

[1] The Mayor's Fiscal 1971 Operating Budget and Programs, City of Philadelphia, p. 1.

[2] An illustration of a three-step breakdown from major program to subprogram and into program elements, drawn from the material on the city of Philadelphia, is presented in Appendix B.

C. Judiciary and Law Enforcement

D. Convservation of Health

E. Public Education

F. Cultural and Recreational

G. Improvement of General Welfare

H. Services to Property

J. General Management and Support

They are typical of the concept as it was developed by other state and local governments. The interrelationships between the various domestic programs that have been discussed are illustrated in Table 1. Hawaii's eleven programs are used as a base. To provide additional information on major program structures, two governments not represented in case histories, Montgomery County, Maryland, and Sparta Township, New Jersey, have been included.

Other Problems Encountered

With the introduction of a formal analytical approach to the organization's decision-making process, there arises an inevitable tug of war between the new undertaking and the *status quo ante*. As analytical studies are quite new to most organizations, they are frequently viewed as a threat by those holding the established decision-making positions. As stated in the chapter on French experience, "Another drawback arises from misunderstandings and psychological reactions. Traditional administrative circles are generally not prepared for innovation. In particular, the new quantitative techniques are hardly welcome to senior civil servants who are trained mostly in law and the humanities. The new methods often seem a threat to their established way of doing things and, still worse, produces a fear of a shift in the existing equilibrium of power."

This problem occurs not only in government organizations but in business as well. The situation is well described by Charles Schultze. Although he writes about program budgeting in a government context, and many believe that *political* applies only to government, Schultze's words apply equally to commercial and industrial organizations:

> [In the] relationship between the political process and the decision-making process as envisaged by PPB ... I do not believe that there is an irreconcilable conflict. ... But they are different kinds of systems representing different ways of arriving at decisions. The two systems are so closely interrelated that PPB and its associated analytic method can be an effective tool for aiding decisions only when its relationships with the political process have been carefully articulated and the appropriate roles of each defined. ... It may, indeed, be necessary to guard against the naivete of the systems analyst who ignores *political* constraints and believes that efficiency alone produces virtue. But it is equally necessary to guard against the naivete of the

Table 1

Major Programs for States of Hawaii and Pennsylvania, Montgomery County, MD., and Sparta Township N.J.

(Numbers in parentheses refer to Hawaii)

Hawaii	*Pennsylvania*	*Montgomery County*	*Sparta Township*
I. Formal Education	Intellectual Development and Education	Intellectual Development	(Special School District)
II. Health	Health, Physical & Mental Well-being	Promotion of the Individual's Physical & Mental Well-being	Health (II & VI)
III. Economic Development	Economic Development & Income Maintenance (III, V & VIII)	Economic Support, Development & Protection for the Community (III & V)	Community Development (III, V & VIII)
IV. Transportation Facilities Services	Transportation and Communication	Community Transport System	Transportation
V. Employment			
VI. Physical Environment	Protection of Persons & Property (VI, VII & IX)	Community & Home Environment (VI & VIII)	
VII. Public Safety		Protection of Persons' Rights & Property of the Individual (VII & IX)	Protection of Persons (VII & IX)
VIII. Social Problems & Standard of Living			
IX. Protection of the Individual			
X. Leisure Time	Recreation & Cultural Enrichment	Community Recreation & Culture	Leisure Time
XI. Governmentwide Activities	Direction & Support of Services	Management & Supporting Services	Policy Formulation & Implementation

decision-maker who ignores *resource* constraints and believes that virtue alone produces efficiency.[1]

There are always political constraints as well as resource constraints. The decision-maker or manager who avoids either one does so at his own peril. Political considerations can only be formulated in qualitative terms, but as already pointed out, the analysis part of program budgeting is not limited to matters that can be handled in quantitative terms. A great many decisions, often the most important ones, can only be treated in qualitative terms.

In retrospect, it becomes clear that the early program-budgeting efforts were victims of an oversell on analysis. Analysis had indeed provided solutions that otherwise would not have been available, but enthusiasts generalized from their experience and gave analysis an electronic black-box magic. Analysis, when complete, is more effective than just judgment or intuition. However, judgment and intuition are required, together with a lot of work.

Another problem arose from the view that program budgeting was only a management tool and therefore the original exposition carefully avoided political problems. In the political context in which decision-making actually occurs, it is probable that if all the tools of analysis are in use, the resultant knowledge tends to lead even those guided by political considerations to more meaningful decisions. However, program budgeting had to build an analytical capability at the same time that its newness made it vulnerable to attack on the political front; many difficulties resulted from a failure to recognize the obvious conflict between the different interests of the analytical staff and the program operators. As indicated earlier, all of these difficulties were compounded by one additional factor; that was the desire of many organizations to get the new system in and working—*instantly*!

[1] Charles L. Schultze, *The Politics and Economics of Public Spending,* Brookings Institution, Washington, D.C., pp. 16–17, 76.

47

CHAPTER 5

Evaluating Program Budgeting in the 1960s

David Novick

To evaluate program-budgeting experience requires not only an examination of what took place in a specific situation but also an appraisal of what the organization might reasonably have been expected to accomplish if existing practices and traditions had continued. Program budgeting has meant many things to many people and a wide range of diverse activities were initiated under that name. Hopefully, most people now have a better idea of what program budgeting is. Also, they differentiate between an across-the-board and a step-by-step approach in terms of the number of activities programmed, parts of the organization covered, or separate components of the methodology applied. Finally, we know that an organization may try to introduce all program budgeting features at the outset or undertake some parts of the new management decision making system separately or in various combinations.

Some observers have said that a piecemeal approach to the installation of a "system" like program budgeting is a contradiction in terms. That this idea is incorrect can be seen from the experience of the city of Philadelphia, the John Hancock Life Insurance Company, the government of Belgium, and the many other organizations which have in fact taken the road to program budgeting a step at a time. To be sure, greater benefit can be expected more quickly from complete coverage of all of an organization's activities, as was the case with the Ford Motor Company, Montgomery County (Maryland), the state of Pennsylvania, and a long list of other organizations. The choice between the two ways of getting on with the job rests in part on a determination of the amount of improvement that it is worthwhile to seek and, in larger measure, an appraisal of the amount of change that can be effected in the organization's decision-making methods at a specific point in time.

In many cases the choice between the partial and complete approaches cannot be planned in advance. Moving a step at a time usually is a planned procedure, but at times it results from an inability to carry out a complete changeover in a single step. The partial application may be in terms of either organizational units or programs to be covered or the selection out of separate parts of the methodology such as issue analysis or program memorandum.

David Novick

A good illustration of success is the experience of the County Council, Blackpool, England. There, as part of the new approach, the Housing Authority presented a report to the council which required a decision in terms of different results produced by different locations of the housing project. For example:

1. Ability to produce mixed communities
2. Difficulty of access for older people if located on the outskirts
3. Distances of traveling to work
4. Access to libraries, theaters and museums

Looking at a housing project in terms like these is in sharp contrast to prior practice. The traditional approach was a financial statement showing land costs, building outlays, and then a translation into the resultant rent structures.

Success came through a somewhat different application in New York City of program budgeting to housing. There, policy previously had also been developed in traditional terms. The emphasis was on land and construction costs, rents, and a one-neighborhood-at-a-time approach. Program budgeting first brought citywide interdependencies into the policy determination. Then rent payments under social welfare were added to the housing-considerations context, and so on into a number of other new and interrelated activities. One of the major concepts introduced was to consider the relationship between rent control on the one hand and housing deterioration and abandonment on the other.

New York City and Blackpool County Council experience are testaments to the idea put forth by France's minister of defense in advocating the introduction of program budgeting in his country:

> .... The problems of all modern organizations, and above all, in government, are tightly tied one to the other. To isolate each of these problems in order to settle them independently ... is neglecting the interdependencies and inter-actions, that is to condemn the organization to a bad decision.[1]

Evaluating these interrelationships means that not only are the decision-makers taking a new and different viewpoint but also that they require and should demand new kinds of information for their deliberations.

Thus a new kind of thinking and appraisal is required by

1. Decision-makers
2. Managers and operators, or the administrators and civil servants responsible for the kind and quality of information to be considered
3. Stockholders or voters affected by the determination.

Measuring Program Budgeting's Progress

To evaluate any system for planning, programming or budgeting requires

[1]Editorial by M. Debré, minister of defense, *Bulletin interministériel pour la Rationalisation des Choix Budgétaires, No. 2*, December 1970.

suitable criteria for measuring success. As of 1971, program budgeting was introduced in a great number of different shapes and forms, and timetables varied widely. Such conditions make it impractical to seek criteria for appraising the utility of what progress was made. However the following list of objectives can serve as a measurement.

Objectives Sought By Program Budgeting

Group 1. Impact within the Organization

1. Total package, that is, development throughout the management of an awareness of the need for clear identification of objectives, an active search for alternatives, the quantitative measurements of program results and costs, and analysis which includes appropriate treatment of both short— and long-term as well as direct and indirect impacts.

2. Development of an analytical capability adequate to cope with major issues that must be resolved in developing programs.

3. Impact on decision-making processes through analytical studies.

4. Development of an awareness of the need to think in new terms without overemphasizing formal procedures or the role of analysis.

5. Demonstration of the program-budgeting approach in a limited area carried out with sufficient success to make other parts of the organization want to copy it or imitate it.

6. Impact of program budgeting thinking on: (a) The way in which information is presented to superior authorities (b) The way in which documents are specifically produced for shareholders or voters.

7. Impact on the decision-making process through "full cost" analysis of the project to demonstrate whether the output is worth the input requested.

8. Addressing "important" problems and formulating better questions by decision-makers. Evidence of better decisions or, at the very least, of better questions.

9. Evaluation of whether program budgeting has an integral part in resource-allocation processes rather than being layered on an existing decision process.

10. Evaluation and adjustment of secondary effects that are generated; for example, adding or deleting data series maintained.

Group 2. External Impact of Program Budgeting.

11. Development of an awareness of the interaction of organizations and operations through thinking in program terms; for instance, recognition of the impact of a health program in the Ministry of Education.

12. Development of an awareness by "outsider" groups of the need for dealing in terms of output or product rather than solely of inputs as in the traditional pattern.

David Novick

13. Substitution of cost-benefit analysis for the trial-and-error practice of adding a little bit more if an operation is going all right or continuing an established operation until it is patently undesirable.

14. Change in the substance and frequency of communications among agencies and between the budget office and line agencies; for example, discussion of problems rather than line-item costs.

Professor F. C. Mosher, in his response to a question on the U.S. federal government's progress in program budgeting asked by the Fifteenth International Congress of Administrative Sciences provided the following list of measures of success:[1]

Forcing, or at least encouraging, more clearly defined and thoughtfully considered statement of objectives;

Forcing the development of indicators and quantitative measurements of outcomes of governmental programs;

Encouraging the development and installation of better systems for gathering information about both costs of programs and their effects.

Examples of the subjects of analysis and brief descriptions of a few of them are contained in Appendix B.

Later in reply to another question, he said:

There is no question that in many agencies PPBS has encouraged a broader and longer range view on questions of public policy and resource allocation than existed theretofore. In some ways, its achievements have been negative. It has raised questions that hadn't been asked, elicited comparisons that wouldn't have been made, forced answers—accurate and perhaps sometimes inaccurate—that wouldn't have been offered, drawn attention to gaps in relevant information that would have been ignored, encouraged the development of criticism of social programs and evaluation.[2]

There is no disagreement with such a statement concerning the need for analysis in making decisions. Dispute arises, rather, over the extent to which the improvements in the decision-making process should be tied to the budget activity. Although in theory it can be argued that such a tie is not required, it is doubtful that analysis can be made effective unless it influences decisions that are really made for keeps. That means putting dollars on the line. In most organizations that occurs only as part of the annual budget process. Program budgeting, therefore, brings analysis into planning-programming-budgeting and binds them together with a common thread—the need to get out next year's budget.

[1] *New Aggregated Systems for Planning Programming Budgeting,* Fifteenth International Congress of Administrative Sciences, 1971. *U.S. Reporteur,* Frederick C. Mosher, p. 7.
[2] *Ibid.,* p.21.

It is in reaching budget decisions that an organization's policy is made and put into effect. Historically, these were in terms of administrative units. object classes, and line-item details like number of jobs and remuneration to jobholders. Obviously, in such a system, the budget determination is restricted to how things should be done and does not consider whether or not they should be undertaken at all.

The balance of this book contains the case histories of organizations in various stages of developing their program-budgeting activities as of the end of 1970. They relate chiefly to government experience, with the exceptions noted in Chapter 3. As explained there, information on program budgeting in the private sector is not generally available because of the reluctance of businessmen to publish on this subject.

One of the reasons for undertaking this volume is to provide an account of events outside the United States since there already is a growing literature about the activities of the federal, state and local governments in the United States. Program-budgeting literature has started to appear in French, German, Spanish and Japanese, as well as English.

CHAPTER 6

Programme Budgeting
in the Australian Federal Government

by S. G. Herring

Assistant Secretary, The Treasury
Australia

The Commonwealth of Australia was formed in 1901 by the federation of six states which were former British colonies, and the general style of government and executive and parliamentary control of expenditure are based on the British model. The budgetary methods now employed have, therefore, been derived from the British pattern, with parliamentary control of expenditure and the concept of "stewardship" as the under-lying bases. Accordingly, the federal budget has traditionally emphasized the organizational structure of government and the types of resources purchased by the government; for example, staff, buildings, and office equipment.

In common with the experience of other countries, the continuing growth of the public sector in Australia, the increasing complexity of the public's demands on the federal government, and the problems of obtaining resources to meet these demands had led to continuing efforts to improve management techniques and the nature and extent of information available to the government upon which its policy decisions can be based. In recent years, the documentation accompanying the treasurer's budget speech and the information available to the government in its budget deliberations have been extensively recast and improved. Perhaps the most significant development has been the construction of a national accounting classification of federal budget estimates. This was first published in 1963-1964 and is designed to relate the federal government's demands for goods and services to the overall national demand-supply position.

The current interest in programme budgeting in Australia could then be portrayed as a continuation of these efforts to improve management techniques and the information presented to the government to assist it to formulate its policy decisions. To this end Treasury officers have kept abreast of developments in budgetary and management techniques in other countries, including developments in programme budgeting in the United States of America and Canada. At the beginning of 1968, a senior Treasury officer was seconded full-time to review available literature on programme budgeting in Canada and the United States and "output budgeting" in the United Kingdom. In June 1968 it was concluded from the preliminary investigations that these developments were worthy of intensive study and that a small team of officials, whose expertise would cover the fields of economic policy, budgeting, accounting, and management, should be set up.

The Study Team

Following consideration of the preliminary study, a three-man study team consisting of two Treasury officers (one each from the economic policy and accounting areas) and one man from the management-services area of the Public Service Board was sent overseas. The purpose of the visit was to discuss with government officials and others, in the United States, Canada, and the United Kingdom, the concept and practice of programme budgeting in these countries in order to test the impressions gained from a study of available literature. A preliminary discussion was held with New Zealand Treasury officials who had already undertaken overseas studies. Following the visits, a report was prepared in May 1970 summarising overseas experience and discussing the potentials of programme budgeting for the Australian federal government.

The report noted that developments in the countries visited arose from the inadequacy of the traditional one-year input-oriented estimates and budget for the analysis and planning of government expenditure. A form of budget covering only one year does little to throw light on the significance of expenditure decisions, the effects of which may be spread over many years. Nor does the traditional approach direct attention to the relationships between activities with similar purposes. Further, the name, or even the apparent mission, of a department is not sufficient to describe what it does, and estimates classified in such terms as salary, running expenses, and capital projects do little to reveal the real functions performed by departments. Despite the improvements that have been made in Australia's budgetary procedures, it was evident that problems which led other countries into programme budgeting were inherent in our own system.

The study team also took particular note of the development of forward estimates by the United Kingdom government—to the point where five-year forward estimates of revenue and expenditure have been published. Although the development of these estimates has not been within a programme budgeting system, the study team believed that the development of estimates along those lines was compatible with a programme budgeting system.

It was also observed that in all three countries visited, the budget cycle was considerably longer than in Australia. In the three countries visited, preliminary budget-year strategies are developed more than a year before the government presents its expenditure estimates, and it appeared that much more time is allowed for consideration, by the executive and the central budget agency, of the estimates in general and of particular issues. Under current practice in Australia, budget estimates are prepared and decisions reached over a much shorter period.

The study team devoted considerable time to analysis of the quite different strategies adopted in implementing programme budgeting and in the adjustments that users of the system have found it necessary to make. It was clear to the study team that there is no universally "best" way of implementing programme budgeting. Rather, the team concluded that each government must consider the emphasis which should be given to the various elements of programme budgeting in any particular political, economic, and cultural setting: each country should consider what are its main needs and what steps can be taken which are not beyond the capabilities of the staff and other resources available to it. Should the Australian federal government decide to implement a programme budgeting system, it seems clear that any such system would have to be tailored to Australia's own particular circumstances and requirements.

At the time of reporting, there had been no decision by the Australian federal government on the application of programme budgeting throughout the federal government. Within individual departments the main developments so far have been in the Department of Defence and its associated departments, and within the Post Office.

The Australian treasurer has, however, referred to the need for a better appreciation of the extent to which the government's freedom of action in relation to budgets of future years is being restricted by expenditure decisions already taken. Preparation of longer-term forward estimates, soundly based, are considered to be of value in meeting this problem and in giving the government a better appreciation of the overall budget situation from year to year. The treasurer has indicated that he sees the main value of forward estimates as providing a wider body of knowledge and a better framework in which to make new policy decisions. The treasurer has also referred to the style of expenditure classification generally adopted in the traditional form of budget. which often gives little indication of the purposes of expenditures. He has indicated that the Treasury will need to explore new classifications under which forward estimates can be arranged.

The Defence Departments

This is a group of departments concerned with defence policy, supply, and the administration of the defence forces. There are five Departments of State in this group; namely, Defence, Navy, Army, Air and Supply.

During 1969 the Department of Defence sent a small group of officers to the United States of America, the United Kingdom, and Canada to study the techniques that had been developed for the application of systematic analysis to defence programmes, and the department began to develop a programme-budgeting concept for the Australian Defence Services. The development of the system was continued during 1970, when the department announced that systematic analysis had been applied to proposals put forward by the Services for major equipment and that analysis was being further developed and complemented by the introduction of processes for a "Five-Year Rolling Programme."

The new Five-Year Rolling Programme is a further stage in the implementation of programme budgeting. It aims at the production of a programme which identifies the major objectives of the Defence Forces—antisubmarine warfare, air defence, and so on—and assigns all the costs, research and development, capital expenditure, and operating costs associated with each activity over a period far enough into the future to show, to the extent practicable and necessary, the full resource needs.

The processes of the Five-Year Rolling Programme are:

1. The starting point in the Five-Year Rolling Programme system is the strategic guidance based on intelligence assessments and projections and military, political, and economic objectives. It provides the basis for the formulation of the Services' plans for the development of the force structure.

2. Before decisions can be made on the further development of the Australian forces, it is necessary to know what resources are already committed, and what the capabilities existing or now under development are. Consequently, the Service Departments are required to make five-year projections of resources and capabilities assuming no new decisions on major equipment were taken.

3. The Service Departments prepare proposals for new equipment to be acquired during the programme period, using the strategic guidance provided to them and taking into account their assessments of technological developments and the necessary replacement of capabilities which will go out of service during the Five-Year Programme. The Service Departments also provide an indication of those very large replacements or additions foreseen as requiring decision in the years six to eight ahead. The Services are expected to argue cogently for their proposals and demonstrate that the proposed solution has been reached after a thorough validation of the need and a proper examination of the alternative courses open.

4. The Services' proposals are reviewed in the Department of Defence so that common criteria may be applied in the analyses of the cost and effectiveness of the proposed equipment system both within and between Services. Decisions leading up to an annual announcement of new projects are

made against a context of strategic objectives, the implications of decisions already taken, and the other proposals put forward as requiring decision in future years. This will ensure that decisions on new projects will not shut out higher-priority items.

5. A basic draft Five-Year Plan will be formulated from the Services' projections of capabilities and resource needs to which will be added the new proposals for minor equipment. Variations to the proposed Five-Year Plan will then be formulated after consideration of the latest strategic guidance and other relevant factors. The variations may take a number of forms; for example, different levels of capability and cost, emphasis on particular areas or aspects of defence, or retiming of proposals.

6. The basic plan and the variations on it are then reviewed at high level. The capabilities provided in each of the alternative plans and their costs are weighed against strategic, political and economic considerations, and one plan is endorsed. The Service Departments then make any necessary changes in detail to this plan, taking into account the latest information on costs, delivery schedules, and so on, but not introducing changes of policy. At the same time, the Department of Defence will prepare a submission to the Cabinet.

After the Cabinet decision, the cycle will begin again. The regular review process will provide for analysis in greater depth of the Services' proposals. There will be up to five or more years warning of impending decisions on major equipment proposals, and long-range studies can be commenced well in advance of having to make the decisions. These studies will continue throughout the year at a steady level. This will make the best use of scarce analytical resources and will allow the studies to be done in appropriate depth, without a flurry of analytical activity in the months before the budget is submitted. The five-year look into the future will also assist in setting priorities on studies.

The Defence Department recognises that the introduction of the new management techniques and procedures will not be easy or quick. The experience of the United States, the United Kingdom, Canada, and many other countries, is useful, but Australia cannot merely copy their systems. Our particular problems demand particular solutions. In its early days the Australian system will concentrate on the essentials.

The Australian Post Office

In 1969 a committee was established within the Post Office to define and develop a management-information system to meet the needs of the Post Office. The need for system changes was associated with an increasing emphasis on the role of the Post Office as a business, rather than as a government department. The committee recommended that a programme-budgeting system be introduced, in a form specially tailored to Post Office information needs. Subject to further feasibility trials which are now in progress, the system will be introduced on a national basis in July 1972.

On the premise that the outputs of the Post Office are the provision of various services, the programme structure comprises twenty-seven service programmes—twelve postal-service programmes and fifteen telecommunications-service programmes. As an example, under telecommunications, three programmes—grouped under the heading "Telegraph Services"—will be: The Public Telegraph Service; Telex Services; and Telegraph Private Wire Services. All costs and all earnings will be allocated to the service programmes so that cost of provision of a service may be related to the revenue it produces. Along with investment analysis, there will be indicators designed to measure the extent to which each programme is meeting the demand for services and to measure standards of performance. Associated with the system will be the preparation of five-year plans.

The new procedures will, in the initial stages, operate parallel with existing management-control systems. A field investigation is now being carried out to develop the details for a programme budgeting system. These studies, for example, endeavor to sort out the very difficult problem of distributing common costs to different service programmes.

The Post Office expects that the programme structure based on services will be extremely useful to top management, and that determination of long-term strategies for the Post Office will be assisted. Management will be able to apportion funds in such a way as to obtain the balanced network growth desired, and it is hoped that managers at all levels will be encouraged to think in terms of outputs.

Conclusion

With the introduction of the Five-Year Rolling Programme for expenditure on Defence Services, the Defence Department expects that the government will be in a position to make more informed decisions on defence expenditures in the future because of the availability of estimates over the longer time horizon. It will also be in a better position to allocate resources and control the flow of expenditure. A similar situation should exist in relation to the Australian Post Office following the proposed introduction of a programme-budgeting system in 1972.

CHAPTER 7

Program Budgeting in Austria:
An Essay in Persuasion

by Egon Matzner

Scientific Director, Documentation Center of Urban Studies, Vienna.
Consultant to the Federal Minister of Finance, Austria

and Karl Vak

Director, Municipal Savings Bank and Dataservice, Ltd., Vienna.
Advisor to the Austrian Chancellor

The public sector in Austria is quantitatively of greater significance that in most non-Communist mixed economies. Of the 1970 gross national product, the central state, the *Länder*,[1] local authorities and a number of smaller public authorities control or influence roughly 38 percent, the dominating agent being the central state. The greater part of total public expenditure is allocated to public consumption and public investment; that is, mainly to the provision of "public goods" to the private sector. Next in order of importance is the transfer of capital and income to the private sector.

The sheer size of public expenditure gives public budgetary decisions a great allocative impact. It is thus both natural and urgent for allocative aspects to be included in the decision-making process. Despite this urgency, public authorities do not make systematic use of analytical methods directed at securing a more efficient allocation of public funds. Program budgeting is not yet applied. This is true, too, for methods of project selection at the sectoral or micro level; for example, cost-benefit analysis. However, elements of program budgeting are included in the government proposal for a new *Bundeshaushalsrecht* (Budgetary Statute) presented to the Parliament late in 1971. Those responsible for this new legislation are using PPBS concepts as their base.

[1] The Austrian Federal State comprises nine states or *Bundesländer*.

Egon Matzner and Karl Vak

The budgeting system still in operation in Austria is of a traditional or "object" type.[1] Its two main functions are (1) to authorize departments to spend money on specific items, and (2) to provide a basis for responsibility to the Parliament, through its auditing agency. While aspects of stabilizing policies and income redistribution can easily be included in traditional budgeting methods, aspects of economic efficiency cannot. The main deficiencies of the present system can be summarized as follows:[2]

1. A too-narrow orientation to aspects of control:

2. No formulation of operational objectives which could be related to alternative programs measured in cost-benefit terms (i.e. neglect of planning aspects);

3. Annual budgets, longer-term aspects being widely neglected;

4. A neglect of future expenditure occasioned by present programs;

5. The predominance of departmental or institutional autonomy and the failure to take into account the interdependence of expenditure programs.

Current Changes

In recent years there has been widespread criticism of the system of budgeting in Austria. The chief criticism is that the budget covers only one year at a time and that data is inadequate.Only recently has the problem of efficiency in the modern sense been brought to the fore. The Social Democratic party, which came into power in 1970, drew up an economic program that, for the first time (outside of a purely academic context), proposed the application of quantitative criteria (in particular cost-benefit analysis) in the selection of projects in the infrastructure.[3]

Before 1969, information about a more comprehensive system of planning, programming, and budgeting was not widespread in Austria. The diffusion of information regarding this social innovation came from three sources: (1) the universities; (2) experts with modern university education from within the Social Democratic party,[4] and (3) the newly established Documentation Center for

[1] c.f. D. Novick, "Introduction," *Program Budgeting: Program Analysis and the Federal Budget,* 2nd ed., Harvard University Press, Cambridge, Massachusetts, 1969.

[2] For a more detailed analysis, see E. Matzner, ed., "Grundzüge eines modernen Budget-Systems," in *Materialien zum Seminar Programmbudget-Techniken,* Documentation Center for Urban Studies, Vienna, 1970, as well as W. Weber and R. Windisch "Okonomische und institutionelle Gesicht-spunkte rationaler Haushaltsplanung," in *Das öffentliche Haushaltswesen in Österreich,* Vienna, 1970, No. 1-2.

[3] In March 1970 the Social Democrats won the election and formed the government, following the conservative People's party which had held a majority since 1945.

[4] At university level, G. Poll presented a paper on program budgeting as an instrument for promoting efficiency in the public sector, in a seminar organized by E. Matzner at the School of Social Science in Linz. Further publications by the same author are an article, "The Planning-Programming-Budgeting System," in *Finanznachrichten,* October 1969, No. 401 and "Ein Allokationskonzept für den öffentlichen Sektor: Das PPBS," June 1970, an M.A. thesis, School of Social Science, Linz. At the University of Vienna, W. Weber and R. Windisch prepared a comprehensive study which included program budgeting.

Urban Studies.[1] In particular, the contributions by K. Vak, W. Weber, and R. Windisch contained concrete proposals regarding the application of program budgeting in Austria. The most interesting sectoral analysis, which resulted in a proposal for a target-oriented program for national health policies in Austria, was recently presented by E. Gehmacher and H. Strotzka.[2]

There is in general a time lag before social innovations are put into practice. It would therefore be premature to expect public authorities to put program budgeting into practice less than a year following the circulation of information about it. There is, clearly enough, a propensity to utilize this new concept. The proposed new budgetary statute already mentioned is based on PPBS thinking; if passed by Parliament, it will move in the direction of program budgeting not only the central Austrian government but also the Länder and other public authorities.

At the *national level*, the new Austrian government has pledged itself to improve administrative efficiency. Administration itself is construed as a service to the public. This approach is very close to that of program budgeting. Seminars will provide information on the principles of this approach to members of the government as well as leading civil servants and officials. Proposals for the reform and reorganization of the administration of government bear the stamp of program-budgeting thinking. It is perhaps the first time that a discussion of governmental reorganization has been dominated by the considerations of how to choose and implement objectives rather than by legal arguments. Even if the government should not adopt this organizational reform, the manner of handling the problem in itself constitutes a major innovation in Austria.

At the *departmental level*, two ministries are interested in program budgeting: (1) The newly founded Ministry of Science and Research intends to apply it in planning its legislative and expenditure program, and (2) the Ministry of Finance is preparing a ten-year investment program for the central government sector. The ten-year program will be redrafted each year, using sophisticated methods of project selection and comprehensive planning.

At the *local level*, officials in Vienna were invited to comment on the applicability of program budgeting in that city. On the whole, the response was positive. A committee of officials and experts in special fields was proposed. Other towns are also studying the possible advantages of the program budgeting system.

[1] In November 1969 the Documentation Center for Urban Studies invited leading officials from local authorities to a seminar on program budgeting. David Novick gave a lecture on the principles of program budgeting. K. Vak discussed problems of its application in Austria. The papers were mimeographed and edited by the Documentation Center for Urban Studies (c.f. second footnote on p. 2).

[2] E. Gehmacher-H. Strotzka, "Die Erarbeitung eines Nutzenvektors für eine Neukonzipierung der Gesundheitspolitik," momeographed, Vienna 1970. (Paper presented to the Seventh World Congress of Sociology in Varna, Bulgaria.)

Evon Matzner and Karl Vak

The Linz School of Social Science included the subject of program budgeting in courses on public finance; program budgeting was also presented to a student audience at the new course for regional planners[1] at the School of Engineering (University of Vienna) starting with the fall term 1970.

Present Outlook for Program Budgeting

During the next two years, the application of program budgeting will remain within the outline presented. Pilot studies will probably be elaborated for special sectors (e.g., education, health, transport).[2] One of the newly founded social-research institutes will also probably focus interest on this new method, thus functioning as a center of communication between analysis and administrative staff in government organizations. A development along these lines would be most useful. At present, it is impossible to implement more ambitious programs owing to the inadequate number of experts capable of applying the methodology.

While program budgeting is regarded as a major vehicle for increased efficiency in the public sector, progress of a less systematic nature can be made outside it. Thus, key elements of program budgeting; for instance, thinking in such program terms as objectives, targets, programs, alternative costs, and effectiveness, will gradually tend to penetrate the decision-making process in the public sector itself. This tendency will certainly be promoted by the increasing number of social scientists expected to assume administrative responsibility in the years ahead.

[1] R. Wurzer, "Uber die Ausbildung von Stadtebauern und Raumplanern-Probleme und Moglichkeiten," in: *Berichte zur Raumforschung und Raumplanung,* No. 4, 1969.

[2] Vak, *op. cit.* p. 60; and Weber and Windisch, *op. cit.,* p. 83.

CHAPTER 8

The PPBS Experiment in Belgium

by E. Poullet

Secretaire Permanent au Recrutement
Institut Administration-Universite
Brussels, Belgium

In general, PPBS was undertaken in countries where methods of public management are fairly advanced. These countries had at the outset some experience with the various elements which make up PPBS, such as forecasting of expenditure trends, estimating project costs, and control over realisation. For them, the essential problem was to integrate these various approaches into a single system.

This was not the case in Belgium. This country must be included among those which still have a very traditional budgeting system. It is also characterized by an inability to control the growth of public expenditure. These two points need brief comment.

Belgium is one of the few countries which still has a capital budget, called the "budget extraordinaire." The ordinary or current budget deals with recurrent expenditure financed through taxes, while the "budget extraordinaire" treats what are called exceptional expenditures for projects ranging from motorways and public buildings to military equipment and even low-cost housing financed by means of government loans.

In spite of a considerable use of borrowing, the ordinary budget is frequently maintained in balance only by the use of tricks, the most serious of which is the transfer of expenditure from the ordinary budget to the extraordinary budget and the postponing of actual payments. Resort to such expedients can only lead to serious financial crises, which usually occur when a conjunctural overturn coincides with a change of government. It is then decided to wipe the slate clean by an effort to reduce expenditures and an increase in taxation. Usually, only the increase in taxation materialises.

In the face of this inability to control public expenditure, the method of budgeting remains traditional. Political decisions are taken empirically case by case under pressure from events and special interest groups. They are nearly always concerned with things to be done and rarely with the objectives to be attained, so that there is rarely a confrontation of alternative policies in terms of cost and effectiveness.

The drawing up of budgets is a matter of recording the financial consequences of the decisions taken. Budgetary negotiation and expenditure control aim essentially at minimizing the budgetary repercussions of decisions already made. Execution is often rendered inefficient by spreading the implementation over an always longer period of time and reducing the resources made available. It is only on rare occasions that past decisions are revised on the occasion of the budgetary decision or that it results in a policy choice.

The decision-making process is only indirectly influenced by the budget. In effect, the annual difficulty of presenting a budget that balances acts as a brake with respect to new decisions, whatever their ultimate utility is in comparison with current activities. Inevitably, the brake on new decisions becomes weaker at the end of the legislature's session.

Finally, the situation is made worse by the fact that the legislature, under pressure from special interest groups, guards against a later reduction of the resources allocated to a certain activity by including in the laws a series of parameters regarding the expenditure. This ultimately leads, other things being equal, to a rate of increase in expenditure which in certain areas is greater than the rate of increase in public revenues.

It would be too simple an explanation to attribute all of the weakness in the methods of budgeting to the lack of control over public expenditure. Both budget and expenditure-control problems have in fact a common cause— weakness of the politico-administrative system. On the one hand, the executive branch is weak when faced with pressure groups which can, in many sectors, bring leverage to bear on the level of expenditure. On the other hand, the administration is restricted purely to a role of execution. The minister, being in practically every case a member of Parliament, is the one responsible for running his department, and he does so through a personal staff. The top civil servants, who are permanent, have no independent decision-making power that would permit them to introduce modern management methods and give a certain continuity to their department's policy.

Reasons for The Program-Budgeting Experiment

The "Institut Administration-Université" was entrusted by the government with the training of senior civil servants. The Institute came to the conclusion that training in modern management methods was useless unless the political authorities paid more attention to it. Therefore, after the major financial crisis of 1965-1966, when the Institute had occasion to hold a colloquium attended by both leading civil servants and ministers, it was decided to explore the possibilities of budgetary reform. It was in this context that the author of this paper advocated the introduction of PPBS in Belgium.[1]

Some months later, the Institute was asked by the government to explore the proposed method of PPBS in two departments: Agriculture and Public Health. The purpose of the politicians was essentially to avoid unexpected increases in expenditure and to promote economies. The civil servants responsible for financial management, however, felt that changes in budget methods would bypass the real cause of the trouble in public finance: the mentality of a political authority unable to resist pressure groups.

The Institut Administration-Université knew that it was engaged in a long-term education process in which the attitudes of the people responsible both politically and administratively would have to be changed. In the eyes of its advocates in Belgium, program budgeting is not merely a procedure but also an instrument of change which could ultimately transform the whole politico-administrative system.

Strategy for the Introduction of PPBS

With this objective in mind, the main pitfall to be avoided was to introduce new procedures that did not have a vital impact on the decision-making process. Hence there was a need to put the system into operation only after those politically responsible had sufficient understanding of how it worked and had made a decision to use it in decision-making. This, in turn, required efforts to create an awareness of the need for more rationality in public management both in political circles and in public opinion in general. Such efforts were also necessary to give PPBS a foundation strong enough to carry a step-by-step implementation through the hazards of political life and through the negative attitudes that result from resistance to change.

At the present time, studies of PPBS are being pursued in five ministries; two others are awaiting to start with it. In addition, under the auspices of the Administration for Scientific Policy, the Institut Administration-Université is in charge of introducing the system in about fifteen scientific offices.

Since the main concern is for real impact on the decision-making process through the active use of the method by those politically responsible, the Institute made a rather sharp distinction between two stages in the implementation of the system:

1. Preparation of tools: program-structure, program-budget, multiyear program

2. Utilisation of these tools by the political authority in the annual budget process

---

[1]Cfr. E. Poullet, *Program Budgeting—Instrument de la direction par les objectifs dans le secteur public,* Institut Administration-Université, Bruxelles, 1967, p. 87, with an annexe, *Bulletin Nr. 66-3,* October 12, 1965, from the Bureau of the Budget, Subject: PPB.

This last means basing the annual budgetary procedure on program decisions rather than on authorisations of expenditure. This would be the case only if a program budget (or still better, a multiyear program) were decided upon as an adaptation of the previous year's program budget (or multiyear program), using for this adjustment simplified memorandums (sometimes called "issue papers"). Each of these two stages deserves a brief comment.

1. The Institute attached the greatest importance to the drawing-up of the first program structure. This procedure involves several months of joint work by the Institute's researchers and the chief department administrators. It is necessary to make the latter think in terms of goals, concrete objectives, and the alternative ways of attaining these, instead of legal terms and previous regulations.

Drawing up of the program structure helps to make explicit the objectives that are implicit in the department's ongoing activities. It also leads to a regrouping of these activities in a manner that will collect and present information adequately for future political decisions.

2. The Institute insisted that the planning-programming-budgeting system should become effective only when the annual budget procedure was carried out in terms of programs. It was aware that it emphasized "programming"[1] while in other countries the emphasis was on either "planning" and its tools (such as system analysis) or "budgeting" and its performance norms.

There were several reasons for this stand. As has been explained, one of the main concerns was the lack of control over the growth of public expenditure, hence the desire to designate within what financial limits political authorities would have to work. Since the available means were scarce while the needs were unlimited, their choices could become real only if past decisions and new initiatives competed annually for the allocation of resources on the basis of cost-utility comparisons. To avoid questioning past decisions and to try instead merely to reduce the cost of past decisions has provided very little opportunity indeed for choice.

Another reason for the emphasis on programming rather than planning or budgeting is the scarcity in Belgium of analytical capacity, adequate statistical information, or norms and control of realisation. In emphasizing "programming," the Institute hoped to stimulate a demand for planning that would be operational; for instance, oriented towards proposals for reallocation of resources either to respond to the emergence of new priorities or as a means of achieving greater effectiveness. The Institute also believed that programming will develop a greater concern for the implementation of the programs and the

---

[1] The dividing line between planning and programming is somewhat differently placed in Belgium than it is in the United States. In the Belgian terminology, the annual readjustment of the multiyear program through which political choices are made and resources are reallocated is included in *programming*.

control of the results obtained, concern that is at present lacking among those politically responsible.

PPBS Impact on Administrative Organisation and Personnel Policy

The attitude of the Institut Administration-Université towards organisation and personnel problems was closely connected with the strategy described above.

The Institute was reluctant to see too close a link between organisation and program-structure. Since it was concerned that program-structure should continuously adapt to the needs of political decisions, it did not want to excite the rigidities and pre-conceptions of individuals that are inherent in organisational problems. It also wished to avoid fixed objectives as a consequence of the organisational structure. In sum, the Institute believed that organisation should be functional and fairly stable while the program structure should be flexible and geared to the needs of political decisions. It is left to the program budget to translate the program structure into tasks to be carried out by departments and services, and so assure coordination between them for the implementation of the programs.

As to personnel policy, on the other hand, the Institute desired that PPBS have a profound effect. Personnel needs were viewed as the consequence of the choice of programs and the conditions for their realisation. At present, expenditures on personnel are seen both as a large budget item in need of economies, and at the same time as requiring automatic increases in public expenditure to keep abreast of economic pressures.

In an attempt to end a traditional approach which hinders "planning" for personnel needs, the Institute wanted departments to allocate each individual member of their respective staffs to particular programs, however difficult this was to do. It did not want to accept the fact that a large proportion of personnel expenditure went into support programs. It wished to reach a situation where budgetary decisions were made in terms of programs, and needs for personnel were determined thereby and no longer by *sui generis* decisions. If this prospect materializes, departments would consider it an attractive aspect of PPBS.

CHAPTER 9

Program Budgeting in the Government

of Canada: Origin and Progress

by B. A. MacDonald

Director General, Budget Coordination
Treasury Board, Canada

The form that a program-budgeting system takes in a particular jurisdiction will be very much conditioned by the environment of the jurisdiction. Some relevant environmental factors are the quantity of resources involved in the budget, the traditions of the process through which decisions on the allocation of resources have been reached up until that time, and the bureaucratic structure that serves the government. Canada has had a long period in which to evolve a unique environment and a unique set of traditions that will of necessity mould any theory of management. This environment and these traditions have led to a particular approach to the introduction of program budgeting.

To understand, therefore, what has happened in Canada in the development of program budgeting, it is necessary to have some understanding of the environment into which it was introduced.

Canada is governed according to parliamentary forms and the government per se consists of a Cabinet of ministers drawn from the party having the majority of members in the legislature. Each minister has responsibility for a department and, often, responsibility as well for one or more of the fifty or so specialized agencies, boards, that is corporations, or commissions set up over the years to deal with certain well defined operations that were thought would best be operated outside the structure of departments. There is a strong tradition that public servants shun the limelight and an equally strong tradition that decisions should appear, in the main, to have been made by ministers acting as the elected representative of the people and that accordingly the influence of public servants on decisions should appear minimal. As will be indicated later, this may provide less than the most favourable climate for analysis, and it certainly reduces the amount of publicity that can be given to analysis.

Some few words are necessary on the financial organization of the government of Canada in order to appreciate the bureaucratic structure into which program budgeting has had to take root and strive to grow.

At the present time, to make a great simplification, the Department of Finance worries about revenue and the Treasury Board worries about expenditures. The Treasury Board is a Committee of Ministers of the Cabinet served by a small Secretariat. Until a very few years ago this Treasury Board Secretariat was a division of the Department of Finance, but in line with one of the recommendations of the Royal Commission referred to later, the Board Secretariat became a separate department in 1967. The board was given powers, both general and detailed, for all matters of management in the public service including financial management.

The term *budget* in Canada has traditionally been used to refer to the revenue side of the ledger, and indeed the budget of the minister of finance is always of greatest interest in terms of the effects on taxes. The expenditure budget, to take a term that is acquiring some currency at the present time, is contained within a volume known as the Estimates, which is presented each year to Parliament. This is the product of the Treasury Board's efforts relative to a fiscal year, the final synthesis of its deliberations, and the reference point for its future progress. Because of the context of this paper, the word *budget* when used here will refer to expenditure, and the term *Estimates* will be used for the document in which the expenditure proposals are finally recorded for submission to Parliament.

Another aspect of the organization of the government of Canada having a bearing on the trend taken in the development of program budgeting is that it is a cabinet government where the power to make and influence decisions is in some respects much more centralized and concentrated than in a congressional form of government. This is particularly true with respect to the way things are done, that is, with respect to the procedures and the forms of government administration. The legislature has not often shown a marked interest in the accounting and procedural aspects of budgeting. This relative lack of interest may have delayed necessary change, since that one powerful source of stimulus for change was lacking. It has meant, however, that the bureaucracy has had greater freedom to make changes when moved to do so. Thus changes in forms of budgeting that appear to have been resisted by the legislatures of other countries have been carried through with relative ease.

Budgeting Practices Prior to 1965

The Treasury Board Secretariat first gave serious thought to program budgeting about the middle of the 1960s. At that time budgetary procedure ran along classical lines. To state it very briefly, the budgetary proposals presented by a department (or agency) were lengthy and detailed. They offered explanations of increased requirements for the next year for each of several line items or standard objects of expenditure within each of the larger organizational units of the department. The analysis of budgetary proposals of necessity tends to proceed in terms of the aggregates in which the budgetary proposals are cast; analysis by the Treasury Board tended, therefore, to be in terms of year-to-year increments in objects of expenditure.

A review of the Estimates from about 1900 on suggests that the essentials of this pattern were set about fifty years ago. There had, of course, been modifications prior to the adoption of program budgeting. Almost all of these consisted in raising the level of detail about which the budgetary decision process would be concerned—from the earlier extreme of concern about the salary of an individual employee to concern about the combined costs for a group of employees in the same job classification or from individual expenditures to classes of expenditures. These modifications were made inevitable in the face of the ever-growing volume of expenditures; they did not follow from any fundamental change in philosophy as to what should make up the budgetary process. It is not unfair to suggest that a desire to save money in the cost of printing the Estimates through reducing the number of pages was about as important a factor in such modifications as any change in philosophy.

In the 1950s and 1960s the Canadian governments of the day could afford to do what they wanted to do; they enjoyed many surpluses, and such deficits as were encountered were usually small. As the 1960s got well under way, however, the impact of relatively new welfare programs and various forms of assistance to the provinces began to be felt, frequently in quite large deficits. This, and the accompanying growth in the total volume of expenditures for all purposes, heightened dissatisfaction with traditional methods of deciding on the distribution of resources and created a desire for new approaches.

The Glassco Commission

It had become customary to attribute all change in management practice in the federal government of Canada over the last decade to a Royal Commission on Government Organization set up in 1960, known for the surname of its chairman as the Glassco Commission. The commissioners, who were drawn from outside the government, employed management consultants and others from the private sector to discharge the mandate given them, which was "to inquire into and report upon the organization and methods of operation of the departments and agencies of the Government of Canada and to recommend the changes therein which they consider would best promote efficiency, economy and improved service in the despatch of public business." If the commission were indeed the father of program budgeting, then program budgeting would seem to be the child of a very casual relationship. The commission, by its terms of reference, was told to direct all its passion to matters of efficiency and economy. The one reference to budgeting was concerned with "making more effective use of budgeting, accounting and other financial measures as means of achieving more efficient and economical management."

The report of the commission did indeed concentrate on matters of efficiency and economy. Like its counterpart the Hoover Commission in the United States, the Canadian Commission in its report never came to deal in a positive way with the stuff of program budgeting—objectives, planning, systems analysis and effectiveness, and the problems of resource allocation peculiar to government. There is an overall air of innocence about the recommendations of the commission that suggests the natural distaste of the business community for government and a belief that the adoption of sound business practices would cure the mismanagement the commission claimed to have discovered.

However, the commission did something most essential for the introduction of program budgeting: it provided a climate for change. The announcement, the investigations, and the report of the commission served to disturb a somnolent environment which if left undisturbed would have probably smothered any attempt at change. The activities of the commission set in motion a process of change which has yet to terminate. The momentum was given first by the announcement that there was to be a comprehensive investigation of the practice of government; it was increased by the probing questions of investigators as they sought to find out the "whys" of contemporary practice; and it was further stimulated by the report. In particular the recommendations of the commissioners relative to accounting practices led directly and indirectly to revolutionary changes in the methods of recording and reporting costs. Their newer methods answered at least some of the data needs of a program-budgeting system as the methods they replaced would have been unable to do.

First Steps

In any event, in this climate for change created by the Glassco Commission and in response to the evident inadequacies of existing prewar-style budgetary decison methods, the Treasury Board Secretariat began in 1965 to study what was known of program budgeting in the United States. The concentration of program-budgeting interest in the defence field in the United States was found disappointing, since defence expenditures bore a much smaller relationship to total expenditures in Canada. However, the essential idea of gathering costs according to operations or services (programs) carried on in pursuit of some stated objectives was seen as being of value regardless of the field of application. It was certainly deemed more appropriate to contemporary needs than the gathering of costs according to objects of expenditure and organizational units alone. The necessity for a program structure, for definite objectives for the

74

programs in this structure, for projections of program costs beyond the new year—all these aspects as well were seen as valuable and capable of adaptation to the Canadian environment.

Since what was desired was a budgeting system to apply to all departments and agencies, not just defence, the possibilities for the application of the more esoteric methods of quantitative analysis were difficult to judge in the Canadian context. They were made the subject of some inconclusive special studies while implementation of the other aspects was begun.

A half-dozen departments were asked to put forward, by the spring of 1966, and for the fiscal year 1967-68, five-year forecasts of their expenditure requirements for each of what they conceived to be their programs, to state objectives for these programs, to present cost breakdowns in terms of homogeneous program elements called activities, to present supporting analysis containing some numbers, to supply tentative measures of effectiveness and, in general, to follow the "book" as it was then understood. In the following year this procedure was enjoined upon about twenty six departments and agencies, and in the next year and all subsequent years upon all departments and agencies who draw resources from the treasury through the formal budgetary process. It is probable that consideration will be given to increasing the scope of the system to cover some or all of the self-sustaining fund operations and the corporations owned by the government whose financing lies outside the scope of the program-budgeting system.

This attempted universality of application, this concentration on the allocation of the whole store of resources among competing programs, and an intimate linkage with the legislative appropriation process are the key elements in the approach to program budgeting taken by Canada thus far. These elements have been dominant almost from the first and have been responsible for the noticeable progress made, though doubtless the concentration on universality and the accommodation to the appropriation process has necessitated some sacrifice in sophistication.

However, beginning with the fiscal year 1970-71, the expenditure budget laid before Parliament is to all appearances a "program budget" in one sense of the term; that is, the appropriation structure of the legislature in providing funds is exactly the program structure followed by the departments. The information carried in these Estimates is in terms of program breakdowns. The Estimates also contain statements of program objectives and description of the activities (subprograms or program elements) that are supposed to indicate what is to be done towards the attainment of these objectives. Each department or agency has to have at least one distinct parliamentary appropriation (vote, in Canadian terminology) and it was accepted that the appropriation structure and the program structure should coincide. For this reason and for other accommodations made to align the program and appropriation structure accommoda-

75

tions whose descriptions here would consume an inordinate amount of space, the Estimates show some very peculiar "programs." In the main, however, the program structure is a sensible division of the operations of departments and agencies into aggregates for which objectives can be developed, which can be costed, and whose pertinence to national goals appears both significant and worthy of assessment. There is much to be done in the way of clarifying the objectives that appear in Estimates, and there are programs that may owe more to long-standing organizational influences than fundamental analysis. But improvements are made regularly, and it would appear that what might be called the presentational side of program budgeting, as opposed to the analytic side, is well advanced and likely to make much more progress.

The organization of government into departments and agencies is a product of current and past considerations that are only partly the same as those which would dictate a good program structure. Thus the structure of departmental programs has certain deficiencies which in the Canadian approach have been compensated for by the construction of another classification into the functions of government. *Government* programs are distinguished from *departmental* programs: Two more activities related to the same objectives of government are considered to belong to the same functional program, though each may belong to programs of different departments.

It would be unfortunate if the case for this approach were overstated, but from a central analytical point of view, the adoption of a classification of expenditures that ignores the distribution of operational responsibilities in an attempt to group together all costs of government associated with the same objectives, explicit or implied, has served to lend greater clarity to resource allocation. The functional classification which brings together under one heading all programs that have to do with, say, health and welfare and under another heading all programs having to do with economic development and support, does not allow for inspired or mindless decisions that the growth in one case shall be precisely, say, 75 percent over the previous year and in the other, say, 180 percent. However, projections of the trend in the many social-welfare programs in which the federal government is the sole agent or in which it is the principal source of funds to the provinces can promote searching inquiries as to whether there is the proper mix between these two main drives and can stimulate inquiry as to whether the projections in the welfare area are capable of being realized unless something more can be projected in the economic area.

Analysis—Progress and Prospects

It is not possible to offer as much evidence of progress in analysis as has been offered of progress in the presentational aspects of program budgeting. There are two kinds of evidence for analysis: published papers and good decisions that can be shown to have been arrived at on the basis of analysis.

Dealing with the first of these, the restrictions of confidentiality in the Canadian government do not inspire the publication of either good or bad analysis regarding important decisions. Dealing with the second kind of evidence, it is not possible, at least for this writer, to cite a clearly documented instance where a decision to undertake program A rather than program B or C was arrived at on the basis of analysis alone or even on the basis of analysis predominantly.

The importance of analysis was stressed every bit as much as the importance of good program structures in the first, and to date the principal, Canadian policy paper on the subject, "Planning Programming Budgeting Guide." A number of officers were added to the Board Secretariat because of their qualifications to promote analytic methods, and departments were encouraged to establish small units of analysts. In a few instances, Treasury Board officers and cooperative departmental representatives have brought cost-benefit analysis to bear in a realistic way at the project level, and it may be demonstrated in some of these instances that decisions of more than trifling moment were at least supported by the findings of the analysts. Nor have all the areas of application penetrated so far been within that traditional purview of cost-benefit analysis, natural resource development.

Speaking subjectively, mostly for lack of evidence to the contrary, it would appear that the immediate impediment to progresss in analysis is the general absence from departmental budget-making circles of junior officers qualified to conduct analysis and senior officers who really want it conducted. Program decisions to spend money for this rather than for that appear to evolve mainly in a qualitative way, from general policy statements of the government and through departmental papers where numbers serve at best to bolster decisions already reached intuitively.

However, the prognosis is generally favourable. The program structure evolved so far is in a constant state of improvement through the joint efforts of the departments and the Treasury Board Secretariat. This structure provides a framework in which decisions are made and within which questions are asked. The questions are answered only in part by the flow of information called for at each of the several states of the budgetary cycle. The process of getting the information together in the departments and of examining it at the centre had laid bare the weakness of some implicit assumptions on which some programs have been based. Thus objectives are being reexamined, and the need for new information is being exposed. The realization of the need to use new and old information more profitably through analysis should follow.

Although it is fair to say that the Canadian system was designed for and has been operated in the interests of the centre rather than for the departments, it does not appear to be regarded unfavourably by the departments. At progressively higher levels as the years pass, more senior officers of departments are becoming involved in the system. Most have come to view the spring Program

Forecast Submission not as a tiresome imposition of the Treasury Board but as the key document for the presentation and assessment of departmental plans. Again, annoying gaps in knowledge are exposed to view and the arbitrariness of basic program assumptions are brought to light in a way that creates a demand for analysis.

Conclusions

A rate of progress can only be assessed in terms of the time consumed. The process by which resource-allocation decisions are reached in Canada began to move in the direction of a program-budgeting system in 1966. The first fiscal year to feel any effect was 1968-69, and at this time of writing late in calendar year 1970, the latest year affected is fiscal year 1971-72, beginning in April 1971. This points up an important restraint on the speed of progress. Most of the fundamental decisions on the budgetary allocation for a given year have to be made almost twelve months in advance in the beginning of that year. The *design* of the process by which these decisions are going to be reached has to be completed months in advance of that. The design of a budgetary cycle for a fiscal year has then to start some eighteen months in advance of the beginning of the year.

In the period since 1966 there have been only three opportunities to change the process ahead of the time at which fundamental decisions are made, and in that period the process has been changed out of all recognition from the one that preceded it insofar as the presentational aspects are concerned. At least the same period of time may be required to see the fruition of the growing interest in analysis that is becoming apparent at this time.

CHAPTER 10

Development of Program Budgeting in the Canadian Department of National Defense

by J. C. Arnell

Assistant Deputy Minister (Finance)
Department of National Defence
Ottawa, Canada

The development of a program-budgeting system for the federal government of Canada has already been described by B. A. MacDonald (Chapter 9). The Department of National Defence, like all other components of the Canadian federal public service, has been attempting to implement this system as it is being defined. In as major an undertaking as this introduction of a new concept of management decisions, it is probably more difficult to modify an existing system of programming than to introduce an entire new system. Such has been the situation in the defence department.

Until the unification of the Royal Canadian Navy, the Canadian Army, and the Royal Canadian Air Force into one Canadian Armed Force in 1964, each service had undertaken planning, programming and budgeting activities on its own. These tended to be unrelated one to another, rather than parts of a whole. As a result, it could be said that there was no overall defence programming. A further problem was the fact that these programs were capital-oriented and concerned themselves almost exclusively with recording plans for the acquisition and operation of new capital equipment. Individual service programs tended to identify a need for more capital equipment, which in turn would require additional resources to operate it—more than there was any hope of funding out of their likely share of each year's budget. As a result, many "program decisions" were taken on the basis of financial constraints in the course of assembling the annual budget, instead of at an earlier phase where they would have been based on the priority of individual requirements.

At the time of the integration of the armed services, it was accepted as a matter of principle that the preparation of the annual budget should flow directly from a properly approved five-year program. To this end, provision was made for an integrated defence program which was intended to display every component of the new force structure requiring financial support.

As might be expected, the first attempt to construct this single program consisted of the consolidation of the rather incompatible existing programs of the three armed services. If there had been any doubt beforehand, it soon became clear when this was done that the three individual programs bore very little resemblance to the balanced defence program that should have existed if the Canadian Armed Forces were to meet the requirements of current defence policy. The most striking thing about this new document was that it was little more than a detailed statement of the time-phased plans for the procurement of new capital equipment. No attempt had been made to relate either personnel or operating and maintenance costs to capital equipment. Since this had not been done in the previous three service programs, it was just not possible to do anything more at the time of integration, even though these costs represented about 80 percent of the total defence budget.

Program Budgeting Steps

The obvious first step towards program budgeting, therefore, was to analyze the pattern of resource consumption, both manpower and money, in the newly integrated Canadian Armed Forces. Only in this way would it be possible to determine actual priorities assigned to different military activities at various levels of command. There was considerable pressure to use the functional command structure, which had resulted from integration, as the basis of this analysis. This was resisted on two grounds. The first and obvious one was that field commands were administrative entities, whose purpose was to ensure that approved operational plans were fulfilled and whose structure could be changed without necessarily changing the activity pattern. The second and more subtle one was the desire to identify the costs of all support activities. In the past, many such activities have been administered by the operational commands without their resource costs ever being properly identified. For example, the three military colleges in Canada have each been supported administratively by a different command, none of which could give a complete accounting of the money or the manpower expended in this educational activity.

For this analysis, a list of ten operational and twenty support activities was drawn up. On the operational side, there were such activities as air defence, mobile general-purpose ground combat, and maritime warfare surveillance, while the support activities had such divisions as command, control and administration, material supply services, and officer training. Each of these activities was made up of a number of military entities, such as the major fleet units, squadrons of aircraft, battalions of infantry, and radar stations on the operational side; and the service colleges, supply depots, bases, communications squadrons and recruiting units on the support side. These were each identified by unit name and were considered the smallest subdivisions or program elements of the Canadian Armed Forces organization. These program elements were all input-oriented in that they reflected what resources were available for assignment to a given activity. For this reason, the activities themselves were called *capability activities.*

Because the commands are functional, the operational activities can, in the main, be equated to them. The rest of the activities cover those areas of resource allocation which in one way or another are necessary in support of military operations, but which in the past have received little scrutiny or analysis as to level of resource consumption. For departmental management, it was considered essential to have the same amount of detail regarding the programmed resource consumption in these latter activities as had traditionally been maintained for operations. In other words, we recognized the need to manage the man-oriented activities as well as the equipment-oriented ones. This was to be achieved by the subdivision of the total available resources into the program elements as described above.

Forward Planning

There are now approximately nine hundred separate military entities or program elements, each of which has a table of organization for both military and civilian personnel in the establishment with respect to rank or grade and numbers, together with a corresponding table of authorized equipment. These program elements can be costed with respect to personnel, operations and maintenance, and capital. Once these basic data have been assembled, they are useful for forward planning, for programming, and for financial-management analyses.

Even while the capability activities were being analyzed in order to establish the existing resource allocations, it was appreciated that a new approach must be made to forward planning. Because armed forces are maintained by a government to be available for a military emergency, there are really no recognizable limits or constraints as to the size of the force or the amounts of equipment that should be provided for each task which can be identified as a possible requirement in an emergency. Thus, a defence program will always tend to be badly over-programmed unless very specific higher-level policy guidance provides the constraints necessary to hold the program within acceptable resource limits. These involve subjective judgment as to the degree of risk entailed by not providing for a given eventuality within the time-frame of the program. Thus, the policy guidance should establish the required level of output capabilities for which the military force structure is to be designed and resources allocated.

J.C. Arnell

The development of policy guidance is particularly important for a middle power such as Canada, situated as it is between the two nuclear superpowers. The major military threat is that of a large-scale nuclear attack on North America, and is the direct result of Canada's geographical location. In addition, Canada's centres of population, industry, and commerce logically form part of the major target areas for such an attack on North America, because most of them are concentrated along the St. Lawrence and in the lower Great Lakes regions. Virtually all of them are close to the Canada—United States border, so that the two economies are well integrated.

Faced with the impossibility of providing for the defence of Canada unilaterally, it has been the policy of the government to cooperate with the United States in the joint defence of North America since the Ogdensburg Agreement of 1940 and to provide forces for collective security in Western Europe as part of the same defence since the signing of the North Atlantic Treaty in 1949. This approach to defence opens up the problem of what kinds and levels of armed forces it is appropriate for Canada to contribute in each instance. Analysis can be of assistance in delineating current and future military threats, by indicating the risks associated with various military responses to these threats by the alliance as a whole, and by assessing the costs and the military effectiveness of particular force elements and specific weapons and equipment. There is, however, no way in which either the desirable level or the structure of Canada's armed forces can be derived by such analysis, since the major and only significant direct military threat to Canada is one with which Canada is incapable of dealing.

In this situation, Canada has a choice of leaving the deterrence of nuclear war entirely in the hands of the superpowers, or of contributing to this deterrence through collective security arrangements in those areas which are appropriate. As participation is the preferred policy, the posture Canada adopts depends on such considerations as the share of national resources to be devoted to Canadian security, the degree to which the government wishes to be involved in the development of collective strategic policies and plans, and sovereignty considerations with respect to the presence of allied forces on Canadian territory.

In the past, the provision of adequate policy guidance was the weakest link in our management system. This weakness was not so much from intent as from a lack of appreciation of the importance of such guidance by management. In developing this aspect of programming, we have been very conscious of the outside influences during the formative stages of a defence program. An example of this is to be found in the recent review of defence policy by the Canadian government. In support of such a review the officials of the departments concerned had to provide information that reflected a tempering of diplomatic concepts and national concerns with an infusion of military realities to produce viable defence forces which were acceptable to the government within the framework of political facts and financial considerations.

Policy Guidance

Quite apart from special policy reviews such as that just mentioned, there is a continuing need for reexamination of existing plans and policy at the official level, both within the department and between relevant agencies. For both these types of reviews, it is important that the necessary guidance for military planning is meaningful to politicians, specialists in foreign affairs, military men, and treasury officials alike. Such guidance is drawn from existing defence policy and is developed within the Department of National Defence, in consultation with the Department of External Affairs and other agencies. The provision of policy guidance must be one of the initial steps in decision-making, as it is the key to the whole process. Its nature is such that it requires the personal involvement of top management; it simply cannot be left to staff action.

The first step in developing policy guidance for the Canadian Armed Forces was to establish the military objectives against which the programming was to be done. As the 1964 White Paper on Defence had discussed the future roles for the military, it was a simple matter to draw on this document and derive the following six objectives from it:

1. Ensuring internal security in peacetime
2. Ensuring territorial integrity in peacetime
3. Contributing to North American defence
4. Supporting defensive alliances
5. Supporting UN peace-keeping activities
6. Providing military assistance.

The nature of these objectives was such that they only identified the broad fields within which some military operational capability was required. The next step was to specify the tasks to be undertaken to give meaning to these objectives. Thirteen tasks or required capabilities in output terms were identified. Typical of this list were: aid to the civil power, surveillance of coastal waters, and countering bomber attack.

It is important that the tasks selected can be weighed militarily against the political judgments which are inherent in the decisions respecting objectives. Some quantification is necessary at this stage in order to indicate the output level against which to do force planning. For example, some indication of the anticipated threat to internal security must be given in order to establish the probable size of military response which might have to be provided in the event of an urban outbreak. Similar guidance is required for each of the tasks listed.

This is as far as we believe that the guidance step should be carried, because in effect this list of tasks is really the output capabilities with required response levels against which the military staffs have to produce a series of realistic and achievable force structures. The force components which will be developed by this process are the lowest level within the military planning function and which, when consolidated, produce the structure of the Canadian Armed Forces. As such, this is the second half of the interface between the required capabilities (tasks) arising out of the policy guidance and the actions necessary to meet them. This is the point at which the thought pattern must change from being *output (program)-oriented* to being *input (performance)-oriented*–that is, from being concerned about "what is to be done" to considering "how to do it." It is important that the force structure planning at this stage be undertaken in direct relationship to the required output and without allowing either existing force structures or other outputs to influence the result.

Once the forces required to meet all the stated tasks have been defined, it is necessary to examine the extent to which these forces will actually be provided in the program. It is recognized that in peacetime, military forces have unused potential and are therefore available to undertake more than one task, provided the requirements do not occur simultaneously. In this way, an actual peacetime military force can be assigned the responsibilities of an emergency force two to three times its size. Of course, in the event of an emergency requiring the full-time use of the force in one or more roles, augmentation plans must be implemented to provide the additional force to meet those other roles previously assigned to the committed force. It is important that size and cost of this additional force be readily available, for it forms part of the cost to the government of meeting the emergency role.

Program Budgeting in Operation

Concurrent with the above work on the defence program, major changes were being made in the form in which the government's annual budget (the Estimates Blue Book) was to be presented to Parliament. The first step in this direction occurred in February 1969, when the Blue Book for fiscal year 1969–70 was tabled in Parliament in the traditional format of standard objects of expenditure and when a few weeks later individual departmental budgets were tabled in the planned new form of estimates showing the same budgetary figures recast into programs and activities. This was done to prepare the members of Parliament for the following year when the actual change was to occur.

The preparation of this document for the Department of National Defence came at the end of a protracted debate with members of the Treasury Board Secretariat (who are responsible for the government's overall financial program) regarding the program and activity structure for the department as a whole, and for the Canadian Armed Forces in particular. At first, the Treasury Board staff were insistent that the Canadian Armed Forces' activities should be allocated among six separate programs, each of which would be funded from a different parliamentary vote. These programs were to be similar to the objectives already listed–support of NATO, defence of North America, etc. We were able to convince them that the multiple nature of the tasking of the military forces was such that under their scheme a sudden change in the international scene, such as the ejection of United Nations Emergency Force from Egypt a few years ago, could result in such forces no longer being eligible to draw funds from the parliamentary vote in which they were included and, with no other provision having been made for them, it might not be possible even to pay the salaries of such troops when they returned to Canada without supplementary funds being voted by Parliament for this purpose. As a result, it was agreed that for at least the next few years the costs of the Canadian Armed Forces would be met out of a single appropriation, which meant treating all military activities as one program.

As a result, this single program was subdivided into six *program activities*, four of which reflected the roles of the Canadian Armed Forces as already discussed, while the other two covered general support services and a statutory item providing for servicemen's pensions. This program represented all of the departmental budget of $1,815 million, except for some $77 million. These residual monies were related to five distinct civilian activities within the department and were consequently identified as separate programs, each with its own parliamentary appropriations. These were:

Departmental Administration (Management and Control)
Defence Research
Mutual Aid (in support of NATO)
Civil Emergency Measures
Defence Construction (1951) Limited.

This last program related to a crown corporation which manages the capital construction program for the Canadian Armed Forces.

In the 1970–71 Blue Book of Estimates, the program activities of the Canadian Armed Forces' share of the budget and the allocated funds were as follows:

Canadian Security ($753.5 million)
North American Security ($207.2 million)
Military Contributions to NATO ($111.6 million)
Support of International Peace-keeping, etc. ($12.9 million)
General Military Support Services ($553.1 million)
Military Pensions, etc. ($221.0 million)

The development of this new form of budgetary presentation has pointed up the differences in the type of information sought by different levels of management. At the governmental level, considerations of defence tend to revolve around two aspects of the subject. One is that concern about the magnitude of Canada's defence effort is generally related to the size of defence expenditures, with little or no reference being made to the actual size or type of forces maintained. The other is that the discussion is always in terms of roles—withdrawal of troops from Europe, maintenance of air defence, increase in national surveillance, etc. Thus it makes sense to present the defence budget to parliament in the new form discussed above. It is imperative that the programming system be responsive to the need to provide information regarding the use made of our financial resources, our manpower, and our physical plant in these terms.

On the other hand, for the purely departmental purposes of operational planning, personnel management, control of operations, and the like, it is desirable to subdivide the total program into performance-oriented operational and support activities. This permits the assessment of the forces allocated to each in terms of performance objectives. Again, the programming system must be responsible to the information needs of this approach.

Although it may appear that these two approaches are conflicting, actually they are two aggregations of the program elements for two quite different purposes. For example, during the 1968 defence policy review, the government was concerned about Canada's total contribution to NATO defences in Europe and was interested in the amount of money required by the Air Division and Mechanized Brigade Group based in Europe to cover all the activities necessary to maintain a high degree of operational capability; it was not interested in how that capability was achieved nor in the individual efficiencies of the contributing elements which supported this capability. However, within the department, given the responsibility for maintaining such forces in Europe, we must be able to examine each contributing activity separately, from the recruiting organization through the training and logistics streams to the actual operations in Europe, and to measure the success of each in meeting the objectives of the relevant program elements on a basis of their individual performance.

The real test of these programming concepts came when the Prime Minister outlined the new defence policy on April 3, 1969, following an exhaustive policy review. While the roles assigned to the Canadian Armed Forces in the 1964 White Paper were all retained, their priority was changed. The new policy assigned first priority to the protection of Canadian sovereignty in place of contributing to collective security in Europe, with the joint defence of North America in cooperation with the United States being retained as second priority. This type of policy change created more difficulty in rewriting the policy guidance than a brand-new policy would have done.

Defining the role of the military in something as intangible as the protection of sovereignty tends to be subjective and input-oriented. Under the National Defence Act, the department has the responsibility of providing for Canadian security. While this is an essential ingredient of sovereignty, sovereignty itself is much broader and includes the maintenance of law and order and the control of access and movement in Canadian airspace, on the land, and on or under the territorial or adjacent waters. Much of this latter is exercised through the promulgation of the necessary regulations and the provision of the means to ensure compliance. This is normally done through civil agencies, which are assisted and backed up, when necessary, by military security forces. These latter are equipped to detect and identify possible intruders into the airspace and waters of national interest.

Summary

It was clear that with its new policy the government was seeking an increased military input in an area that traditionally was the responsibility of such federal departments as fisheries, transport, and the Royal Canadian Mounted Police. However, there was no indication given as to what new output capabilities were being looked for from the Canadian Armed Forces. The immediate reaction of the military was to attempt to restate operational priorities, which appeared to be in line with the new policy, before any analysis had been done to determine whether new outputs were required and if so, at what level. This showed once again how subjective or input-oriented military-force structure planning tends to be unless adequate policy guidance outlining required levels of output capabilities is provided beforehand.

To help develop this policy guidance, a joint working group of representatives of the defence department and the central agencies concerned with overall policy was established to clarify the role of the Canadian Forces in the protection of Canadian sovereignty. Although the working group accepted that the April 3, 1969 government policy statement had identified four roles in order of priority, it recognized that these were mutually supporting, so that a given force structure could meet the needs of two or more of them on an "as available" basis. This group was able to agree on a program objective and subobjectives related to the sovereignty role against which output capabilities could be developed in consultation with the civil agencies involved and recommended to the government as the basis of the future defence program.

With this work completed, we are once again confronted with a wide range of choices in the types and amounts of military capability which should be maintained to meet this newly defined objective and subobjectives related to sovereignty. As this is written, an attempt is being made to apply some quantification to the required capabilities in order to permit the modification of the five-year program forecast to reflect the new direction of defence policy.

Incomplete though our system of program budgeting is at the present time, it has proved its value in a period of great change in Canadian defence. This change was not only one of priorities, but also one of force structure. Program reductions have been implemented which will result in significant reductions in military and civilian personnel strengths over two or three years. Without the fledgling system it would not have been possible to define the necessary changes in force structure in any realistic way to meet these reductions. The principles of the system as outlined above thus have been tested and found to be valid, and we are now moving towards its full implementation.

CHAPTER 11

Planning-Programming-Budgeting in the United Kingdom Central Government

by J. M. Bridgeman

H. M. Treasury
London

The development of planning and resource allocation systems under the title "PPB" has been but one of a number of developments in the improvement of the control of public expenditure in the United Kingdom in the last fifteen years. Indeed, the role of PPB systems has so far been relatively modest. On the other hand, some of the other developments, notably the public-expenditure survey system, have applied at least some of the concepts advocated by the proponents of PPB systems, and it is necessary to have some understanding of these wider developments if our work on PPB is to be put into context. This paper therefore outlines those developments before describing the approach which has been adopted to PPB, and the results which have been achieved so far.

There are of course numerous differences between the political and administrative structures in different countries which will influence the way in which their systems of public-expenditure control develop. But there are three points where the United Kingdom differs from some other countries, notably the United States, and which have had a considerable influence on the way in which our public-expenditure system has developed. First, while Parliament has to vote the annual Estimates, the party system in the House of Commons is such that it is virtually unknown for Parliament to amend the Estimates put to it by the government. This is not to say that Parliament does not have a significant influence on the pattern of public expenditure, but it is exercised in various indirect ways at the formative stage of determining the pattern of public expenditure, and not through variations in the government's proposals once they have been laid before the House. Second, successive Governments since World War II have used taxation and public expenditure as instruments in their management of the level of demand in the economy. Finally, central government has sufficient influence over expenditure by local government (in part because of the arrangements for grants from central government to local government, and in part because of more direct controls) that it can realistically plan for the total of central and local government expenditure and not just for its own expenditure. (Chapter 12 on programme budgeting in the Department of Education and Science develops this point further.)

Development of the Public-Expenditure Survey System

During the 1950s there was increasing and fairly widespread dissatisfaction with the existing systems of control and public expenditure linked to the annual Estimates. In particular, it was felt that the annual Estimates provided an inadequate time scale for the consideration of programmes with long lead times, and that there was no comprehensive framework within which expenditure could be judged as a whole. Individual programmes still tended to be considered "on their merits".

A number of steps were taken during the 1950s to meet the shortcomings in particular areas. From the mid-1950s a major roads programme extending over several years was developed. Subsequently all public sector investment programmes were examined together and, in order to put these investment reviews into perspective, from 1957 onwards the first steps were taken in developing a five-year economic assessment for the economy as a whole. From 1958 five-year defence costings were introduced; these were later extended to ten years. But the integration of the individual developments did not happen until after the report of the Plowden Committee.

The Select Committee on Estimates undertook in 1957-58 an examination of the Treasury control of expenditure. This drew public attention to some of the shortcomings just referred to and called for the appointment of an independent committee to carry out a more detailed and more expert inquiry. This recommendation led the government to set up the Committee on the Control of Public Expenditure under Lord Plowden in the summer of 1959. A major recommendation of the report, published in July 1961, was that: "Decisions involving substantial future expenditure should always be taken in the light of public expenditure as a whole, over a period of years, and in relation to the prospective resources."[1]

This report led to the development of the present public-expenditure survey system. Under this, departments have to put forward each year their estimates of the cost of carrying out existing agreed policies for the next five years costed at current prices. The totals so arrived at are set against an assessment of the likely course of the economy over the next five years, in order tq provide a framework

---

[1] *Control of Public Expenditure,* Her Majesty's Stationery Office, London, Cmnd 1432.

for decisions by the government on the future totals of public expenditure, on their allocation between the main expenditure programmes and on particular policy decisions which will have significant effect on that allocation. These decisions result in a five-year expenditure programme. In general, the decisions on the first three years are in more specific terms than those for the final two years.

The system has been progressively improved and developed. For example, the inputs into the various programmes are classified by the economic category—for example, transfer payments, purchases of goods and services—so that allowance can be made for the fact that the same amount of expenditure in different programmes can have a markedly different impact on the economy. The forecasts now include a "wedge" for contingencies to allow room for changes in policy or costs which cannot be foreseen. Allowance is also made for the fact that, while the forecast is at constant prices on a common basis with the national income forecasts, there will be a movement in the relative prices involved in public-expenditure programmes and in the economy generally.

Two particular features of the system are worth noting. First, it covers all expenditure by the public sector regardless of the spending authority and how it is financed. This means that expenditure, by both central government and local government, is included, and that payments between the two cancel out. Second, the figures, when presented to the ministers, are organized into broad functional programmes, for instance, defence, transport, housing, and law and order. This functional classification crosses departmental boundaries to some extent, although account is taken of the needs of control and so of departmental organization. It would probably be fair to say that the functions relate to services rather than objectives, and so do not strictly meet the specification of a programme budget. Notwithstanding the fact that the classification is inevitably something of a compromise, it has been found that it does give ministers a useful basis on which to make major decisions about the size and pattern of future expenditure.

The public-expenditure survey process is itself internal to the government. However, on a number of occasions since 1963, brief descriptions of the future pattern of expenditure which would result from the government's decisions on the public-expenditure survey were published as White Papers. In 1969, the government announced that it intended to publish an annual public-expenditure White Paper, setting out in considerably greater detail than had been done in the previous ad hoc White Papers, the pattern of future public expenditure. The first such White Paper was published in December 1969. The purpose of the White Paper is to give Parliament, and also the public at large, an opportunity to understand the government's intentions for public expenditure and to debate them. The new government elected in June 1970 has said that it intends to continue this series, and the second White Paper was published in early 1971.

J.M. Bridgeman

The Introduction of PPB in the Ministry of Defence

As in the United States, defence was the first field in which PPB was applied in the United Kingdom. The forward-costing system in the Ministry of Defence mentioned above had been based on projection of inputs. But it was decided in 1964 that the Ministry should adopt a system similar to the McNamara system in the United States Department of Defense. The programme budget, known in the Ministry as a functional-costing system, was closely modelled on the programme structure then in use in the Pentagon. This can be seen from the following list of main programmes:

Nuclear Strategic Forces
European Ground Forces
General Purpose Combat Forces: Army
General Purpose Combat Forces: Navy
General Purpose Combat Forces: Air Force
Air Mobility
Reserve and Auxiliary Formations
Research and Development
Training
Production
Repair and Associated Research Facilities in the United Kingdom
Contingencies
Other support functions
Miscellaneous Expenditure and Receipts
Special Materials.

These programmes are divided into subprogrammes, groups, and programme elements in the normal way. There are over six hundred of the last, which consist of such things as Leander class frigates, infantry battalions in BAOR and Lightning Squadrons.

The functional-costing system itself rapidly proved its value in the series of reviews of defence policy which were carried out in the following years, primarily because the programme elements were in the same "language" as that used by the military planners; it therefore facilitated very considerably the costing of alternative force structures which were under consideration as part of the reviews.

The development of functional-costing systems was matched by the development of the use of analytical techniques to evaluate alternative weapon systems and other alternative defence strategies. Much of this work was carried out at the Defence Operational Analysis Establishment, which brought together analytical staff previously dispersed in the three service departments.

The Ministry of Defence functional-costing system and the associated analysis has been seen as a means of improving the department's own internal planning and resource allocation procedures. But the annual Estimates presented to Parliament are still basically on an input basis, because the Ministry consider it better to base their day-to-day budgetary control on inputs such as manpower, weapon systems, and central purchases of petroleum, than on a programme and subprogramme basis. However, when the Defence Estimates are presented to Parliament, the accompanying White Paper includes an analysis by programme and subprogramme of the expenditure in the coming year.

PPB in the Civil Departments

The public-expenditure survey system imposed on departments a requirement to look at the implications of their programmes and policies for expenditure at least five years ahead. It therefore encouraged them to improve their own internal planning and resource-allocation systems, and most did so in varying ways. Departments also developed work on cost-benefit analysis and cost-effectiveness analysis on a fairly large scale. However, by 1966 the success of the PPB system in the Department of Defense and of the functional costing system in the Ministry of Defence, and the knowledge that the United States federal government had decided to extend PPB to all civil programmes, caused the Treasury to consider how far such systems might usefully help the civil departments to carry further the developing of their planning and resource-allocation systems. We had already obtained some of the benefits which others looked for in PPB from our own public-expenditure survey system. Moreover, there was a considerable problem in that it was considered if a PPB system was to be of use to a department, it must have the same coverage as the programmes in the public-expenditure survey for which that department was responsible. This meant that it would have to cover the total public expenditure on those programmes irrespective of whether it was incurred by that department or autonomous bodies such as local authorities. It was therefore decided that there was insufficient evidence to justify the immediate introduction of PPB systems, either in a single department or right across the board, but that instead a number of feasibility studies should be carried out in departments before committing the departments concerned to the introduction of the system.

The first two studies were in the Home Office and in the Department of Education and Science. Both these studies started, given the Ministry of Defence analogy, with seeing how far it would be practicable to develop a planning and resource-allocation system on PPB lines for the departments as a whole. As Mr. Brierley will show in Chapter 12, this is the way in which the Department of Education system in fact developed. In the case of the Home Office, however, it proved desirable to adopt a rather different approach.

First, it was found on closer examination that the range of activities for which the Home Office was responsible was so wide, and many of the services were so relatively self-contained, that the advantages of a system going right across the Home Office would initially be very great. It was felt that analysis was likely to make little contribution to the allocation of resources between the Police Forces and the Fire Service, for example. It was therefore decided that the development work should be confined to one of the principal services for which the Home Office was responsible, namely the police.

Second, the relationship between individual police authorities (of which there are some forty in England and Wales), who provide a 50 percent grant towards the cost of their services, was such that the majority of resource-allocation decisions are taken by the chief constables of those authorities in relation to the particular need for their areas, rather than centrally. It therefore seemed that a PPB system could be of most value if it were developed initially for use in the local police authority areas, and only subsequently aggregated to provide a system at the national level. The aim in designing the system was to provide managers at the various levels in the police system with better information about the resources they controlled, bearing in mind both the cost of producing information and the dangers in quantification which can only too easily be concealed.

The system was first developed on an experimental basis with three police authorities. The programme structure which evolved divides expenditure into about eighty programme elements, grouped into nine major programmes.

1. Operational:
   Ground Cover
   Crime Investigation and Control
   Traffic Control
   Additional Services
2. Support:
   Management
   Training
   Support Services
3. Overheads:
   Pension
   Accommodation

The programme structure was related closely, but not exclusively, to the organizational structure of the force, in order to overcome the problems of allocation of joint costs. The programme elements were units of identifiable police activity or activities. This had the considerable advantage that it enabled costs to be identified in terms of centres of responsibility, and so that the system could also be used for management-control purposes. At the present time the system has either been introduced or is being introduced, in twelve police authorities. It is envisaged that it will be progressively extended to the others.

The first two feasibility studies have therefore been sufficiently encouraging to lead to the development of two somewhat different types of PPB system for the respective services, education and the police. But almost all the effort so far has gone into the development of the information base, mainly on the costs side. At this stage, therefore, we have not yet any substantial experience of the use of PPB systems for civil-expenditure programmes. The first local police authorities are now building up their experience of its use. As Mr. Brierley's chapter shows, we shall shortly be getting such experience at the national level for education. A significant amount of analytical work is also being done in both areas, but it is not at present directly linked into the PPB system.

Notwithstanding the absence of direct experience in the use of PPB systems for civil programmes, a number of departments have been sufficiently encouraged by the experience of the feasibility studies in these two areas to start studies of their own. The most recent, and probably the most significant, addition to the list is the Department of Health and Social Security in respect of the health and welfare programmes. This will include the totality of expenditure on the National Health Service.

Programme Analysis and Review

The Conservative party had shown considerable interest in new methods of planning and controlling public expenditure while they were in opposition. When they came to power in June 1970, the new government invited a small team of businessmen to carry out a study of a system for regular reviews of programmes embodying detailed analysis of existing programmes in relation to their objectives, and of major policy options on them. It was intended that the system should be a natural extension of the public-expenditure survey system, supporting the departmental submissions in that system. The Prime Minister announced in January 1971 that the government had now approved the introduction of a system of "Programme Analysis and Review" on lines proposed by the business team.

Reviews of expenditure programmes have, of course, been carried out in the past. Some of these reviews have been full and careful analyses which (where the subject matter allowed) considered the objectives of the particular area of policy, measured as accurately as possible the inputs of resources and outputs obtained, and presented alternative courses for decision with full supporting information about the effects of each of those courses. However, the new aspect of programme analysis and review, as the government is applying it, is that these features will be applied systematically and regularly to a wide choice of programmes from across the whole field of government. There will be closer consideration of the objectives of programmes, more attention to the relationship between expenditure incurred and returns obtained, and wider review of alternative ways of achieving the objectives. The aim is to get better value for public money and to achieve a more selective approach to the use of public expenditure.

95

CHAPTER 12

Programme Budgeting in Education in the United Kingdom[1]

by J. D. Brierley

Department of Education and Science
London

The development of programme budgeting in the United Kingdom central government has been described in the chapter just preceding. In brief, the successful use of this method in the United Kingdom Ministry of Defence prompted the question of whether the approach could be adapted for use by the civil departments, and a number of feasibility studies were mounted of which one of the first was in the Department of Education and Science.[2]

Two general considerations suggested education as a field in which the use of the programme-budgeting concept as a tool for the allocation of resources might be profitable. First, during the mid-1960s, major changes in the scale and scope of the responsibilities of government departments concerned with education brought about the assumption by education ministers in 1964 of responsibility for the universities, for civil science, and for government support of the arts. The second main factor was the sheer growth of central and local government spending on education (as defined in pre-programme-budgeting public-expenditure analysis) which increased, in money terms, from £1.2 billion in 1963-64 to some £2.3 billion in 1969-70; expressed as a percentage in relation to the gross national product, the increase is from 4.4 per cent in 1960-61 to 6.2 per cent in 1969-70.

---

[1]The educational responsibilities of the Department of Education and Science cover primary and secondary education in England, further education and teacher training in England and Wales, and university education in Great Britain. This study has been published as Education Planning Paper No. 1, *Output Budgeting for the Department of Education and Science,* Her Majesty's Stationery Office, London, 1970.

[2]This study has been published as Educational. Planning Paper No. 1, *Output Budgeting for the Department of Education and Science,* Her Majesty's Stationery Office, London, 1970.

J.D. Brierley

A planning branch was set up in the Department of Education and Science at the end of 1966 to look at, among other things, the longer-term planning of resource allocation in education. Work was begun on higher education, using developments in educational models. But it was soon realised that this work should be related to the whole field of education (but not include leisure activities and research, the other main areas of policy concerning the Department of Education and Science). The programme-budgeting system for education is now being developed but has not yet been adopted as a fully operational tool. The main purpose of this chapter is therefore to sketch the programme structure proposed and some of the main problems which have so far been encountered; two concluding paragraphs set the work in the more general context of policy formation.

The Structure Proposed

The new system would cover expenditure on education both by the central government and (which is by far the largest part) by local authorities. It needs to be stressed that in the United Kingdom education is a national service locally administered: Responsibilities are diffused widely among many organisations outside central government, and to a considerable extent initiative rests in the hands of local education authorities and other bodies. The role of the department itself is, to a large degree, to exercise a planning function. Its management role in the education system is small and its positive influence is exerted mainly in the longer term and by indirect means; for example, in authorising capital-investment programmes and in planning the supply of teachers for the schools. The programme-budgeting system for education has been designed as an instrument for planning, not for management, and the department's use of it would have to take account of the balance of responsibilities among its partners in the education service.

The programme structure devised for education, which is fully set out in *Output Budgeting for the Department of Education and Science*, may briefly be described as follows. A two-dimensional structure is proposed to analyse according to (1) the groups for whom education is provided and (2) different factors affecting changes in resource allocation. The first dimension is by educational level, the major programmes being:

1. Compulsory education
2. Nursery education
3. Education for the fifteen-year-old (this level is separated out because of the particular problems associated with the raising of the statutory school-leaving age to sixteen in 1973)
4. Education for the sixteen- to nineteen-year-old.

[1] *Op. cit.,* chapter 5 and appendix 2.

5. Higher education below degree level
6. Higher education courses leading to a first degree or equivalent
7. Postgraduate education
8. Educational infrastructure.

This grouping is related to age at the lower end and to educational level at the higher end, for instance first degree level courses and postgraduate work. The transition between these two types of grouping is made under "Education for the sixteen to nineteen-year-old": This major programme would cover both the level of work usually considered appropriate for the sixteen-to-nineteen age group and also work of a lower standard done by students over sixteen and work of a comparable standard done by students over 19.

The second dimension distinguishes the main factors affecting educational expenditure, as follows:

Existing Pattern and Scale of Provision[1]

Maintenance of the existing pattern and scale of educational provision at each level. This is further analysed into:

Provision for present numbers;

The additional provision required for population growth;

Provision (where appropriate) for additional resources required because of the movement of families from one area to another.

Cost Reduction

Reduction of the cost of provision while maintaining existing standards of output. This group is intended to cover savings in the use of resources achieved by increased efficiency without any reduction in standards.

Improvements such as

Increased participation: the resource consequences of changes in the proportions of given age groups receiving education.

Changes in the proportion of the group in different types of institutions or taking different subjects.

Changes in the standards and quality of accommodation.

Changes in staffing ratios.

The resulting two-dimensional programme structure is illustrated by the chart following.

A programme structure of this kind focuses attention on the main variables which determine changes in the amount of resources allocated to education. They range from exogenous factors such as population growth to factors which are the subject of specific policy decisions of ministers, such as improved staffing ratios in the schools. The system was designed to build on data which were already available to the department in one form or another. The forms of analysis in

---

[1]Total resources, expressed in money terms, actually available to sustain or develop the education service, or any part of it (or allocated in advance—future provision).

	Existing Pattern and Scale of Provision			Cost Reduction at Existing Standards	Improvements		
	Existing Numbers	Population Change	Population Shift		Participation Rates	Staffing Ratios	Etc.
Compulsory Education							
Nursery Education							
Education for the 15-year old							
Education for the 16- to 19-year old							
Higher Education (below 1st Degree)							
Higher Education (1st Degree)							
Postgraduate Education							

current use by institutions (nursery, primary, secondary and other schools, further education establishments, colleges of education,[1] universities) are provided for through additional dimensions derived from the same data base.

The programme structure described above is intended to be stable over a period of years and to act as a frame of reference for development of policies over that period. In any given period and at any given time, development of the education service tends to be shaped by a number of specified objectives. The structure which has been devised forms a framework for these special objectives of policy, and where appropriate they are identified in the fine structure (the third and fourth digits) of the programme elements. Whether separately identified or not, the resource implications of each such objective need to be brought out clearly in the relevant analyses. Such a structure adopts a rather different categorisation of objectives from that which one would expect to be mentioned in discussion among, for example, parents or teachers about the objectives of education. But it produces a system which makes sense for its purpose, which is to enable those responsible for policy to look more rationally than hitherto at the choices facing them, choices between the competing claims for the allocation of resources at the major strategic level.

Problem Areas

Three problem areas may be referred to: They relate to the information requirement, to some practical and conceptual problems of costing, and to the assessment of output.

The main difficulties on the information side have concerned the establishment of unit costs for pupils and students. With a system such as that proposed, based on educational levels rather than on institutions, the available data require considerable manipulation before they can be allocated among the various programmes, and additional information is required to guide the allocation of the basic data. It is in this process of allocation that many of the main problems arise; for example, in determining the proportion of university costs which is attributable to research rather than to teaching. Once available, the expenditure figures have to be reconciled with those used for the department's existing forecasts of educational outlays. Existing methods embody a variety of conventions which help to weld together different departmental forecasts into projections of public expenditure as a whole; but these conventions may be difficult to reconcile with other requirements of the programme-budgeting system. Looking ahead, it is hoped to transfer some of the work to computer operations and to increase the extension of the programme budget beyond the

---

[1] "Further education establishments" are institutions maintained by local education authorities which provide a wide range of courses, many of which lead to professional or vocational qualifications. "Colleges of education" are institutions of teacher education.

time scale of five years (its initial duration) since many educational trends and choices require a longer period for their full assessment.

The second main problem area, costing, covers a range of practical and conceptual problems which are discussed at some length in *Output Budgeting for the Department of Education and Science.*[1] Here it is sufficient to point out that difficulties arise in particular in relation to the measurement of the production foregone (opportunity cost): (1) because students are in education instead of in the labour force, (2) the measurement of other resource costs, (3) the establishment of marginal rather than average costs, and (4) the time at which certain types of cost (e.g., capital or superannuation) should be brought to account. More study is needed of this range of problems.

The assessment of the "output" of education raises difficult issues.[2] It is generally easy enough to set against the forecast expenditure figures projecting pupil or student numbers, staffing ratios, and the like. But numerical targets of this kind need to be related to a higher order of objectives of the education system. It is desirable, for instance, to understand the relationship between improving staffing ratios by so much and the results of such action as demonstrated by improvements in the pupils' achievements. The techniques of the rate of return approach to education and of cost-effectiveness analysis need also to be explored.

As first steps towards tackling these problems, the department and Her Majesty's Inspectorate are examining: (1) what would be involved in devising national tests of reading ability, (2) the earnings of a sample of qualified people in an attempt to relate earnings to higher education, and (3) a pilot cost-effectiveness study (mounted in association with a number of local education authorities) of the educational provision made for a particular age group. A main objective of this last study will be to examine the methodology of cost-effectiveness analysis in the educational situation.

Programme Budgeting in Education Planning

The programme budgeting system for education was designed on the understanding that it would help the department to play its part in the Public Expenditure Surveys and in longer-term studies of the use of resources by the public sector. The Public Expenditure Surveys include arrangements for the preparation of costed options for additional or reduced expenditure in different programmes; analysis within the programme budgeting system is seen as a way of developing and systematizing work on the costed options. Such work is well geared to the development of the new government's recently announced plans[3]

---

[1] *Op. cit.,* Section 4.3.

[2] But not necessarily more difficult in education than in many other areas.

[3] *The Reorganisation of Central Government,* Cmnd 4506, London, Her Majesty's Stationery Office.

for more comprehensive analysis and review of public-expenditure programmes in ways which will enable them to be related to the general strategy of the government.

Within the department, the programme-budgeting system for education is now being brought to an operational stage as a means of studying the problems involved in working out the scheme devised in the feasibility study. Much work has been done in developing a programme budget for education from the forecasts made for the 1970 Public Expenditure Survey. It is intended to continue this process and so develop a new tool for use in forthcoming revised departmental arrangements for resource planning. These are designed to integrate more closely (at the highest levels) the various elements in the department concerned with policy, finance, and planning.

In conclusion, it may be mentioned that a number of local authorities and one or two universities in the United Kingdom are studying the applicability of this method to their responsibilities. It is, however, too early at this time to report on these developments.

CHAPTER 13

Programme Budgeting
in English Local Government

by R. H. R. Armstrong
Professor, University of Birmingham
England

The growing interest in programming budgeting in English local government must be viewed in the context of a number of important developments. During the past five years a series of changes in approach to management in local government have occurred, all of which have contributed to creating a climate favourable to the introduction of radically new systems and techniques.

Until the Maud Report[1] on the management of local government was published, local government tended to be seen as a process of administering a collection of services imposed or permitted by statute, and having little or no connection with each other except that they were largely financed from a common source. By placing the emphasis upon the need for a unified decision-making structure, with the introduction of some means of coordinating policy-making and management, the report triggered off a wholesale reexamination by authorities[2] of their committee structures and decision-making processes. The most obvious changes came in the form of reductions in the number of committees and the appointment of chief executives responsible for the overall management of the authority's affairs.

Concurrent with the Maud Report was the Mallerby Report[3] on staffing in local government. Although the Mallerby Report had little direct effect on the activities of individual local authorities, it influenced the establishment of the Local Government Training Board. A major concern of the Training Board has

---

[1]*Management of Local Government,* Her Majesty's Stationery Office, London, 1967.
[2]See Glossary at the end of this chapter, p. 110.
[3]*Staffing of Local Government,* HMSO, London, 1967.

been management training. More recently, the Skeffington Report,[1] dealing with public participation in the planning process, and the Royal Commission Report on the reorganisation of local government have added to the ferment of discussion.

Added to these public events have been a number of other less publicized changes. Increased emphasis has been placed on the need for "rolling programmes" in certain areas, for example, road construction. Coupled with concern about the rate at which debt charges have been growing, this has led to a search for methods of forward financial planning and control. The professional associations, to which most senior officers belong, have been considering the relationship between their professional expertise and the managerial role.[2] The undertaking of work on programme budgeting by various departments of central government[3] has focused attention on the approach, partly because in some quarters there is a fear that it will increase central control over local government activities.

Approaches to Programme Budgeting

As might be expected, such a variety of influences has led to an equal variety in the approaches being adopted in introducing this new management tool. These approaches can be classified according to three sets of factors:

1. Origin of the initiative for the introduction of program budgeting—whether it has come from within the organization or is the result of intervention by an outside body such as consultants

2. The degree of formality, in terms of a programme structure, being given to the approach

3. The breadth of approach—whether an attempt is being made to cover the whole or only some section of the activities of the authority.

At this stage, however, it is impossible to attempt a final classification on the basis of these factors as most authorities describe what they are doing as either "experimental" or "a feasibility study." Whatever the final position may be, it is unlikely that these "experiments" and "feasibility studies" will leave the decision-making process in local authorities unchanged.

Each of the three factors mentioned will be discussed briefly to illustrate the contrasts that exist.

Initiatives

Up to the present, the contrast has been between those authorities

---

[1] *People and Planning*, HMSO, London, 1969.

[2] Correspondence and articles in the journal of the Institute of Municipal Engineers have contributed to a debate throughout 1970.

[3] For example, the work undertaken by the Home Office in relation to the police.

attempting an approach to programme budgeting as the result of an internal initiative and those where the impetus has come as the consequence of a report prepared by consultants. A further consideration entering into the situation may be of considerable importance in the future; that is the setting up of working parties by national bodies representative of given professional or other interests in local government to examine the programme budgeting approach.[1] The influence of the professional associations in local government is considerable, and could make this third source of initiative the most significant in the years ahead.

It is often difficult to pinpoint the exact origin of internal initiatives. While it is possible to guess at the origin in many instances, the source of the formal initiative may often have been dictated by "political" considerations. However, it seems significant that the majority of larger authorities adopting the approach are ones in which a chief executive has replaced the traditional clerk as the senior officer of the authority; this has been the case in the Greater London Council, Coventry and Gloucestershire. The appointment of a chief executive has often followed the setting up of a policy committee charged with the responsibility for determining the overall or long-term strategy to be adopted by the authority. Thus in these cases programme budgeting tends to be seen primarily as a means of securing coordination.

In other cases the fact that the authority is new has probably been an important influence. Thus in Teesside, formed by the amalgamation of a number of authorities, there was a felt need for a means of looking at the problems and activities of the new unit as a whole. This element is present in the case of the Greater London Council, which is still in the process of defining precisely the scope of some of its functions (e.g., strategic planning) and the nature of its relationship to the London boroughs.

Changes in political control during the past two years have been a factor insofar as a new party in power will tend to welcome new approaches with more enthusiasm than one which has been entrenched for a long period. The advent of the Conservative party as the majority party, after sometimes as long as thirty years in opposition in an authority, has given impetus to a search for ways of controlling the rate and extent of increases in expenditure.

The outstanding cases of the approach being introduced by consultants are the city of Liverpool and the London borough of Islington. In many other authorities there is evidence to suggest that consultants are moving increasingly towards suggesting the introduction of at least elements of a programme-budgeting approach.

[1]The Institute of Municipal Treasurers and Accountants has set up a working party to examine and report on the problems of introducing programme budgeting into local government.

Formality

Much of the discussion surrounding the introduction of programme budgeting into local government is concerned with the question of defining a programme structure for an authority. There are some people who would like to see a programme structure worked out centrally so that all authorities adopting the approach would be using a common basis. This attitude is not widespread, however.

No matter how formal the programme structure being adopted, there are few signs as yet of any attempts to replace the traditional financial budget with a new budget structure based on the programme heads, though in some cases this is the avowed objective. In both the Greater London Council and the city of Liverpool the stated intention is to run the two systems in parallel for a period of up to five years.

More significant in the case of Liverpool has been the introduction of organisational changes to match the programme structure adopted. Each programme area has been matched with a director responsible for planning and administration of the activities placed within it. The programme structure adopted by Liverpool is composed of seven heads: (1) Housing, (2) Education, (3) Personal Health and Social Services, (4) Environmental Health and Protection, (5) Transportation and Basic Services, (6) Recreation and Open Space, and (7) Arts and Culture. Four departments have been designated as central to all the activities of the authority and do not come within the programme structure. They are: Clerk and Chief Executive, Treasurer, Planning, and Land & Property Services.

The process of analysis is only starting in both London and Liverpool. In both cases a unit has been set up in the Clerk and Chief Executive's department to carry through analysis and maintain contact with programme directors.

Less formal is the approach in Gloucestershire, where the programme structure being worked out is seen as a basis for discussion and as the starting point for more detailed analysis of selected activities. No organisational changes have been made, but a working party composed of representatives from different departments has been set up to undertake the preliminary work.

In many authorities the approach is completely informal, depending entirely upon the fact that senior officers who have studied programme budgeting are using the approach to "inform" the reports they are preparing for submission to their committees. This approach is becoming very widespread and corresponds to an "issue paper" approach. It is particularly important in the smaller authorities where specialist resources are not available for large-scale efforts.

Breadth

The major dispute concerning the introduction of programme budgeting is over the question of whether the attempt should be made to cover all the authority's activities in the first place, or only selected areas. The formal approaches mentioned above favour the across-the-board approach.

Derbyshire has, by contrast, chosen to use the new method in an attempt to analyse the operation of their library service, and then to extend the approach, if it appears useful, into other areas of activity.

The across-the-board approach is favoured mainly because of the framework for coordination it provides, whereas the approach through a specific area is dictated by caution and a desire to see what resources may be needed and how quickly it is possible to gain some "pay-off."

In this connection, the Institute of Municipal Treasurers and Accountant's working party on programme budgeting leans towards an "across-the-board" approach in the first place, as it is considered desirable to provide a framework within which later studies in depth can be conducted.

Conclusion

Programme budgeting has already had more influence in local government than any other approach or technique introduced in the postwar period. It is too early to say whether this early flush of enthusiasm will produce lasting results. All the indications are that whatever the specific results from particular experiments may be, local government decision-making is undergoing a radical reappraisal in the light of the insights provided by the programme-budgeting approach.

(See Glossary on following page)

Glossary

Writing about programme-budgeting activities in English local government, I have used the language of our country. Since this may not be identical with usage in other English-speaking countries, or to the usage of persons outside these areas, the following glossary of terms is provided.

Authority—Unit of local government in England like city, county or school district in the United States.

Council—Total body of elected representatives for any one authority.

Committee—A group of elected representatives responsible to the council for specific aspects of the authority's activities.

Clerk—An official who is chief legal officer of an authority.

Senior officer—An official who is professionally qualified and responsible for advising committees and elected members. Co-equal to the clerk in professional terms.

Official—A paid officer as contrasted to an elected member. He is a professional and, in United States practice, could be called a civil servant.

Professional organization—Examples are the Institute of Municipal Treasurers and Accountants, the Institute of Municipal Engineers, the Society of Town Clerks. Their closest counterparts in the United States are the American Bar Association or the American Medical Association, for example.

CHAPTER 14

An Appraisal
of Program Budgeting in France

by Patrick Bréaud

Inspecteur des Finances, Direction de la Prevision,
Ministere de l'Economique et des Finances

Jean-Louis Gergorin

Ecole Nationale d'Administration [1]

To understand the motives for the introduction of program budgeting in France, it is necessary to look at some general features of the French bureaucratic system, and also to summarize the National Planning System. The latter was a first step toward the rationalization of the decision-making process in government.

Some Specific Aspects of French Public Administration [2]

Important characteristics of the French bureaucratic systems are: (1) its high degree of centralization and the important part played by the Ministère des Finances; (2) its management by professional civil servants who are carefully selected once and for all at an early age and are separated into legal categories called "corps", each corps monopolizing specific administrative tasks; (3) its centralization—that is, the local governments have very limited power since practically all decisions are taken in Paris or by the Prefets (the government delegates in the provinces).

The most significant feature of the government administration in Paris is the predominance of the Ministère des Finances over the other Ministères. The Ministère des Finances include Direction du Budget (Bureau of the Budget),

[1] The authors want to thank especially Michel Crozier, Centre de Sociologic des Organizations, for his advice and guidance.
[2] See Michel Crozier, *The Bureaucratic Phenomenon,* University of Chicago Press, 1964.

111

Direction du Trésor (Treasury), Direction des Impôts (Tax Division), Direction de la Comptabilité Publique (Public Accounting Division) and Direction du Commerce Interieur (Domestic Commerce Division). The predominance of the Ministère des Finances results from tradition on the one hand and the part it plays in the budgetary process on the other. It is due also to its supervision of the disbursement of obligation authority by the operating agencies.

The budgetary process in France is not too different from the American one. The operating agencies send requests on what they consider to be their needs to the Direction du Budget and the latter discusses each proposal with them. In fact, the discussion is limited to new proposals, since the so-called "services votés" (appropriations voted in former budgets) are only rarely reviewed.

A lively bargaining takes place between the two contending parties. The operating agencies usually ask for more than they really expect and the Direction du Budget has a propensity to refuse systematically all new proposals. The reason is that available resources are very small indeed compared to the total of new budget demands. In case of unresolved conflict, the decision is taken first by the Directeur du Budget, and then by the Ministre des Finances. For very important matters the issue may go to the Prime Minister, and ultimately to the President of the Republic.

These discussions often can be said to be near-blind ones. The criteria of choice are not rational, since the input classification of the budget structure does not afford a clear idea of the objectives, and the bargaining mechanism favours sprinkling resources among everyone. The psychological atmosphere is altogether bad, since the Ministère des Finances historically tries to prevent the new expenditures proposed by the operating agencies, and the operating agencies believe the Ministère des Finances does not give them an opportunity to develop a consistent policy.

The Ministère des Finances closely supervises the implementation of all government policies through the system of financial control. There is in each operating agency a financial comptroller who is under the direct authority of the director of the budget. He has to countersign all the expenditure vouchers. (In theory, he checks the conformity of expenditures by the agency to the obligational authority it received. In practice, this can amount to a veto. This was not intended as a management-control system, since its purpose is to see that financial orthodoxy is respected, and not the check on how the aims of the national policy are attained.)

Top government officers in France, as well as middle-grade and lower-grade ones, are not political appointees but professional civil servants grouped in closed-up categories called "corps". These have a monopoly on some tasks and appointments. These civil servants are a very elite group, carefully selected through the system of the "Grandes Ecoles". They are divided roughly into two categories according to the type of training they received. Most of them have a law or humanities training and are graduates of the Ecole Nationale d'Administration (National Academy of Public Administration). The others are alumni of the Ecole Polytechnique or some other scientific Grande Ecole and have an engineering degree. The first group run the Ministère des Finances and most of the nontechnical ministries; the second manage the Ministère du Developpement Industriel (Industrial Development), the Ministère de l'Equipement (Highways, Housing, and Urban Development), the Ministère des Telecommunications (Communications), the Ministère de la Defense (Defence Department) and the Institut National de Statistiques et d'Etudes Economiques (National Institute for Statistics and Economic Studies) of the Ministère des Finances. In spite of the partitioning between the two groups, a certain competition takes place between them, and group conflict generally is more important than individual competition.

The National Planning System

The five-year plan can be considered as a first approach to the rationalisation of decision-making in the French government and has three main characteristics: It is a macroeconomic forecast; a program of major public investments; and a forum for discussions on past and proposed policies. The idea of having a plan developed as early as 1946. The responsibility for the plan falls upon a Commissariat au Plan which is under the direct authority of the Prime Minister. The Five-Year Plan is developed by the Commissariat au Plan with the collaboration of committees of competent people from various government organizations, business and trade, and the universities.

The plan is, first of all, a macroeconomic forecast of the national accounts of the country at the year $n + 5$. By using Keynesian-type models and (for some years) computer simulations, one can see attainable growth objectives and determine the tools in economic policy that must be used if full employment, price stability, and equilibrium of commercial balance are the goals. This projection indicates also the general allocation of resources; for example, the division between public and private expenditures, savings and consumption.

The plan is also a five-year program of public investments, but is different from the planning and financial components of the American planning-programming-budgeting system. It is essentially a physical program of major investments with a detailed financial schedule. Moreover, there is no systematic link between the budgetary process and the plan.

Finally, the plan allows for a complete re-estimate of all the various policies of the government every five years. Many new ideas and proposals for reform spring from the searching criticism which takes place during the discussions of the committees. The procedure of the plan is much more a synthesizing work than an analytical one. The aim is not to end with alternative proposals along with their cost and effectiveness, but rather a general consensus, which is inevitably a compromise.

The Introduction of the RCB

The factors just enumerated gave rise to the idea of the Rationalisation des Choix Budgetaires, or RCB, which springs from a recognition of the need to find solutions to two problems:

1. Demands for public goods are constantly growing, but for psychological and political reasons, the present level of taxes cannot be raised. This makes it necessary to find a means for better resource allocation to rule out superfluous expenditures and concentrate financial support on the more effective programs.

2. A link between the government's policies defined by the plan and the budget must be created. It also should effect a better understanding of the activities of the operating agencies.

Two groups of interests united to launch the RCB. One was the civil servants with an engineering training in the Ministère de 'Equipement, the Ministère de la Defense and the Direction de la Prévision (Forecasting Division; i.e., systems-analysis staff) of the Ministère des Finances. They were looking for a means to develop rational methods in decision-making and management that would allow them to increase their effectiveness through better use of their competence in quantitative methods. The other was made up of top civil servants from the Ministère des Finances—especially Direction de Budget—who felt that the budgetary process as previously described could not be maintained without damage to national economic growth and the resulting threat to their own position.

With these conditions, the introduction of RCB in France was made possible by the example of PPBS in the United States. Starting in 1964, upper-middle-grade civil servants from the Ministère de la Defense went to the United States to study program budgeting. They convinced the Ministre de la Defense of the desirability of creating a program-evaluation staff and of undertaking the evolutionary implementation of a planning, programming, and budgeting system. In the same way, upper-middle-grade civil servants from the Ministère de Equipement and the Ministère des Finances went on missions to the United States. After four years of development of the idea at that level, top people from the Direction du Budget and the Ministère des Finances took great interest in it, and in January 1968 suceeded in convincing the then Ministre des Finances, M. Debré, to experiment officially with the new system in a number of departments.

Main Features and Implementation of the RCB System

The name itself—Rationalisation des Choix Budgetaires—has an historical background which is characteristic of French administration. Whereas the Defence Department entitled its effort 3 P.B. — Planning-Programming-

Preparation of the Budget—the first title thought of in the civil administration was O.D.P., for "optimization of public expenditure". This laid stress on two different approaches to the decision-making process: procedure and general coherence of the system from a central point of view, and analysis to provide for the best possible allocation of public resources.

Neither view seemed sufficiently comprehensive or realistic. The title which was finally chosen, with its emphasis on budgetary impact and reference to France's well-known philosophy, covers most elements of systems analysis and program budgeting. The definition of RCB proposed by Ph. Huet,[1] is: a systematic search, applied to public action, by the use of all the existing techniques of calculus and analysis, or prevision and organisation. It aims at implementing public policies effectively at the many different levels of government.

Description of the System

After a period of various approaches, owing to historical factors or characteristics of the different departments, there is now a relatively clear agreement on a number of concepts deriving mainly from economic analysis and PPBS, and a willingness to concentrate on the process of public decision itself.

Analytical studies were the first approach. They were called "études-pilotes" (test studies). Their objective was to demonstrate the ability of the cost-benefit techniques in the public field. At the same time great emphasis was given to the elaboration of objective-oriented program structures, applied as well to a given policy as to a service. These first efforts (with a few exceptions) had little impact on the course of action. They lacked roots in the budgetary process and were not clearly linked to the management process.

An important development was the emergence of the program concept in two different forms:

"Programme finalisé" (objective oriented), was used mainly in policy planning and analysis, and related to specific indicators at various levels, including social indicators;

"Programme d'action" (output oriented), allowed for a comprehensive description of public activity and related total costs clearly to end product or service.
The "programme structure" tool also was used to analyze and strengthen the management of local services, the organisation of a large department (such as education), and to display the key devices of defense policy.

Finally, the "RCB method" is now clearly composed of three parts, closely related to one another. Program budgeting is the keystone since it is at the same

---

[1] Directeur Général, Head of the "Mission R.C.B.," who is in charge of introducing the new methods in the Ministère des Finances.

time the framework for analytical studies and the information base for a management control system. All of that sounds very much like the United States approach, but we have adapted it to the psychological, political, and civil service needs of France.

Implementation of the Operations

From the very beginning, a number of important principles were stated by administrative and political authorities as the basis for developing RCB.

The first principle may be called that of "willingness": It must be clearly understood that *no* imperative regulations will be imposed upon departments or services. In fact, it is clear that the initial condition of success is the complete assent of the head of a given department or service, and his belief that the existing decision process is unsatisfactory. Moreover, there is no question of imposing new methods or processes on complete departments, through imperative and detailed memorandums; such a way would be both inconsistent with the cental tendency of RCB, and ineffective in most cases.

From this basic principle there immediately derives a second one: The introduction of RCB must be selective and progressive, taking advantage, at each level, of the opportunities and extending, if necessary, along a span of several years to completion. This principle means that different approaches are not only inevitable but even desirable, provided coordination and cooperation can take place in a timely fashion.

The third and last principle can be summarized as the necessity for teamwork, from the institutional, technical and even psychological points of view. This point is particularly important in France, where individualism is a deeply rooted factor.

Naturally, each department has followed its own way in the process of developing RCB, according to its needs and its basic features. The Ministere de l'Equipement for example, experimented with nearly all the approaches described above.[1] The Ministère de la Defense has, from the outset, oriented its work towards a general PPB system. Some of the departments which have more recently gone into RCB, like Ministère de l'Intèrieur, have emphasized improvements in management.

The present situation can be summed up as follows:

Analytical studies (on road safety, medical prevention, energy prices, public transportation, etc.) have found budgetary outcomes. The demonstration phase

---

[1] See also S.A.E.I. "La R.C.B. au Ministère de l'Equipement et du Logement," *RCB: Bulletin Interministériel pour la Rationalisation des Choix Budgetaires*, No. 3, March 1971, and "La R.C.B. dans les Administrations," the first government-wide report by the R.C.B. Commission, R.C.B. No. Special, la Documentation Française, 31, Quai Voltaire, Paris 7, 1971.

has come to an end. Almost every Ministère now has a program for developing RCB in which analytical studies play a major part.

Program budgeting is becoming effective in three departments: in the Ministère de la Defense, the next five-year military plan has been expressed in program structure; in the Ministries of Education and Equipment, a good part of the 1972 budget discussions will take place along the lines of the new method.

Improvements in management are, by now, mainly at an experimental stage. The Ministères of Poste, Equipement, Intèrieur, and Finances are the more advanced in this field.

Some Sociological Characteristics of the Process

In addition to these historical developments, some general features of the process are worth mentioning:

1. RCB developed essentially at a central level, with little or no interaction with local authorities, is a phenomenon that can be easily understood in light of the general structure of administration in France. Steps to change that direction are now being taken. Moreover, it is hoped that the rational method developed by the central agencies will be extended to local communities.

2. It is unusual in the history of administrative reform in France since the first world war, that RCB had essentially an administrative origin. The government sponsored and encouraged its development, but the original impulse came from public administrators rather than as a response to political pressure.

3. Unlike PPB, RCB developed without tight links with universities or private research institutions. French universities are not readily prepared to provide for an advisory service to public agencies. The government in turn only rarely entrusts universities with research work.

4. RCB was developed by the departments for their own various uses. The Ministère des Finances encouraged this tendency. However, in the beginning, the operation was not considered, as it is now, as a way to change the relationships between financial and operating departments.

Problems and Outlook

The development of RCB has now reached the point of leaving the experimental stage and entering into effective use. Difficult problems will have to be solved in the near future.

The shortage of qualified analysts must be emphasized. The existence of trained analysts, working at the right place, is a prerequisite of success. It is not an accident that departments most advanced in RCB are those which have at their disposal numerous officials with engineering degrees. From this point of view, the more traditional ministries suffer a serious handicap, which is not easily overcome. It is difficult to attract highly competent analysts to public aministration, and at the same time minimize turnover from "rich" departments towards the others, and vice versa. The level of public salaries does not compare favourably with that of the private sector, and the procedures of recruitment into the public service are not adequately flexible.

Misconceptions and psychological resistances are another drawback. Traditional administrative circles are generally not prepared for innovation. In particular, the new quantitative techniques are hardly welcome to senior civil servants who are trained in law and the humanities. They see new methods as a threat to their established ways of doing things and, still worse, to the existing equilibrium of power.

Organisational problems also tend to become critical. It has already been mentioned that RCB initially was developed in the economic and research services of the various ministries. With its extension to the operating services, the need for coordination of procedures is often viewed as a new constraint. A hopeful step was taken at the end of 1970 with the creation of a consultative committee composed mainly of representatives of each department and presided over by the minister of finances. One of its major tasks may be to establish a new kind of dialogue between budgetary authorities and the nonfinancial organizations.

Hopes and Pitfalls of the RCB

Development of the RCB system methods originated from the belief that the traditional processes of decision-making and administration were not well fitted to current needs. Objectives were difficult to attain for two reasons. First, the legal status of the French civil service makes it difficult to introduce a performance control system with incentives towards efficiency. Second, civil servants trained in humanities generally lack skill in the use of quantitative methods. Moreover, the development of the RCB system is hindered by the gap that exists in France between university and administration. The result is that analytical studies are entrusted to the research staffs of the ministries, which are inevitably prejudiced, or to profit corporations whose view of administrative problems and of the general interest is not properly oriented.

The development in France of independent "think tanks," either in the universities or as nonprofit corporations, may be the next step in the development of program budgeting and techniques of rational decision-making in government.

In France as elsewhere (with perhaps a still more perceptible "pesanteur sociologique") success of the new methods depends on the possibility of achieving change in habits and minds. If that change is not sought and organised from inside the government itself, the pressure of collective needs, which calls for efficiency in the public sector as in the rest of the economy, will inevitably force it.

CHAPTER 15

Programme Budgeting in Ireland

by Tomas F. O'Cofaigh

Department of Finance
Ireland

In considering the status of planning, programming, and budgeting in Ireland prior to the current developments in programme budgeting, it is necessary to distinguish between national economic programming and fiscal budgeting. A series of national economic programmes has been published by the Irish government, starting in 1958. They have included, among other matters dealt with, projections of central government expenditures, both capital and current, and comment on the likely availability of financial resources to meet them. These projections have not been rolled forward annually, nor have they represented binding commitments.

Ireland's traditional fiscal budget shares the common international feature of being prepared on an input basis only and, up to now, has looked only one year ahead. It does distinguish between current, or consumption, expenditure and capital, or investment, expenditure. Since 1966, multiyear fiscal budgeting had been attempted in a limited way on the capital side. This took the form of projections for three years ahead for public capital expenditure. The projections were in greater detail than those of the national economic programmes, but they have been of limited effectiveness and have not been published.

A decision has now been taken to project central government current as well as capital expenditures for three years ahead, to roll both sets of projections forward annually and to apply them with determination to secure the forward control of expenditure. The projections, of necessity, will continue to be prepared on the same basis as the annual expenditure. This is as an input-oriented budget to be used as an interim measure until programme budgeting can be developed.

The Need for Programme Budgeting

Annual expenditure on the current budget is equivalent to about 30 percent

119

of gross national product and expenditure on the capital budget, or what is termed the public capital programme, accounts for about 50 percent of gross domestic fixed capital formation. The influence of such a large volume of public-sector expenditure from a demand management point of view on the generally development of the economy, particularly in the growth context, is highly significant. The excessive growth of expenditure in relation to resources and the growing complexity of government services has turned the attention of the Irish government to the desirability of giving a longer perspective to decisions affecting the allocation and management of national resources.

Irish experience, of course, is not unique in this respect. Growing awareness of the problem has been a phenomenon of the 1960s in many countries. In Ireland, the importance of "forward looks" in the field of public expenditure was receiving steadily growing attention over the decade, as the development of multiannual budgeting indicated. Study of the new concept was also undertaken as part of the general examination, but this remained essentially theoretical until 1967.

Programme budgeting emerged as a practical issue in that year as a result of an appraisal of the expenditures in the public capital programme. The appraisal was directed to considering the cost of the expenditures in relation to the economic and social benefits which they yielded or might be expected to yield to the community. And, so far as practicable, it was to employ techniques of a cost-benefit or cost-effectiveness type. The appraisal highlighted at an early stage the absence of systematic procedures for defining objectives, identifying and quantifying expected costs and benefits, projecting costs and benefits annually and globally for a reasonable period ahead, and for continuous review and updating of progress. It drew attention to the prospects of remedying these deficiencies if the various procedures involved in the programme-budgeting system could be adopted, and suggested that the study of programme budgeting being made by the Department of Finance should be put on a practical experimental basis. This suggestion was accepted and the Irish government's Third Programme for Economic and Social Development, published in 1969, carried a statement to that effect.

Action Taken to Develop Programme Budgeting

The Irish developers of programme budgeting benefited from the experience of the United States federal authorities, and they also took into account the reactions to the system in Canada and in European countries such as Belgium, France, Norway, Sweden and the United Kingdom. The central unit set up in the Department of Finance in early 1969 to carry out practical experimental investigation of the new system commenced by choosing two government departments for experiments in depth.

This course was taken in preference to attempting to introduce programme budgeting simultaneously in all government departments in the light of the difficulties experienced in the global implementation of the new method in the United States federal agencies. There was also, of course, the difficulty of securing adequate skilled personnel to do the work involved. In this the Irish and Belgian approaches have been very alike. It was recognised that the form of programme budgeting to be developed and the emphasis to be placed on the particular aspects of the system should reflect specific national needs. This would necessitate closer, in-depth, examination than is practicable under a global application—even though the partial approach may involve deferment of the advantages of a generally applied system for allocation of resources.

Pilot experiments in programme budgeting commenced in the autumn of 1969, with the full cooperation of the ministers and officials concerned, in the Departments of Education and Lands (Forestry Service). The selection of the education area reflected the emphasis in recent years on the development of educational planning in Ireland and the existence in the department of a special planning unit. The Forestry Service not only had the advantage of being directed by a planning-conscious staff but also was a relatively self-contained activity, strongly investment oriented and therefore amenable to programming.

Work Programme

The programme-budget studies in the education and forestry areas are still in progress (end-1970). They are being carried out by a working group consisting of officers from the Department of Finance programme-budgeting unit and from each of the two departments concerned. The initial design of the systems for each of the two departments was seen as involving the following stages:

1. Formulation of the overall policy objectives of the department;
2. Listing of existing activities of the department;
3. Design of programme structures with existing activities grouped to give expression to objectives as defined;
4. Identification of output measures and commencement of design of management information systems;
5. Translation of available data to fill, as far as possible, the cost and output cells for the elements in the programme budget;
6. Projection of a provisional multiannual programme budget;
7. Refinement of 6.

These steps comprise only the first round. Once programme budget systems are installed, their operation will generate further clarification of departmental objectives and more quantified expression of policy targets. Their success will also depend on detailed analysis on a continuing basis of each department's operations, targets, and programmes. The development of computerised management-information systems will be essential to process output measures and control programme performance.

121

Tomas F. O'Cofaigh

A discipline applied in the Irish programme-budgeting studies of education and forestry was to define departmental objectives in relation to *existing* policy and activities. This was to ensure that programme projections could be tied in firmly with the actual (input) budget allocations. The process of identifying objectives and activities has already instigated thinking about alternatives, and the design of programme structures will consciously encourage this development.

Problem Areas

Different countries place differing emphasis on the features of programme budgeting which appeal to them. This in itself indicates that problem areas will differ from country to country. It is fair to say, however, that the Irish approach is to attempt to "milk" the system of its potential benefits on all fronts—resource allocation, analysis and decision-making, management control, and improved personnel performance. The usefulness of programme budgeting as a means of improving forward resource allocation was perhaps uppermost in the minds of those promoting programme budgeting in the early stages. This was seen as a fundamental need by the Department of Finance; but it was obvious also in the early days of the study that the system had a great deal to offer in the field of management and control. It was this aspect of the system which held the main attraction for the other departments since they were not concerned directly with the macro-allocation of resources.

Only slightly less important than the resource-allocation potentialities of the system, in the view of its promoters in the Department of Finance, was the emphasis it placed on analysis. This is not to say that analysis in some shape or form was not a run-of-the-mill feature of departmental work; but the system laid emphasis on institutionalising it, as it were, by building it into all decision-making and requiring its development in depth. It is only too obvious, of course, that analysis, even in depth and using all available techniques of quantitative measurement, does not supply a complete answer. There will always remain a subjective element, which perhaps increases according as the decision becomes more general in its impact on the community. Quantitative, if possible, in-depth analysis of programmes and policy issues is seen as reducing the subjective element in decisions and as leading to their being better informed. If sufficient lead time is allowed, major issues can be studied in sufficient depth to provide useful information for budgetary decisions. It may take time to develop acceptance of the discipline of basing decisions on explicit analysis. Issues which require major decisions very often cannot wait for analysis!

Operational Difficulties Encountered

One would expect to find opposition to change a major element of difficulty but, so far, this was not the Irish experience. In fact, the appeal of a system which promised a basis for forward resource allocation and better management control has had an early and favourable impact on top management. There is a move to extend the area of development of programme budgeting, and the practical studies are being introduced in other Irish government departments as rapidly as staff resources permit. It is rather a truism that programme budgeting will not succeed unless it has the active support of top management and care has been taken to ensure that this will be forthcoming before work commences in any department.

Another very real difficulty has been how to give departmental staffs an adequate operational knowledge of the system with the limited number of "trained" personnel available; these persons themselves were "learning by doing." Expectations are that, after an initial pioneering period, the numbers of trained personnel will increase rapidly so that the pace of development can be accelerated.

Assuming that the results of the pioneer efforts in the selected departments are such as to confirm the feasibility of making the system generally operational, it would be unrealistic not to anticipate a difficulty, first as regards marrying the new system with the existing system and, secondly, in dealing with the organisational implications of programme structures. As regards the first of these difficulties, common sense indicates that it may well be necessary to keep both systems running in parallel for a time with crosswalks between the two.

It is to be expected that there will be a reaction on organisation and personnel as departments are brought to think of their activities in terms of programmes and sub-programmes.

Reorganisation could be a serious problem but would be better sidestepped for as long as practicable. If highlighted and met head-on, it might provide a focus for opposition to the new procedures. On the other hand, if the implications are permitted to emerge in a pragmatic way in the course of operating the system, the reorganisation proposals may come from the organisational units themselves.

In order to derive the full benefit of the sytem in the management area it is necessary—and it is the intention in the Irish effort—to align the subdivision of government policy objectives with the personal objectives of line managers. The sense of personal involvement which can and no doubt will be generated will have a payoff in the form of improved management performance—apart from the individual satisfaction which will be derived. The Irish version of programme budgeting distinguishes between that system and the technique generally known as MBO or "Management by Objectives". MBO in the Irish context is seen essentially as a technique for improvement of management performance and will be developed in departments as a follow-up to the installation of programme-budgeting systems. In this way the idea of personal identification with the achievement of policy objectives, and therefore of programme outputs, should be secured. The regular progress reviews will secure that this process of personal identification will continue.

Inadequacy of data on which to base costings and measures of performance included in the first programme budget is a problem. Often, where information is available, it is not in manageable form for use in the programme budget. A certain amount of arbitrary allocation of costs by reference to statistical aggregates may be necessary until a suitable management-information system is developed.

The important thing is to use whatever tools, techniques, personnel, data, and so on, which are at hand. If deficiencies are identified, this in itself is progress since they can then, if significant, be remedied over time.

CHAPTER 16

PPBS in the Japanese Government: Necessity, Preparation and Problems[1]

by Yasuto Fukushima

Professor, National Defense College

Although the Japanese national government has not officially installed the planning-programming-budgeting system, the Bureau of the Budget in the Ministry of Finance took the initiative in late 1967 and began to study program budgeting. It also (unofficially) established a policy and took the following steps to make it possible to introduce this new management system:

1. Organized a group to work on PPBS;

2. Instituted a training program for executives and administrators for work in PPBS;

3. Requested that each ministry prepare case studies in several areas;

4. Requested that each ministry establish its objectives and develop a program structure to achieve those objectives;

5. Encouraged private institutes to improve their analytical ability, and

6. Studied the PPBS activities in the United States and other foreign governments.

To gain as many advantages as possible of the underlying techniques and methodology of program budgeting, the Bureau of the Budget set up the Inter-Agency Conference of PPB Officers (Deputy-Assistant-Secretary class) in all ministries and agencies (fourteen in all) in November 1968. It continues as the driving force in all of the new activities. System Analysis Units consisting of several staff members were established in the Economic Planning Agency (1968), the Defense Agency (1969), the Ministry of Construction (1969), the Ministry of

[1]The author is sincerely appreciative of the cooperation of Mr. Taroh Kaneko, budget examiner (former chief, Research Section), of the Bureau of the Budget, Ministry of Finance. The paper does not represent official government views.

Finance (1969), the Ministry of Transportation (1970, the Ministry of Agriculture (1970), and the Ministry of Labor (1970). Study groups were organized in other agencies and ministries.

All agencies except the Ministry of Foreign Affairs have applied systems analysis to a few selected subjects each year since 1968, and they submitted the results of their analyses to the Ministry of Finance. Some of these have been put into the annual budget-making process by the Bureau of the Budget.

A number of training courses for government officials were conducted by the Bureau of the Budget. These included a one-week course for 45 high-ranking officials (assistant-secretary level) in May 1969; a one-week course for 35 middle-management personnel (deputy-assistant-secretary class) in June 1970; a six-month course for 47 younger staff members in September 1969; and another four-month course for this last category in September 1970.

The Bureau of the Budget also sent 15 government officials to planning-programming-budgeting training courses conducted by the U.S. Civil Service Commission in 1969 and in 1970. Several Japanese government representatives attended the PPBS course conducted by the U.S. Navy Management School at Monterey, California, in 1970. Our Bureau of the Budget invited 30 scholars, mainly economists, to a two-day program-budgeting symposium in the spring of 1970. In addition, each government agency has given a number of its own PPBS orientation lectures for general education purposes for its staff.

Many Japanese government agencies have attempted to design an informal program structure for their use. The personnel who attended the six-month course referred to above were asked to develop program structures for their particular agencies as part of their course work.

The development of the analytical ability of private institutes was encouraged through subsidies from the Bureau of the Budget. Starting in 1969 the Ministry of Finance, as well as other government offices, studied the results of their counterparts in the U.S. government in the use of PPBS. One indirect result was the introduction of computer systems. The Fiscal System Council, a special advisory group to the Ministry of Finance, took under consideration the adoption of PPBS by all government agencies. Sometime in the future, the council will make its recommendations to the ministry.

The Need for PPBS in Japan

News of the Pentagon's management revolution was promptly received in Japan, and the basic idea was presented in detail in the April 1962 issue of the *Journal of the National Defense College.* Program budgeting did not seriously capture the interest of the Japanese government, however, until a group of leading Japanese businessmen visited the United States—the Management Information System Mission. Upon their return to Japan early in 1968 they recommended to the Japanese government the adoption of this new management idea. By that time, however, the Bureau of the Budget, on learning of President Johnson's order in August 1965 to all U.S. government agencies, had established the six activities outlined at the beginning of this chapter.

It is generally said in Japan that the Ministry of Finance is more powerful than other ministries because it has the authority for preparing the budget. However, the year-by-year increase in recurring costs of government operations has limited the flexibility available in fiscal policy. One result was that the Ministry of Finance recently adopted the integrated budget principle to avoid the supplements that had come to dominate the process. This means that all expenditures for the year involved are incorporated into one—the initial—budget and there are no supplements to it. Nevertheless, factors such as price rises and irrational political pressure have made it difficult to maintain this principle in actual budget operations.

Planning and Budgeting Processes in Japan

As was the case in the United States, there has been an incrementalist, muddling-through, arbitrary-budget-ceilings, etc., approach. Although the Japanese people are said to have good intuition and mathematical abilities for coping with management problems, the scope of government activities was so enlarged in recent years that such traits alone were no longer sufficient for management. This meant that the government did not plan adequately for what ought to be done before considering how it was to be done.

Japanese government management takes the form of a "bottom up" rather than a "top down" approach. In this management system, leaders are not required to show objectives clearly so that their staffs can plan how to achieve these objectives. The annual budget is not developed through systematic analysis, but instead, a budget ceiling is set politically. Therefore, irrational political pressures affect the budget-making.

The effectiveness of expenditure activities has not been properly challenged. Although some agencies had five-year programs, these were made along vertical rather than horizontal lines. Such five-year programs were not flexible because the budgets and their duration were rigid. Thus, it was clear that some deficiencies existed in the national government planning and budget-making process, and it was believed that adoption of the PPB concept could improve them.

Problems and Prospects

At the present time, the government faces difficulties relative to the introduction of PPBS. The top management in each agency have not yet fully recognised the necessity for PPBS. Some of the middle managers who have substantial power in the government management hierarchy as it now operates are attracted to the existing budgeting system because it leaves room for their discretion.

There also is misunderstanding and resulting resistance among some officials. They feel that PPBS will be used by the Ministry of Finance mainly for reducing their budgets. Some feel that PPBS is based on operations research and the extensive use of computers and will result in cutting many people out of their jobs. They ask, what good is cost-effectiveness analysis if it has a very limited function? At present, no agency as a whole is prepared or willing to adopt PPBS.

The nondefense areas of government have not had a long experience in systematic analysis. The number of young analysts is gradually increasing, but the number is still not large enough. Traditional data are mainly input-oriented, and bureaucratic conservatism may make line organizations hesitate to provide authentic or reliable data to the central staffs. Each agency tends to reveal only favorable information. The government feels it must identify areas that can or cannot be analyzed.

The essence of PPBS lies in the concept of "program". However, since many programs have many purposes and extend over more than one organization, there are not only interagency level but also intraagency and multilevel program structures that are not easy to design.

Furthermore, the reaction of the Diet is well known. The government may have to consider if the new budget-planning process should be introduced under the name of PPBS or if, from a psychological viewpoint, it should be identified by some distinctive Japanese title. It is important that the form of PPBS should be adjusted to the characteristics of the Japanese people and traditional Japanese management practices. This is especially important since the effort will not succeed unless the majority of officials have a strong incentive to introduce it. Indeed the introduction of such a new system cannot be arbitrarily enforced.

Conclusion

For program budgeting to succeed in Japan: First, there must be strong leadership in the government by the Prime Minister and cabinet ministers. Probably more important in Japan, understanding and cooperation of middle management is indispensable; Second, it seems better not to introduce the concept in a drastic way but, rather, to do it piecemeal; Third, although the Japanese people in general might be impatient to see results, the people involved in instituting this new management tool must realize that it will be a long and very difficult avenue to travel before satisfactory results are realized.

CHAPTER 17

Introduction and Development
of Programme Budgeting in New Zealand

by J. R. Battersby

The Treasury
New Zealand

The decision to introduce programme budgeting in New Zealand stems primarily from the work of a study group formed in 1966 to examine Treasury procedures for planning and controlling government expenditure. In its terms of reference the group was asked to "pay particular attention to the link which will need to be established between planning and programming over the longer period for both capital and current expenditures and the present procedures for approvals, delegation of expenditure authorities and investigation of financial proposals by Treasury."

The study group reported in December 1967 and recommended that "attention be given to the classification of public expenditures by their function with a view to developing functional programmes of government activity and systems for controlling costs and performance in these programmes." Following adoption of the study group report by Treasury, a special section was established early in 1968 to develop and introduce the reforms necessary for the operation of the systems recommended.

Present Financial Management System

The Estimates of Expenditure tabled in Parliament as part of the annual budget are made up of a number of "votes". Generally, each government department controls one vote showing details of its estimated expenditure for the current financial year. Some departments, however, control two or more votes. The two major reasons for this are:

1. Some departments have activities falling within different ministerial portfolios and a separate vote is prepared for each; for example, the Social

Security Department, beside controlling its own "Vote: Social Security" within the portfolio of the minister of social security, also controls "Vote: War Pensions" within the portfolio of the minister in charge of war pensions.

2. The public accounts system requires that expenditures funded from loan money or trading activities be clearly distinguished from expenditures funded from current revenue. A department which has some activities funded from loan money and the remainder from revenue therefore requires a separate vote for each; for instance, the Ministry of Transport controls "Vote: Transport" containing its normal operating expenditure funded from revenues, and also "Vote: Airport Development" which contains expenditure on airport construction funded from loans.

Events leading up to the tabling of the annual estimates and budget can be summarised as follows:

October

Departments submit forecasts of expenditure for each vote for the following financial year and two further years.

December

On the basis of the departmental forecasts, adjusted to take note of possible price rises, for example, wages increase or policy changes such as increases in social security benefits, Treasury reports to government on the expenditure outlook for the following year (i.e., commencing next April 1). At the same time Treasury usually recommends to government an overall expenditure limit to be used as a guideline in framing estimates for the year.

January

Government decides on its expenditure guideline for the year.

February

Departments are requested to submit estimates bid for the financial year commencing April 1.

March-April

Estimates bids are subject to detailed scrutiny by Treasury, which recommends vote allocations to government.

May

Government decides on allocations to each departmental vote. Departments prepare estimates in accordance with this allocation.

June

Budget and Estimates for the year are tabled in the House. Salient features of the present precedures are:

1. Annual estimates are tabled three months following the commencement of the financial year to link with the parliamentary year.

2. Departments prepare estimates bids with the assistance of reliable information as to actual expenditure for the current year.

3. Although three-year forecasts are called for in October, only the first year of the forecast is used for decision-making purposes and then largely for the setting up of expenditure guidelines. There is no integration between the forecast information and estimates bids received four months later.

In addition to the three-year expenditure forecasts collected in October each year by Treasury, the New Zealand government has operated a system of five-year works-programming since 1949-50.

The Works Programme is assembled and operated by the Ministry of Works. Departments supply details to the Ministry (in December of each year) of their building and construction requirements for the following five years. It is designed to facilitate consideration of the effect of government activity on the building and construction industry, to plan forward building and development proposals in the government sector within the scope of the programme, and to determine the financial resources to be allocated to this phase of government activity.

Whilst the initial purpose of integrating government's building and construction requirements with the resources available still remains, in recent years the Works Programme has been increasingly used for short-term expenditure control. This is because it gathers together one major element that can be varied without too severe disruption if expenditure has to be limited. Cash allocations for Works Programme purposes are approved only for the first year of the programme, and no attempt is made to set allocations for ensuing years, although the level of future commitment is noted.

The New Financial-Management System

Development of the General Approach

The New Zealand Treasury has always maintained contacts with similar organisations in other countries, particularly Canada, the United Kingdom, and the United States. Experience gained in introducing programme budgeting was therefore readily available and influenced the particular changes now being made.

Following the Treasury decision to introduce programme budgeting early in 1968, it was realised that progress in developing the system could only be made if:

1. Government endorsed the Treasury decision;
2. The data base was linked with the Estimates of Expenditure, the budget and Parliament's control function;
3. Procedures were developed for actually employing long-term expenditure forecasts in resource-allocation decisions;
4. A comprehensive education programme was instituted.

The first step was therefore to recommend to government that programme budgeting should be adopted. The outcome of this was that in August 1968 the Prime Minister advised ministers that the system was to be introduced and sought their cooperation in dealing with the procedural changes proposed. This advice gave recognition to government's intention and ensured department cooperation and assistance to Treasury.

The Estimates of Expenditure and the Government Accounting System

One of the first tasks of the special section established in Treasury was to review the information needs of government, and the manner in which they could be met. One basic difficulty that had never been satisfactorily resolved when a computer-based accounting system was introduced in 1961 was the lack of financial data available for planning and control within departments. The system had been designed largely to meet parliamentary requirements by analysing expenditure in input form for each vote.

The study of information needs revealed that there was a continuing need for information by input, by output (or activity), and also by responsibility within each department. It was also desirable that the system should be capable of supplying information in economic terms. The continuing information requirements have now been met by the introduction of SIGMA, System of Integrated Government Management Accounting.

To assist in meeting the need for economic information, it was also decided that each transaction would be identified as to its economic category under the U.S. System of National Accounts (SNA). It also was decided that a standard input code would not be developed, as the time taken to design a code and the necessary continuing administrative procedures did not seem to be offset by any material advantages. However, to ensure uniformity it was decided that departmental codes should organise objects of expenditure into standard expenditure groups (SEG) which were identified as:

Personnel
Travel, Transport, and Communications
Maintenance, Operating Upkeep, and Rental of Property and Equipment
Materials, Supplies, and Services
Other Operating Expenditures
Capital
Grants, Contributions, Subsidies, and Other Transfer Payments

Advances, Loans, and Transfers to Other Votes and Accounts

The classification followed the grouping most useful for financial, political, and economic purposes in segregating current, capital, and transfer expenditures.

The new accounting code to provide the data base for programme budgeting could have been introduced without alteration to the Estimates of Expenditure format. It was felt, however, that more impetus would be given to the introduction of the new system if some change was made, especially if this change concentrated on providing information to Parliament on each departmental activity programme.

The main section of each vote is "Activity Programme" which gives expenditure details for the major activities of the department. For example, in the Estimates of Expenditure the Department of Health major activity programmes are:

Administrative Services
Dental Services
Hospital Services
Maternal and Child Health Services
Medical Research
Public Health Services
Welfare Services

The information on activity programmes given in the estimates is supported in each department's reports by detailed information for sub-activities and for input items within standard expenditure groups. As well as linking with the information system that will meet government's financial planning and control needs, the new format has been shown to have distinct advantages for parliamentary purposes. It emphasises the work that departments are doing and forces politicians and administrators to think in terms of output rather than inputs as in the past.

Although the introduction of the new format may appear to be a relatively simple task, several problems have arisen that have not been dealt with satisfactorily as yet. For instance:

The definition of activity programmes proved more difficult than envisaged in some cases and has inevitably led to a compromise between programmes useful for evaluation purposes and programmes useful for departmental responsibility purposes. For some departments still to change to the new format it is also apparent that activities may have to be defined in intermediate rather than final output terms to meet organisational requirements.

Some departments have had difficulty in specifying objectives precisely in the programme statements which accompany each departmental vote.

Government Decision-making

Although three-year forecasts of expenditure have been collected annually

133

since the early 1960s, except for the first year of each forecast period, these have not been used to any great extent. One reason was that the forecasts were prepared for departments as a whole rather than based upon the separate departmental activities. It therefore proved impossible to relate forecasts back to the demands being placed upon the various activities of each department. Another reason was that collection and analysis of them were never placed on a formal basis within the decision-making system. In addition, no procedures existed for relating forecasts made in October to estimates bids prepared in the following March. The result was that very little attention was paid to the forecasts by departments as the annual estimates process was seen to hold prime place in decisions on expenditure

To achieve the degree of integration necessary and also to emphasise the importance of long-term forecasts in the resource allocation decision, New Zealand has adopted a procedure operated successfully by the United Kingdom government. In May 1970 the New Zealand government approved the formation of a Committee of Officials on Public Expenditure (COPE) to operate along the lines of the United Kingdom Public Expenditure Survey Committee (PESC).

The committee comprises the permanent heads of major spending departments, with the secretary to the Treasury as the chairman. The committee is required:

1. To survey government's expenditure requirements over the long term (i.e., up to 5 years); and

2. To analyse the effect on government's policies if total expenditure is to be kept within the constraints imposed by government's economic and financial objectives.

Initially COPE is concentrating on producing realistic costs of existing policies for each departmental activity and in July 1970 asked departments to forecast needs to March 31, 1974. Departments were to distinguish for each activity between:

1. Variations in requirements due to the implementation of existing policies at existing levels of service;

2. Variations due to improvements in the standard or quality of service; and

3. New policies likely to be approved and have financial effect during the forecast period.

Little emphasis is placed on new policies at this stage as the prime purpose of the COPE exercise in fiscal 1971 is to establish basic costs that are a proper expression of existing government policy. To assist the committee in scrutinising forecasts, departments have to supply a statement of policy objectives being followed at present and to justify variations in forecasts by reference to demand changes.

The forecast information is required in exactly the same form as used for estimates and departmental control purposes, that is, by standard expenditure groups for each departmental activity. One aspect of the system now being introduced is the provision for updating forecasts. To ensure that the forecasts are realistic on a continuing basis and that the forward-estimates position is kept in kind, it is necessary to amend forecasts to allow for changes in policy, demand for services, and prices. Without this regular updating, forecasts would quickly show a wide divergence from estimates bids for the forecast years, and would therefore tend to be regarded as a separate exercise from the annual estimates procedure and thus not be given the attention required.

The timetable of the new system being developed is envisaged as:

September

Departments submit forecasts of policy costs for a forward period of five years, supported by demand data justifying expenditure changes.

October-November

1. Forecasts are assessed for realism by COPE.
2. Government advises COPE on its expenditure guideline for the coming years.
3. COPE analyses the effect of policies of keeping within government's expenditure guideline.

December

1. COPE reports to government on its policy costs over the forecast years and the effect on policies of keeping within the expenditure guideline.
2. Treasury reports to minister of finance on possible policy variations to meet the guidlines.

January

Government decides departmental expenditure levels for the following year (i.e., commencing April 1) and tentative levels for subsequent years.

March

Departments submit estimates bids for the financial year framed in accordance with government's decision on expenditure levels.

April

Following Treasury scrutiny of departmental bids, government decides estimates allocations for the year.

May-August

Departments review policy assumptions and roll forward activity-programme forecasts on the basis of allocations approved for current financial year and government's decisions on expenditure guidelines for subsequent years.

The Officials Committee procedure is designed primarily to ensure that government obtains objective advice on its policy costs. It is also hoped that COPE will in time be able to display in broad terms any options open to government if expenditure variations are necessary. The very nature of COPE, representing as it does the major departmental interest, precludes it from making recommendations. Further, it is doubtful whether COPE will ever conduct any serious analysis of programmes; this is seen as more of a departmental task, although COPE could advise government on any areas where analysis would be desirable.

As a part of the process of introducing programme budgeting over the past two years, the government has been given financial information in functional terms. This, coupled with the use of the new estimates format, has resulted in more awareness of the issues involved in resource.allocation problems. For instance, there is now an increasing tendency for politicians and officials to recognise that new programmes can often be introduced only at the expense of existing programmes.

Education for Programme Budgeting

If the introduction and development of the new system was to be successful, it had to be accomplished by a comprehensive education programme to provide an adequate supply of trained staff. The education programme commenced in 1969 and to date has included:

1. The retraining of existing staff through a series of short (i.e. one-half day) appreciation courses for administrative staff and longer (i.e., one-half week) more intensive courses for specialist financial staff. About a thousand employees have attended these courses to the present time.

2. The strengthening and reorganisation of courses in government finance at the university level.

Introduction to Specific Departments

As well as the work being done in dealing with the overall resource-allocation problem, a full programme-budgeting system is being introduced into the Ministry of Defence. A detailed accounting system has already been introduced to analyse expenditure into programme elements. The Estimates of Expenditure have also been drawn up in "activity" form to show the tasks of the Ministry more clearly:

Programme I.   General
                         Defence Administration
                         Cadet Forces
        II.   Forces for Overseas Deployment
                         Forces in Southeast Asia
                         Other Forces

III. Provision of New Zealand Support Base
Administration
Command and Communication
Supply Support
Technical Support
Training
IV. Ancillary Tasks
Hydrographic Survey
Aid to Other Countries
General
V. Research

Work is now under way in costing out and aggregating programme elements to form the Integrated Defence Programme, and costing systems are under development. It is also planned to commence a pilot study on determination of performance and effectiveness measures as the first step in the development of a management-accountability system.

Already, essential parts of the system which have been introduced have materially assisted management in the Ministry of Defence. For example, in addition to the setting of Defence objectives, priorities, roles and missions, the five-year programme, although still being developed, has already helped:

1. To integrate management effort for each activity;

2. To provide an overall integrated programme for policy decisions on the allocation of resources to roles, missions, and activities;

3. To provide a rational basis for the annual Estimates of Expenditure;

4. To provide Defence with a one-tier system of executive management, with servicemen and civilians fully integrated into this system;

5. To permit a greater delegation of financial authority and decentralisation of activity while giving a more effective control than in the past;

6. To provide a more fully considered presentation of defence needs to government.

Because of the relatively small size of the typical government department in New Zealand, it is expected that a full programme-budgeting system will be introduced only in the Department of Education and Department of Health, as well as the Ministry of Defence. Some other departments may, however, be required to carry out rigorous analysis of programmes and, in fact, in the land use, power, and transport areas, cost-benefit analysis is already an accepted technique.

Future Developments

Besides continuing the reforms to the Estimates of Expenditure and the development of the COPE procedures, it is expected that:

1. Greater effort will be made to develop the use of systematic analytic

137

techniques. Shortage of trained staff has prevented any serious work on programme evaluation, but it is expected that some work will be possible over the next few years in major policy areas such as defence, education, and health. The insistence upon a rudimentary marginal analysis in the COPE exercise should inculcate the need for the adoption of more sophisticated techniques by departments.

2. The education programme will be placing more emphasis on specialist courses rather than on general appreciation courses as at present. The possibility of involving the universities to a greater extent than hitherto is now being explored.

3. When the SIGMA coding pattern and control report system is in general use after April 1, 1971, the larger departments will be required to introduce management-accountability systems to emphasize personal responsibility for programme implementation.

Summary

Introduction of programme budgeting is at an early stage in New Zealand and has centred on two areas:

(1) restructuring the annual Estimates of Expenditure and the government accounting system to provide the data base;

(2) integration of programme-budgeting techniques with the decision-making processes in government.

The former has resulted in an estimates format that highlights expenditure on activities as well as continuing information in the more usual input form. It is expected that all departments will be employing the new format and the attendant SIGMA account code from 1971-72.

Integration of longer-term programming with the "real world" of annual estimates is expected to result from the work of a Committee of Officials on Public Expenditure (COPE) formed to advise government on its policy costs and the effect of meeting likely financial and resource constraints.

In addition to the work being done on the overall resource-allocation problem, several departments are to develop full programme-budgeting systems. The Ministry of Defence is the first to do so and at present is at the stage of introducing a pilot study to attempt to define measures of effectiveness and performance. Other departments likely to start in the near future include Education and Health.

A comprehensive education programme has already operated at the general appreciation level for the past eighteen months and is now entering a second stage. It is now intended to concentrate on specific topics, particularly those concerned with the use of more advanced analytical techniques.

CHAPTER 18

Program Budgeting
R and D at General Electric[1]

by R. W. Roberts and R. W. Schmitt,

Research and Development Center,
General Electric Company, Schenectady, New York

Research and development is sometimes seen as a mystical and unpredictable activity which cannot really be managed other than to find some creative people, give them a budget and a place to work, and hope for the best. They can, of course, be given a list of problems—but it should be no surprise to find them working on something that seems absolutely useless. They are, after all, creative; and if anyone tries to direct them, they will feel stifled and stop producing.

This approach to R & D is part of the folklore of an earlier era. It *may* have been the way General Electric managed Charles Steinmetz some sixty years ago. Perhaps it was the predominant style two decades ago when money for R & D was abundant. But today, when ideas and needs outstrip revenues, management had better adopt a more effective style to continue a flow of new products and techniques from an R & D operation. Today, at General Electric, we use a formal structure for planning and budgeting the activity of our corporate R & D center. The injection of a program-budgeting system has not solved all management problems, but it is making our operation more efficient and productive.

If an R & D operation were viewed as an organization with well-defined goals, limited resources, and an abundance of opportunities, then conventional planning techniques could be used to establish apppropriate programs. Further, since each program would have (as a result of the planning process) clearly stated interim and final goals, together with a detailed budget of resources, it would

---

[1] From an article in the March 1971 issue of *Innovation,* Technology Communication, Inc., New York.

not be difficult to monitor progress. This prescription for R & D management is so simple that one looks immediately for booby-traps—and of course they are there. R & D activity is to some extent unpredictable, and one cannot expect that even a well-planned R & D program will stay as close to its schedule (or its budget) as, say, a manufacturing run. More Important, R & D people are creative and one cannot with impunity impose either goals or schedules on them from above—one must give them a voice in both goal definition and schedule-setting.

Even in the face of these difficulties, modern management techniques can be adapted to the task of managing research and development activity without impairing its essential creative quality. Aside from the obvious benefits of improved management capability, a formalized structure (if it is a good one) provides working communication channels up and down the technical and management hierarchies of an organization and is a useful tool for the exercise of leadership—an intangible but vital element of management.

Principles of Program Planning and Budgeting

We begin by considering some of the organizational goals which compete for the limited budget of resources. These goals can be sorted, roughly, into four types.

Scientific Goals: discoveries; new knowledge, concepts, and understanding; new materials, techniques, and processes.

Technological Goals: inventions; new and improved systems, products, and components; new and improved manufacturing processes and design techniques.

Economic Goals: improvement of economic position; penetration or creation of new markets; increase in existing markets, or in shares of existing markets.

Social Goals: public health, education, and welfare; improvement in the environment and in the quality of life.

For formal planning, the corporate R & D center of an industrial enterprise ordinarily considers only scientific and technological goals. Other sectors of the corporation give their attention to economic goals, and to technological goals as well. Their decisions affect formal planning at the R & D centre only through expressions of the relative desirability of certain goals and, of course, through determination of the total resource budget allocated to the center. Social goals affect the corporation primarily through external constraints imposed by the government, but usually these are transmuted into equivalent economic, technological, or scientific goals.

In R & D management it is useful to think about these goals on two levels, strategic and tactical. *Strategic goals* relate to programs, well-defined segments of activity, and are formulated by interplay between the managers of R & D and the managements of the corporation and its operating divisions. *Tactical goals* are formulated within the R & D organization itself, and relate to what we call program elements.

Strategic goals are expressed in broad (but specific) terms, as for example, "to achieve scientific leadership in the field of long-distance radio communication," or "to develop techniques which will significantly reduce the cost of machining refractory alloys." Tactical goals, by contrast, are as specific as "to achieve an improved understanding of the mechanism of noise generation in an axial-flow compressor.' A well-formulated tactical goal is directly translatable into a goal-directed course of action. Once this has been established, the technical people should be able to carry the ball. If they have the required expertise, and if they are good at coming up with bright ideas, nothing much stands between them and success except hard work and (sometimes) the laws of Mother Nature.

The apparent simplicity of a strategic goal is deceptive. It is a long-term objective which includes, by implication, a large number of technical options from which tactical goals are chosen. Strategic goals must be general enough to be readily understandable by managers outside of the R & D center, who take account of these goals in developing their own operating strategies. At the same time, strategic goals must be precise enough to serve as the basis for generation of appropriate short-term tactical goals by the R & D staff. Further, strategic goals of the R & D center must support the plans and attitudes of the parent organization. If the company wants to market a product better than those available from other sources, strategic goals will reflect the need to stay ahead of the competition in knowledge of the relevant technologies. If, instead, emphasis is placed on comparable quality at lower cost, strategic goals will stress efficient manufacturing techniques.

Long-range goals for an organization cannot be deduced, in simple logical steps, from an agreed-upon set of assumptions and hypotheses. Their invention is an act of synthesis. Use of technological forecasting is sometimes helpful, but we believe the formulation of goals to be essentially a creative activity. Although the difficulties of invention by committee are well known, it is nonetheless necessary to involve all relevant parts of the organization in the goal-setting process if the results are to be a useful reflection of organizational needs and plans.

Planning, of course, involves more than the assembly of a set of goals, even if they are all well formulated. It is up to the managers of the R & D center to avoid being carried away by the mystique of goal formulation and to synthesize around the goals a coherent and unified program which is solidly based on the capabilities of the center and the requirements of the parent corporation. The formal structure of the program planning and budgeting cycle includes nine separate events, which are shown in time sequence in Figure 1.

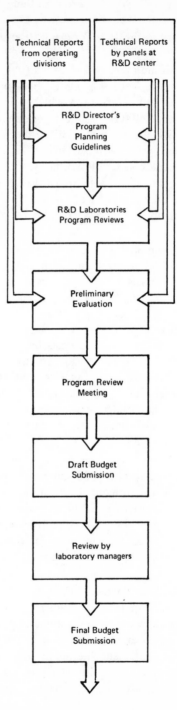

The formal structure of the Program Planning and Budgeting cycle includes nine separate events, which are shown here in time sequence.

We aim for a program of goal-directed activity described in the following terms:

Program element: a single integrated task, aimed at a tactical goal and ordinarily involving not more than five people.

Program: a set of several related program elements, aimed at a common strategic goal and ordinarily involving not more than fifteen people.

Program area: a relatively broad field of activity in which there are a number of current and projected programs with related strategic goals.

Operation of Planning and Budgeting Cycle

This scheme of describing goal-directed activity provides a broad overview of the work at the corporate R & D center. To explain how we actually work our way through the planning and budgeting cycle (in the interests of simplicity and corporate privacy) the process is described in the context of H Corp, a (hypothetical) company which exists only for the purposes of this paper. H Corp is a simpler organization than General Electric, and the system described here is rather less complicated than the scheme used at GE. The underlying philosophies, however, are the same, and H Corp's technique (as described) is a good model of the basic process at GE.

H Corp is an industrial company with annual sales of about one billion dollars. It has several operating divisions and a corporate headquarters. The divisions are oriented towards different market areas and do not compete with each other, but all the divisions are in electronics businesses, and there is a high degree of commonality in their technological interests. Each division has an advanced development department and a number of specialized laboratories, all of which do research and development. In addition, H Corp supports over one hundred professionals at a corporate R & D center of four laboratories whose laboratory managers report directly to the corporate R & D director.

Short-range product-oriented R & D is ordinarily handled by the divisions. Long-range, exploratory, and high-risk programs are pursued by the corporate R & D center, whose business is essentially the extraction of new products and techniques from emerging areas of science and technology. The center does not, however, have a free hand to pursue anything simply because it happens to be interesting. Its activity must be responsive to the needs of the operating divisions and must support their strategies. Using the planning technique described below is one way of making sure that the center's activity is well integrated with that of the rest of the corporation. Merely going through the motions, though, is not sufficient. The system will not work unless open communication channels are available and in use at every level of the organization. Members of the center's staff, both managerial and technical, must *actively* work at the business of understanding the needs, strategies, and goals of all parts of the corporation.

The R & D director is key man in the annual cycle of planning and

143

budgeting the activity of the corporate R & D center, and he works with the following information.

1. An intimate understanding of the plans and problems of the operating divisions and the corporation as a whole.

2. Data, formal and informal, concerning the performance of the R 7 d center during the past year in moving toward its established goals.

3. Formal documents, prepared once each year by the head of each operating division, detailing the areas in which the needs of the division seem to require the attention of the corporate R & D center.

4. Formal reports of panels drawn from the technical and management staffs of the corporate R & D center. Each panel maintains close liaison with a single operating division and prepares an annual report on the status of advanced technical work in that division—and, of course, on its view of requirements for assistance to that division by the corporate R & D center.

The director also uses common sense and more than a dash of creative intuition.

The opening gun in the annual planning and budgeting cycle, which runs for about six weeks, is fired by the director who issues *Program Planning Guidelines* for the current cycle. These are set forth in a short document which goes to each of the laboratory managers at the R & D center. The document specifies three possible levels for the center's budget during the coming year. Expressed in terms of deviation from the current budget, these levels are the director's best estimate, high estimate, and low estimate. In addition, the document lists all current and projected programs (using the term in the formal sense as described earlier) segregated by program areas. Each program is coded P or N to indicate the director's initial judgment that "Present program goals are adequate" or that "New or modified program goals must be formulated." (the reference is to strategic goals). Each program is also coded +, 0, or − to indicate the director's opinion that the level of effort should be increased, held constant, or decreased. The whole document is simple, but it gives the R & D staff a concise picture of the director's thinking. For H Corp it looks something like this:

Estimated Changes in Total Budget:
Probable, +10%; Maximum, +20%; Minimum, −5%.

Program Area: Communications Technology

Optical Communications	P/+
Satellite Communications	P/0
Terminal Equipment	N/0
Signal Processing and Transmission	P/−

Program Area: Instrument Technology

Instrument Displays	N/+
Biomedical Instruments	P/0

Program Area: microelectronics

Microwave Electronic Circuits	N/0
Computer-Aided Circuit Design	P/0
Semiconductor Physics Research	N/−
Electron Beam Devices	N/−

The next step in the cycle is the generation of a set of *program reviews,* one for each program. These are drafted by members of the technical and management staff at each laboratory, but responsibility for their content rests with the cognizant laboratory managers. A joint effort is sometimes required when the program elements of a single program are not all placed in the same laboratory at the center. At this stage, formulation of the tactical goals and allocation of resources to the corresponding program elements is initially carried out at a grass-roots level—that is by people who will later be involved in using these resources (money, manhours, and time) to achieve the goals they have had a hand in formulating.

A program review is a highly condensed formal document containing a wealth of substantive information about the program. The program review for H Corp's imaginary optical communications program consists of six parts:

I. The formal strategic goal of the program is given. Here, also, are brief statements covering the technical content of the program and its significance to H Corp.

II. The schedule and the milestones of each program element are spelled out, giving a look at the microstructure of the program. The schedule, of course, is based on the level of effort implied by the funding recommended in part III.

III. The recommended budget for each program element for the coming year is shown. It also shows the suggested distribution of funds among the program elements for three specified conditions: total budget (for the program) the same as for the current year; up by one-third, and down by one-third. As a basis for comparison, distribution of this year's current budget is also given. It is unlikely that the budget for the R & D center, or even the budget for a single program area, will change from one year to the next by as much as one-third. The funding level of a single program, however, may easily change by this amount.

IV. Brief discussions of the consequences of changing the budget (from the current level) by as much as + one third or − one third are offered.

V. Accomplishments under the program and the significance of each achievement during the current year are presented briefly.

VI. Each of the program elements are described in detail, spelling out the tactical goal and stating who will actually do the work. This part, like II, is based on the assumption that funding will be at the level recommended in part III.

These program reviews are the formal documents prepared for the planning and budgeting cycle. They are not only a digest of important information about the programs, but also a distillation of the creative ideas of the technical-staff members and managers who will be directly involved in the programs. They are the basis for all subsequent discussion and decision-making in the planning/budgeting cycle. The substantive information contained in the program reviews is, however, limited. They could not possibly be used as a basis for decisions by people who had no other information about the programs—managers at some remote headquarters—nor are they used in this way.

After preparation of the program reviews, the next step in the cycle is a *review meeting*. It is called by the director and attended by selected members of his staff and by the laboratory managers. Well in advance of the meeting, each person who will be there is provided with a full set of program reviews (earlier, he will have received a copy of the program planning guidelines) and sets of the formal reports prepared by the operating divisions and by the vice-president's technical panels (listed above as sources of information used by the director).

The review meeting is a thorough examination of the accumulated information about each program, followed by a discussion of the changes that ought to be made. In addition to the detailed consideration of each program, there is usually a discussion of the priorities and factors which affect decisions concerning programs. On occasion the technique of program planning and budgeting is itself the subject of discussion. Most of the meeting, however, is devoted to the programs themselves.

For the first go-around, the director usually selects a single laboratory manager to outline all of the current and proposed work in a program area—even though the activity may involve several of the laboratories at the R & D center. Following this presentation the floor is opened for anyone to ask questions, to challenge the goals, effectiveness or potential impact of a program, and to suggest changes. The spirit of these discussions is critical but constructive (the director is, of necessity, a superlative chairman), and they must lead to a high degree of common understanding of the programs by the laboratory managers, the director, and the members of his staff. It is not uncommon in these meetings to find unrecognized opportunities that can be readily exploited by new combinations of the work and talent of the laboratories.

Even though a high commonality of understanding is achieved, it is too much to expect agreement or consensus to emerge from one of these meetings. The laboratory managers, if they are good managers and leaders, are not indifferent to the impact of the program decisions on their own laboratories. If decisions imply a smaller size or a less important role for his laboratory (in some areas), a laboratory manager will face the delicate task of maintaining the

146

dedication and effectiveness of his organization in the face of ostensibly adverse decisions. He may also face the problem of having to implement decisions about which he has grave personal doubts. We have no magical process for producing good program decisions and avoiding the common problems of managing an organization. What we do have is a methodology that elicits frank discussions, promotes common understanding, and enables us to settle efficiently on a definite course of action.

At the close of the meeting, each man prepares a set of formal program ratings for the director. Three aspects of each program are independently considered.

Impact: the long-term impact of the program on the operation of H corp, on the assumption that the strategic goal of the program will be achieved more or less as scheduled.

Performance: The performance of the laboratories, particularly during the past year, in reaching milestones and achieving tactical goals within the schedules and budgets called for by the program (for a new program, the rating is of course based on an estimate of future performance).

Growth: The desirability of raising the level of funding for the program (for a new program there is no current budget to serve as a base, but the director supplies a bench-mark figure which is used in rating).

The programs are not rated first, second, third, and so on—this calls for more precise judgment than seems warranted. Instead, numbers ranging from 1 for the highest rating to 5 for the lowest are used. Each man at the meeting assigns three rating numbers (based on impact, performance, and growth as described above) to each program. What the distribution of ratings must be and might be is specified, for example, that they approximate a statistician's *normal distribution* (the usual bell-shaped curve). This is done to counter the tendencies of optimists to rate all programs 1 and of pessimists to rate all of them 5.

The staff at the R & D center also prepares a set of consolidated program ratings using the information turned in at the close of the proceedings. This is an average of all the ratings, but in computing it the director's opinions are given a weight of two, laboratory managers get a weight of one, and staff members one-half. The result is biased toward agreement with the director's judgment, which is probably as it should be, since he is saddled with the task of using the information in preparing the final budget request. Here are the ratings that came out of this year's review meeting at H corp.

Consolidated Program Ratings for
Impact, Performance, Growth

Program Area: Communications Technology	Impact	Performance	Growth
Optical Communications	2	1	2
Satellite Communications	1	3	1
Terminal Equipment	4	4	3
Signal Processing and Transmission	3	5	4
Program Area: Instrument Technology			
Instrument Displays	3	3	2
Biomedical Instruments	3	4	3
Program Area: Microelectronics			
Microwave Microelectronic Circuits	5	3	3
Computer-Aided Circuit Design	2	2	3
Semiconductor Physics Research	3	3	4
Electron Beam Devices	4	2	5

Following the review meeting, the director prepares a draft of the proposed budget broken down by programs. There is no formal justification for this step in the cycle, except the old doctrine that "the boss makes the decisions." The draft is circulated to the laboratory managers, giving them one more chance to argue against decisions they do not like, before the formal budget request goes to the top management of the corporation.

As a matter of interest, here is what this year's budget submission at H Corp came to. The first column is the proposed budget (in thousands) for 1971. The second column is the change (in percent) from 1970.

Proposed Budget for 1971
Program Area: Communications Technology

	budget	per cent change
Optical Communications	$560	60
Satellite Communications	910	49
Terminal Equipment	290	45
Signal Processing and Transmission	315	(7.5)
Program Area: Instrument Technology		
Instrument Displays	550	47
Biomedical Instruments	225	80
Program Area: Microelectronics		
Microwave Microelectronic Circuits	450	7
Computer-Aided Circuit Design	780	11
Semiconductor Physics Research	420	(20)
Electron Beam Devices	400	(38)
Total	$4900	14%

The total increase, at 14 percent over last year's figure, is a bit higher than the program-planning guidelines estimate of a 10 percent probable increase. In comparing the final budget submission with the recommendations of the program reviews and with the ratings for growth, there are some interesting correlations. Optical communications, for example, had a recommended increase of 17 percent (from $350,000 to $410,000) but actually received (in the budget submission) an increase of 60 percent because of favorable ratings. Others, with lower ratings, did not fare so well.

Surveillance

Planning, of course, is only the beginning—monitoring must go on eternally. Monitoring of the microstructure of the operation of the R & D center is made possible through the medium of program elements. The director monitors work at the laboratories in several ways.

News Items

Brief one- or two-page descriptions of noteworthy events or achievements are reported by program managers as the occasions arise.

On-Site-Visits

Periodic half-day visits are made to see the activity going on under each program and to discuss it informally with the people who are actually doing the work.

Oral Program Reviews

Formal oral reviews of the status of each program are held at least once every year.

Miscellaneous Reviews

At least once a year, and sometimes more often, progress under each program is formally compared with the detailed schedule in the program-review document.

Technical Reports

Technical reports are prepared, either for external circulation or for distribution within the company, when a coherent portion of the work (not necessarily an entire program element) under a program has been completed. For some programs, progress reports are also prepared at specific intervals.

The management system makes it possible to monitor both activity and expenditure. Indeed, it forces thinking in terms of progress aimed toward explicit ends. As a result, signs of trouble can be detected far earlier than when a manager simply checks on the rate at which his allocated resources (man-hours

149

and dollars) are being used up. On this account, laboratory managers are given a fairly free hand without losing control of the operation. They have complete authority to change the allocation of funds (to the several program elements) within a given program, and deviations as large as 15 percent in total program costs are tolerated.

Conclusion

There is no magic in these operations. In planning, we start by thinking about goals instead of resources, and we try to involve everybody in the planning process. In monitoring, we look first at goal-directed progress instead of at depletion of resources. We find this approach to be a sturdy skeleton on which to hang the rest of the difficult and undescribable task of R & D management.

A creative researcher working on a tough problem often seems to move from thought to thought, from one experiment to another, in a way that is almost unpredictable. Whether or not this mode of operation is essential to a truly creative effort is very much beside the point. It is, in fact, the research style of some of our best people and we cannot afford to destroy this kind of activity by an overly rational planning process. On the other hand, with a laissez faire philosophy we run the risk of dissipating the creative energy of the R & D organization, either by spreading our effort over too many areas or by attacking problems which, however interesting they may be, are not of primary importance to the parent corporation.

The first point is raised by scientists who want to be left alone, the second by businessmen who cannot see why R & D should not be as orderly and predictable as manufacturing.

We feel that the difficulty raised by these two contradictory points of view is illusory. Even our most unpredictable researchers are strongly guided by their perceptions of goals. Most of them welcome discussion and evaluation of their work, and cooperate in coordinating their activity with the broad objectives of the research center. In fact, they do not want to be left alone at all. They simply do not want to be pushed around. There is no basic conflict between technical creativity and a system of formal goal-setting, and the two become compatible when the creative people are involved in the process of goal formulation.

We do not want to leave the impression that our research people always have things their own way. However they are involved in the planning process; and if anybody's views are set aside, it is only after detailed discussion. In the end, issues are sharply drawn and disagreements are brought out into the open where they are not likely to breed disaffection. It takes some effort to shift from simple resource budgeting, "how many dollars is it going to take to pay our bills?" to a formalism in which goal selection is basic to the planning-budgeting process, but we believe it is paying off at General Electric.

CHAPTER 19

Program Budgeting
at John Hancock Life Insurance

by Robert J. Lamphere

Vice President, Corporate Analysis and Planning
John Hancock Mutual Life Insurance Company

Formalized long-range planning started at John Hancock in 1965 with the establishment of an Office of Corporate Planning, headed by a vice-president, reporting to the chief executive officer. The office's first task was to institute a planning cycle which would involve all elements of the company in planning its future directions. The philosophy used was that plans should be made by those who would ultimately be responsible for executing them. The Planning Office, therefore, plays the role of catalyst and coordinator, rather than making rhe plan itself. Another important decision was that plans made by the several departments would be discussed with top management and would be ratified by that group prior to their implementation.

On that basis, a system was established whereby corporate areas such as marketing, investment, and electronic data processing each prepared detailed plans for the ensuing five years for discussion with the Executive Committee. Included in the material were sales and investment forecasts, manpower requirement estimates, operations planning and system proposals. Over time, such planning was gradually integrated with an already existing salary-budgeting system.

In 1965, another top-management decision has resulted in the launching of a major expansion effort. The number of agents in the distribution system was substantially increased and new field offices were established. A separate department was created to look into areas of possible diversification. Over the next several years the company acquired a Canadian subsidiary; established a real estate subsidiary; purchased a group insurance brokerage company; established an international group insurance program (in association with leading foreign insurance companies throughout the world); established a financial services subsidiary to serve professional men and women; and, entered the mutual fund field.

All these activities, but primarily in the field-sales expansion—which went farther and faster than was originally contemplated—brought pressures to bear on the organization. These pressures manifested themselves in terms of decreasing surplus ratios and increasing demands on available manpower resources. One result of these pressures was to lead the top decision-makers to seek better ways of managing the company's resources. Especially needed was the means to call attention to the consequences of various rates of growth and expansion in terms of key corporate-performance indicators.

Consideration of Program Budgeting

This desire to improve the company's resource-management methods led to the establishing of a committee in 1968 to explore program budgeting for possible application to operations at John Hancock. Little was known about the subject at that time except that there was some evidence of successful application in the automobile industry and some government agencies.

Accordingly, the committee set about learning what program budgeting was, what the essential elements were, and if some or all aspects might be adapted to John Hancock. The committee's research included investigation of what appropriate objectives for a mutual life insurance company were, how a program structure might be devised to link operating systems to objectives, and how top management could use a program-budgeting system.

Inasmuch as most of the available literature dealt with the application of program budgeting within a governmental framework, the committee experienced some difficulty in translating these methods into mutual life insurance company operations. Real doubt existed as to whether program budgeting's heavy emphasis on resource allocation, and the close tie between expense budgeting and long-range planning that seems to be required, was appropriate for our company. Furthermore, the committee recognized that establishing measures of effectiveness which could be generally accepted would be a long process without much immediate payoff. Because of the challenges of rapid expansion, the company's most immediate need was for a tool that would evaluate new projects and new methods of operation.

Despite such problems, which embraced both the conceptual and the operational aspects of program budgeting, the committee concluded that there were important features that could be adapted to John Hancock. Accordingly, some of these (in particular, a methodical approach to project planning) were introduced and others were designated for further study and future implementation.

Project Planning and Reporting System

John Hancock first applied program-budgeting methods in 1968 in an

152

operation known as Project Planning and Reporting System (PPRS). The intention was to force careful consideration by top management of how, where, and when company resources should be allocated to projects that are discretionary in nature.

The system was meant to insure that various elements of the company did not initiate new activities and projects which might commit resources to the point that the company could not easily respond to new opportunities which might arise. The system involved a full description of the project, the timetable for implementation, a development of all of the costs associated with it, and a thorough cost-benefit analysis of the results expected. including (when appropriate) a comparison with whatever system or activity it was designed to replace. Also involved was a detailed analysis of alternative means to the same or a similar result.

Although analysis has always characterised the work of the actuaries who figure prominently in all insurance company operations, program-budgeting methods brought new dimensions and new kinds of emphasis to John Hancock's study requirements. Under PPRS the advocate prepared a *project memorandum* which was submitted to a reanalysis staff who raised questions and developed options and issues for executive committee deliberation.

The establishment of the Project Planning and Reporting System had by-products. Among these was the acquainting of various levels of management with the techniques of cost-benefit analysis. An emphasis on the consideration of alternatives and concern for broad objectives in relation to a specific activity also resulted.

Some of the projects considered under this system were relatively small in scope, others related to a detailed systems change, and frequently computer-related activities were involved. Some of the projects were much larger in scope, and involved the company's diversification and acquisition efforts.

Corporate Objectives

An important element of program budgeting is careful definition and articulation of corporate objectives. As one definition of program budgeting states it, the technique consists of "identifying end objectives, designing alternative ways of achieving the objectives, and choosing among them on the basis of systematic analysis.'. Peter Drucker confirms the need for establishing objectives in this way:

It is not possible to be effective unless one first decides what one wants to accomplish. It is not possible to manage, in other words, unless one first has a goal. It is not even possible to design the structure of an organization unless one knows what it is supposed to be doing and how to measure whether it is doing it.

In fact, it is never possible to give a final answer to the question, "What is our business?" Any answer becomes obsolete within a short period. The question has to be thought through again and again.

But if no answer at all is forthcoming, if objectives are not clearly set, resources will be splintered and wasted. There will be no way to measure the results. If the organization has not determined what its objectives are, it cannot determine what effectiveness it has and whether it is obtaining results or not.[1]

Accordingly, the company's objectives have been developed under three main headings. The first category concerns responsibilities to policyholders and other clients. Considerations here are based on legal contracts between policyholders and other clients and the company, since in a mutual company these policyholders also own the company. Out of this contractual and ownership relationship a number of responsibilities arise, including a need to maintain a strong and healthy company over extended periods of time,[2] a desire to assure equity among individual policyholders and among classes of policyholders, a need to keep net costs to policyholders at reasonably low levels through dividend allocations and a wish to maintain satisfactory levels of service to existing policyholders.

The second category deals with responsibilities to employees and agents. This group of objectives covers salaries and employee benefit plans which must be basically competitive in the insurance industry and with other financial institutions; provide opportunities to advance within the organization commensurate with individual abilities; provide educational and training opportunities to assist individual development.

The final category is concerned with responsibilities to the public. It includes such items as operating ethically and morally and in the general public interest with due regard for the fiduciary responsibilities of a large financial institution and recognizing that a large insurance company has certain responsibilities to the societies in which it operates, ranging from the country at large to the states and specific communities where it does business.

As they stand, the category descriptions so far delineated are useful but not sufficient. It will be necessary to further define each of the three areas and to make explicit statements about specific objectives.

Defining objectives and setting goals require a thorough understanding of

---

[1] Peter F. Drucker, *The Age of Discontinuity: Guidelines to Our Changing Society*, Harper & Row, New York, 1968, pp. 190–191.

[2] Eloquent language by the Supreme Court of Georgia in Carlton v Southern Mutual Insurance Co., 72 Ga. 371 (1884) described the responsibility of management as follows: "They must look to the future, as well as to the present and past. They manage a scheme, which will live when they are gone. They must be careful to transmit to their successors, for managing for future insurers and assured, a body politic as healthy and sound as that which they nurtured so wisely and well."

how the firm operates and of the often complex interrelationships which exist among its several parts. One objective of importance, for example, is growth. Growth is important to employees and agents insofar as a dynamic organization implies greater opportunities for the future. Growth appears desirable from the corporate point of view also. The question "What level of growth can be sustained over time?" arises and leads to the question "What will be the financial impact of this or that growth pattern?" Further questions arise such as "How should growth be measured?"

It appears, therefore, that in a mutual insurance company some level of growth is important. It also appears that growth should be measured for each line of business in terms of new sales, insurance in force, and premium income. However, in setting growth goals, one needs to assess their impact on each kind of financial result such as operating gain, changes in surplus, and net costs and to measure the relationships between income and expenses for each line of business. What the firm is seeking then, in the final analysis, is a set of specific objectives, attainment of which will produce the proper balance between growth and profitable operations.

In arriving at such objectives, it is important to be specific, to select goals that are quantifiable so that results achieved in moving toward the goals can be measured, and to elicit top management's agreement on the objectives to be pursued. Then, and probably only then, can it be said that there are corporate objectives. These can then be translated into quantified lower-level goals, various alternative programs to achieve the objectives can be examined, and trade-offs between objections can be considered.

Issue Analysis

A major feature of the developing system at John Hancock which incorporates aspects of program budgeting is issue analysis. Its concern is to identify and resolve major issues which the company faces or will face in the near future. The approach has been to convene a task force of knowledgeable people, usually a combination of junior and senior officers, to undertake a thorough study of an identified situation. The task force follows an organized process and presents a formal report to top management.

The study of issues basically follows a five-step process:

1. Issue Identification

Issues are identified in two ways: (a) at the beginning of the annual planning cycle when all company departments and offices are invited to nominate issues to be analyzed during the coming year and (b) during the preparation and review of area and departmental projections which constitute one of the major items in the Five Year Program and Financial Plan. From this list, top management selects several issues for analysis. The final step in the

155

issue-identification process is the preparation of a paper by an interdepartmental group of junior officers which sets forth the dimensions of the problems involved and outlines the study to be undertaken.

2. *Guidelines for Analysis*

The issue paper is reviewed by an independent group to determine whether the problems at issue are important enough to warrant an in-depth analysis. If the analysis is to be conducted, this group also prepares guidelines which set the scope and structure of the study to be made in a way useful for planning purposes as well as for developing solutions to the problems.

3. *Cost/Benefit Analysis*

The interdepartmental group which originally prepared the issue paper now conducts the study. Explicit attention is given to the company objectives involved, the costs and benefits of alternative courses of action to achieve them, and a recommendation of preferred solutions to the problems, along with the details of implementation and progress reporting.

4. *Review*

The analysis is reviewed by an independent group for comprehensiveness, documentation and substantive adequacy.

5. *Decision*

The report is then presented to the appropriate committee of senior officers which accepts, modifies, or rejects the recommendations.

This process appears to have several beneficial by-products, including further identification of corporate objectives and providing the occasion for decision-makers to choose between conflicting objectives. It also helps to highlight the relationships between organizational elements of the company and, in certain instances, make clear the trade-off between various courses of action which involve more than one organizational element.

The process as presently structured requires the assignment of well-qualified people from various company operating areas to a study group, and requires a substantial allotment of their time, usually for many months. It appears that the benefits of this expenditure of resources are worth the cost. The work of people from different areas over an extended period of time seems to break down some organizational barriers—and the necessity to produce documented factual data plays an important part in developing understanding of the interrelationships among various departments and areas. Such emphasis on a corporatewide perspective is not purchased at the price of submerging minority views. Indeed, fundamental to the review process is the preservation and clarification of disagreements when they exist. Consensus is not a requirement, and minority views are presented together with the preferred options.

An additional value of issue analysis is the formal and analytic process which tends to force a consideration of what the real problems are, how these interrelate with company objectives, and what solutions appear to be viable. It also forces the production of a record which is available as a starting point either for review or for reference when the same or a similar issue comes up again. In essence, the process seems helpful in improving communications in a large organization in a meaningful way. And this takes place not only at the time the task force develops the report but also when the matter is under review at the decision-making level.

A continuing part of this process in the future will be an annual request to operating areas of the company for their opinions on major issues or problems facing the company over the next five years. In this request, operating areas will be asked to think not only of broad company issues but also of problems which bear on their particular area of responsibility. The resulting data provide the reviewing group with input from various segments of the company which will provide insights into both the separate parts and the totality of its activities. Another important occasion for identifying corporationwide issues occurs during the preparation and review of marketing, performance, and financial forecasts for inclusion in the program and financial plan.

The Planning Model

When a number of issues and problems are identified, the complex interdependencies and relationships that exist between and among the many elements of the firm come into view. In seeking to sort out these relationships and in attempting to set appropriate goals and directions for the future, some problems have been identified. Important among these are lack of information on cause and effect relationships, lack of information on the peripheral impact of a decision, lack of methods for quantifying the impact of a decision, and lack of a means for swift evaluation of many alternative courses of action. Each of these areas is integral to a program-budgeting approach to planning and constitutes a significant lack.

One means of remedying these deficiencies, thus permitting greater adaptation of the program-budgeting technique, appears to lie in the construction of a corporate-planning model. The kind of model needed is one which encourages analysis of the relationships and interrelationships between the company, its environment, and key operating variables. A number of the elements of such a model already exist within the company, in one form or another, and in various places for varying purposes. What is required is to pull existing material together, and to determine what additional relationships need to be and can be identified. Finally, each important relationship must be decribed mathematically—and the whole model programmed for the computer. This does not mean that all significant considerations can be quantified. Some just are not quantifiable and must be subject to qualitative analysis.

Such an undertaking is complex and time-consuming, and is apt to be expensive. Despite these conditions, it seems to be a worthwhile endeavor and will provide a means for speedy, more adequate and less personnel-demanding response to many problems. These include such questions as: what are the effects of growth rates, expense margins, operating gains, insurance in force, surplus and assets; of changes in agents' turnover rates, field expansion, insurance-policy lapse rates, pricing, mutual-fund sales, entering the casualty business, investment policy and on and on.

A planning model can facilitate an examination of the effects on corporate results of proposed changes in operation, of differing assumptions about the economic environment, and of alternate strategies and plans. Its output can be an array of these results in some order of relative importance for top management's consideration and decision. In short, a model is a tool to facilitate decision-making by making it possible to simulate the possible outcomes of a wide range and large number of available alternatives prior to the time the decision is made. A model is particularly relevant in the program-budgeting technique because it permits rapid and thorough assessment of the probable results of a large number of alternatives. It is an important element in developing a system which applies certain important principles of program budgeting to an insurance company.

Program Structure

To date, after considerable study, it has been decided not to adopt a program structure for all the activities of the company. There are several reasons. The most important is that efforts to define objectives and set specific goals are still in progress. Even if the goal-setting process were farther along, there is some question of the desirability of cutting a structure out of whole cloth and of the relative importance of creating a traditional crosswalk in an insurance company. Much of an insurance company's operating budget is automatically determined by the amounts of insurance in force and the level of new sales. Budgetary aspects of such vital programs as investments are trivial in comparison to their policy aspects. Top management priorities emphasize deeper understanding of the effects of various policies on key indicators of corporate performance. Therefore, at present, there seems to be a larger payoff from continuing to refine objectives and to define goals, to understand key interdepartmental dependencies, to analyze discretionary projects and companywide issues in terms of objectives, to establish usable measures of effectiveness and to refine marketing and other financial forecasting.

Financial Plan

The ultimate product to be produced will be a Five-Year Program and

Financial Plan. Though the title is borrowed from program-budgeting language, the product will be tailored to John Hancock's needs. It will contain some elements of program budgeting, but it will also bring together and integrate the results of Hancock's whole system of planning.

Presently, the planning documents serve some of the functions in the John Hancock system which program structure serves in other organizations. Better understanding of how various department and area courses of action and their aggregate costs affect measures of corporate financial performance is of paramount concern to top management. The present Program and Financial Plan offers a quantitative summary of how sales, investment, and other important program goals, along with the manpower and salary plans of each department, affect operating results by line of business and other measures of corporate financial performance. In its current form, the plan is constructed from the plans and estimates of individual departments. It is primarily a communications device—displaying the corporate consequences of departmental operations and plans. Obviously, it has great potential for becoming a framework within which departmental plans can be tested for consistency with corporate plans and goals.

The plan also will highlight segments of data with commentary on each aspect. It will assure that all significant trends and changes are covered, important constraints are identified and at the same time will avoid losing the reader in a mass of detail. Complementary to the plan document (actually a part of it) are the major issue analyses and program studies. As the plan evolves over time, it will be responsive to the desires and needs of the top decision-makers.

The further development of the John Hancock planning system will include additional work on corporate objectives, the financial plan, issue analysis, the Project Planning and Reporting System, models, and a reporting system.

Corporate Objectives in the terms described earlier will be used as a framework for meetings with the Executive Committee to secure understanding and suggestions on corporate objectives.

Financial Information now contained in the document "Summary of Department Plans and Other Key Financial Data 1971-1975" will be restructured next year in a more complete financial plan. Information thus generated along with data taken from Issue Analyses and PPRS memoranda will be the bases of constructing the plan. A short narrative will highlight the data, and wherever possible existing goals, problems and constraints will be quantified. This will enable the preparation of the information for the 72-76 period in a more comprehensive financial plan. By 1972, preparation of the 73-77 Program and Financial Plan could well be the vehicle for corporate goal setting, planning and decisionmaking, depending, of course, upon continued progress in defining corporate objectives.

Issue Analysis will be continued during 1971. The major study of the John Hancock individual marketing distribution system already under way will be presented (to the extent appropriate) in the Issue Analysis format. In addition, other new studies will be initiated.

Project Planning and Reporting System will be strengthened to insure that all appropriate projects are prepared in its format. More people will be educated in the system and the conduct of cost-benefit analysis will provide decision-makers with information that is both more complete and thorough in its treatment of options. The reanalysis function will play a part in this educational process and through it we will seek to improve the data being sent back to the project manager and used in memoranda to the decision-making committee.

Planning Model efforts to develop a comprehensive planning tool will continue. This will not be in great detail concerning any line of business or program. Its primary purpose will be to show the interrelationship between the various parts of the company, and how an action taken at one point affects other parts. As its names suggest, it will also assist in long-range planning.

Reporting System needs range from plans and projections made by departments to the Project Planning and Reporting System actions. The president's chart room will be studied in this connection and made more responsive to the system being developed. Further analytical work needs to be done on the time-cost reporting system presently being developed by the controller's department and the Project Planning and Reporting System. Early study indicates problems in comparing costs projected under the PPRS system with data being collected under the time-cost reporting system. This kind of problem needs to be minimized in developing a system in order to facilitate the evaluation of progress compared to plan.

Annual Planning cycles are subject to a calendar constraint frequently not recognized by events. The regular planning system must be refined to determine when changes in existing plans are to be considered and what analytic and procedural steps should be introduced in connection with changes not appropriate to PPRS and which cannot be put off until the next planning cycle.

CHAPTER 20

Application of the Concept
to School District Decision-Making

by William H. Curtis,

Research Project Director
Association of School Business Officials

Early in 1968, discussion began within the educational community and between the members of this community and the United States Office of Education (USOE) about the appropriateness of the concepts of the planning-programming-budgeting system for education. As a result of these discussions, a research project was designed which was to be sponsored and financed primarily by the USOE. It was to be unique in that the users of the system were to be its designers. The usual practice was to have the program-budgeting system designed by those trained and versed in the methodology of system analysis.

The letter "E" was added to the PPB acronym to emphasize the function of evaluation explicitly, rather than implicitly as evaluation is treated in the traditional PPBS concepts. In the summer of 1968, work was started on the national PPBES project under the direction of the Research Corporation of the Association of School Business Officials. This project involved not only the Research Corporation but also the concurrent effort of the Dade County Public School System of Florida. Both were scheduled for completion in June 1971.

The Research Corporation in its acceptance of the contract for the project agreed to be responsible for:

Surveying the field to determine the extent to which school districts in the United States had planned or were planning to adopt the PPBES concept as a new approach in support of decision-making at the local level.

Disseminating information about the concept and its potential for adaptation by local school districts as well as about work on the project as it progressed.

Preparing a conceptual design to serve as a guide for local districts as they

William H. Curtis

attempted to design, develop and implement their own version of the PPBES concept.

The Dade County Public School System agreed to be responsible for:

Preparing an operational design for applying the PPBES concept in the Dade County Public School System.

Testing this design and *disseminating* the results of the testing.

It now appears that a substantial gain would have been realized if the two efforts had been sequential rather than concurrent. Although the integration of both efforts was achieved in the joint report, the ideal situation would have been to have an operational testing of the conceptual design developed in the RC-ASBO effort.

Surveying the Field

The first step taken by the RC-ASBO team was the development of a survey form designed to explore the state-of-the-art of planning, programming, and budgeting in local school districts.

Approximately 2900 survey forms were distributed to members of the Association of School Business Officials. Of the 1800 replies received, approximately 5 percent of the school districts appeared to be involved in some form of program budgeting and 20 percent indicated that their district had plans for adoption of some form of program budgeting. Only 30 percent of the administrators had any experience with PPBES and only 1 percent had any training in this particular field.

The results of the initial survey left considerable doubt as to whether many of the districts (5 percent) were truly involved in the total application of the PPBES concept. Consequently, a second questionnaire was sent to the 5 percent that claimed to be doing program budgeting for the purpose of determining their degree of sophistication in PPBES. In the final analysis only six of the districts seemed to have complete plans for the utilization of PPBES and in no instance was a district identified which had designed, developed, and implemented a complete PPBE system.

As a result of these surveys, it was decided that the field of education was far from ready for this concept from the standpoint of understanding as well as capability for design, development, and implementation. Consequently, when RC-ASBO's section of the 1969 contract was prepared, it placed more emphasis on dissemination of information than was thought necessary at the inception of the project.

Disseminating Information

As a major part of the effort during the first part of 1969, the RC-ASBO team prepared a set of schematics describing the initial conceptual design for the application of the PPBES concept to education. This conceptual design was given wide visibility, especially during the latter part of 1969. It was presented to a national conference of leaders in education, to eight regional conferences for the leadership, at two conferences involving professors and deans of educational administration, and at various clinics throughout the country.

Throughout these early conferences and clinics, the RC-ASBO team was encouraged to adopt a new title for the activity. Consequently, an interim title of Educational Resources Management Design (ERMD) was selected. It was changed to Educational Resources Management System (ERMS) in the fall of 1970.

Three areas were emphasized at the conferences and clinics. These were planning, evaluation and in-service education.

Planning

Prime importance was attached to early involvement of members of the professional staff in the planning process, especially teachers. Also stressed was the need for gaining early support of teacher organizations for the overall design and particularly for the planning process. Discussions frequently emphasized the importance of involving those outside of the professional staff, including students and members of the constituency. Considerable importance was attached to the involvement of middle management and it was emphasized that overall management of education was no longer a unilateral process.

Strong support was given to the importance of the early identification of the needs and problems of a district; the early identification of all of the resources available to a district as well as careful consideration of the allocation and re-allocation process; and the early establishment of long-range goals and broad-based objectives as well as consideration of their feasibility. This segment of planning also emphasized the need for developing greater skills in writing about objectives (both general and performance) and for relating them to programs aimed at target groups.

Evaluation

It was universally felt that the overall process of evaluation was the most difficult problem. Concern was also expressed regarding the present lack of sophistication in this field, the types of evaluation that were suitable for the conceptual design, and the essential reconciliation between required and existing allocation of resources needed to achieve established objectives.

It was emphasized that the evaluating process should be subjective as well as objective; that the teacher's position in the evaluation was important in keeping the focus on the learner; that the evaluative process should be continuous in relation to both long-range and short-range objectives, and that provision should be made for a procedure to evaluate the design itself.

In-Service Education

The need was recognized for state departments of education, institutions of higher learning, and professional organizations to assume a much greater responsibility in providing leaderhip and resources (especially human resources) for in-service education. It was also felt that greater involvement of curriculum personnel was needed both for leadership and to develop a closer relationship with other members of the professional staff. Too much reliance for applying this concept had been placed on school business officials and not enough on curriculum specialists.

Results of the Dissemination Effort

A questionnaire was distributed to participants at most of the conferences and clinics. The participants responded to questions concerning (1) their own views of PPBES and (2) their perceptions of how other groups looked at PPBES.

On the question of adopting PPBES, the educators felt that state legislators generally favor adopting PPBES in education. State legislators and school board members were perceived nationally as ranking high interest in and awareness of PPBES. This favorable attitude was thought to be shared by school business officials, state professional-organization staff members and general school administrators but at a decreasing rate. Principals and classroom teachers were believed to have relatively little interest in adopting PPBES. Educators did not see any of the influential groups as being opposed to adoption of PPBES in education.

Preparing the Conceptual Design

On the basis of feedback from the conferences and clinics, information from Dade County as well as seven other pilot districts, and cooperation from other projects and individuals involved in similar efforts, the RC-ASBO team devoted a major share of its efforts during the latter part of 1970 to the preparation of the final documentation of the conceptual design. The Research Corporation published it in late 1971 but orders in excess of the initial printing resulted in distribution delays.

A synopsis of the contents of the document on conceptual design follows.

The anticipated impact of society's changing expectations on the school system raised the need for a new approach such as the Educational Resources Management System provides, for the utilization of available resources. In the past, few questions were raised about the money put into education. Today, the community is thought to be more sophisticated and to demand knowledge of and a voice in the allocation of resources to the school system. Essential to the effective operation of the new system were an understanding of human development and the environment for learning; the involvement of laymen, students, and educators and a plan for the application of the Educational Resources Management System in the decision-making process for education.

Four processes constitute the ERM System—planning, programming, budgeting, and evaluating. They represent a systematic, ongoing plan for decision-making by which education's resources can be managed. The process of planning was seen to involve identification of needs, problems, and available resources; establishment of goals and general objectives; analysis of existing and proposed new programs, including the consideration of possible alternatives. Planning, in the ERM System, was recognized as a deliberate and continuous rather than a casual and occasional activity. It is both the basis for programming and a beneficiary of its output. The program plan is prepared from information received from each of the other major processes including programming.

Program information is, in turn, forwarded to those working with the other processes, especially planning, to assure that plans are relevant and feasible. Budgeting in the ERM System was seen as covering a series of activities designed to provide the decision-makers with essential information for making selections among the alternatives available in the management of the school system's resources. Evaluation was conceived as a process through which feedback to planning generates the information required to determine whether objectives are attainable or not in light of either identified program or resource limitations or both.

In the view of the RC-ASBO document the most important educational resource was the professional staff. The role of the staff was a critical one in realizing the benefits of the system. Staff was considered to have a relationship to each of the processes of planning, programming, budgeting, and evaluating.

Federal, state, and local interface and interaction have had a potential influence on the acceptance of the Educational Resources Management System by local education agencies. This included variations in state policies and laws, the resulting reporting practices, and their pertinence to the proposed new way of doing business in the school system.

The program-budgeting concept is so new to education that a review of the limitations of the work done and the need for further study and development appeared essential to its successful application. The implied need for change in the preparation of educators and the need for massive in-service education programs dealing with the ERM System were also seen to be factors in the future governance of education.

Even though the primary goal of the RC-ASBO project was the preparation of a *conceptual design*, the field continuously urged the team to include ideas on implementation procedures in the final document. It is planned to develop a section providing insight into problems of design implementation based on experience. The documentation to support this discussion will be in the form of case studies and methodological exposition. The role of analysis in educational-program management and the techniqes of resource and cost analysis will be emphasized.

The pilot school districts (Clark County, Nevada; Douglas County, Colorado; Memphis, Tennessee; Milwaukee, Wisconsin; Montgomery County, Maryland; Peoria, Illinois; Westport, Connecticut) have contributed suggestions for the necessary control and evaluating instruments to be applied in making decisions regarding program implementation. The case studies provide illustrations of many requirements necessary for developing and implementing the system.

ERMS in Education—the Future

The adoption of the ERM System or a similar form of PPBES will have an impact on the school-district staff. The direct support and personal involvement of the superintendent will be essential for success of the undertaking. He will find it necessary to spend more time in the planning process than he does now. Personnel oriented primarily toward curriculum design will exert influence on the allocation of resources to a degree greater than they do now.

Boards of education will be actively involved in approving goals and general objectives recommended for adoption as part of their school-system responsibility. They also will be vitally involved in the determination of priorities.

The implementation of ERMS will necessitate that the skills of the staff at all levels be upgraded. The skills involved are those needed in planning, decision-making, formulation of education objectives, development of alternative programs for achieving objectives, coordinated collection and treatment of diverse data for use in the budgeting process, and evaluating achievement of educational objectives.

The educators viewed the following as representative of conditions and problems likely to pertain when a school system adopts ERMS/PPBS: (1) increased emphasis upon evaluation will result in considerable pressure for more attention to the learning problems of target groups. (2) The school system will have to develop greater capacity for research of an operational nature. (3) The use of the ERM System may suggest internal allocation of resources distinctly different from traditional patterns. (4) More careful delineation of objectives for the learner should result in the discovery of more effective financial support for schools if evidence of accomplishment is provided to them.

The ERMS methodology relates products (outputs) to objectives. It provides increased precision in the identification of objectives for a school system and better correlation of activities and services to specific objectives.

Use of the system will provide a school district with an improved capability to identify, allocate, and use available resources. Decisions presently made by central office administration will be made increasingly in cooperation with principals and teachers. Educators will become more proficient at organizing for effective community involvement in selection of goals and general objectives. Evaluation through the ERM System will result in increased use of available devices for objective determination of educational output.

Overall, the educators viewed the inadequacy of skills, techniques, and understanding of the new methodology as the top-ranking problems in the adoption of the ERM System. Other important problems were negative attitudes and operation and implementation tasks (e.g., coordinating, organizing, communicating, securing two-way involvement, etc.).

The educators recommended that responsibility for providing in-service education to support the ERM System or a similar form of PPBES should be shared among local school systems, state universities, and state departments of education, with the latter to assume prime responsibility for leadership. The least desirable option was for the local school systems to act alone in providing the necessary in-service education for the design, development, and implementation of the new concept. No great distinction was made between options providing for involvement of organizations or professional educators and the U.S. Office of Education.

In conclusion, it seems obvious that the application of the program-budgeting concept to the field of education is a very complex process. Focusing on the learning process and the learner and what happens to him requires the application of design and developmental patterns somewhat different from those of government or business. Therefore, it should be recognized that the outcome of this project and related ones now in process represent only the beginning of the developmental process. Much more in the way of research and development will be needed if the planning-programming-budgeting system concept is to be used effectively by the school districts of this country.

CHAPTER 21

Pennsylvania's Planning, Programming, Budgeting System[1]

by Robert J. Mowitz

Director Institute of Public Administration
The Pennsylvania State University

When Raymond P. Shafer was inaugurated as governor of the Commonwealth of Pennsylvania in January 1967, he inherited a budgeting system which had been revised in the late 1950s from a line-item budget to a "program budget." Budget requests were presented in terms of departments and organizational units, and although some work-load and activities data were included, the interpretation of what was meant by the word *program* was ambiguous. Both the Governor and Arthur F. Sampson, his secretary of administration and budget secretary, were convinced that there was need for improvement in the way in which decisions were made about programs and resources. Shafer had served as Governor Scranton's lieutenant governor and Sampson had served as deputy secretary of the Department of Property and Supplies in the Scranton Administration, and their conclusion that there was a need for a change was based upon experience with the existing system. On February 29, 1968, the Governor's Office of Administration concluded an agreement with The Pennsylvania State University's Institute of Public Administration, giving the Institute the responsibility for directing the implementation of a planning, programming, budgeting system for the Commonwealth. The agreement called for the new system to be installed and in operation by December 31, 1970. This meant thirty-four months to develop, install, and make operational a new decision-making system for the Commonwealth of Pennsylvania.

[1] A detailed description of the Pennsylvania system will be found in the author's *The Design and Implementation of Pennsylvania's Planning, Programming, Budgeting System,* Commonwealth of Pennsylvania, Harrisburg, 1970.

Robert J. Mowitz

Situation in 1968

The decision-making process which culminated in an annual budget in Pennsylvania in 1968 was probably typical of most large industrial states. To call the total process a "system" implies a degree of interrelatedness among the myriad behaviors which did not in fact exist. The fact that an annual budget was printed in a single document created the aura of a meaningful decision process which would be difficult to find if one were to attempt to trace requests for funds to probable effects upon individuals or the environment resulting from the expenditure of those funds. The structure for the budget was provided by organizational units, and "programs" were described at best in terms of activities to be carried out and at worst in terms of monies to be expended. Although larger agencies did in fact, engage in some research and analysis, and many purchased such efforts from universities and consulting firms, there was no systematic way in which the results could be fed into the decision process. In fact, the "product" of a research study was expected to be a report rather than a decision.

In 1968, the Commonwealth did not have an integrated planning system. The State Planning Board, a quasi-independent staff unit, had certain long-range planning responsibilities, for example, the State Development plan, and also engaged in short-term planning, particularly related to capital budgeting. The board was outside the direct chain of command flowing through the governor and his Office of Administration, and there was no systematic linkage between program planning on the agency level and State Planning Board activity, although the board did participate in special projects in substantive areas such as natural resources which eventually contributed to agency program decisions. There was neither a formal nor an informal planning function carried out within the Governor's Office of Administration. Within agencies, planning capability varied a good deal. Larger agencies such as Welfare and Highways had planning units, but the extent of their contributions to program decisions was not always clear, and the agency planners were for the most part remote from the budget decision process.

Given these conditions, it was not surprising that the budget failed to provide the governor with a vehicle for expressing policy and for obtaining program alternatives among which he could choose in order to accomplish his goals and objectives. For example, during his first year in office, the governor made the decision to increase support for work-training programs in order to reduce unemployment. But there was no way in which the reporting system supporting the budget process could readily provide him with information concerning which agencies were then conducting training programs, what target groups were being served, and what level of effort was required for a given degree of success. Afloat on such a sea of uncertainty, policy-making was not much more than an educated guess.

170

Characteristics and Impact of the New System

Although the redesign of the decision process was referred to as a PPBS project (Secretary Sampson had succeeded in lobbying through the Legislature an appropriation of $450,000 for the explicit purpose of "implementing a planning, programming and budgeting system"), the *objective of the project was to develop and install a politically responsive, research-oriented and information-sensitive decision-making system for the Commonwealth of Pennsylvania.* In order to accomplish this objective, three major changes had to take place: a new structure for decision-making had to be developed; new decision processes culminating in an annual budget had to be institutionalized; and a program and financial information system had to be installed to support the total decision process. Each of these changes had an impact upon organizational structure, personnel requirements, and the strategies associated with the budget-allocation process.

Program Structure

In preparing the program-structure instructions, PPBS terminology such as *program categories, subcategories,* and *elements* was employed. But these terms were redefined as they were to be used within the Commonwealth system. First, a distinction was made between goals and objectives. A goal was defined as a desired state of affairs based upon current knowledge and values. It is timeless in the sense that as achievement approaches, goals tend to be restated at a higher level of aspiration or new goals are projected. Goals were thus defined as *values* which are culture-bound and subjective. To make the transition from questions of value to questions of fact, an objective was defined as that which can be described quantitatively in terms of units of desired impacts upon individuals or the environment to be achieved within a given time-frame and employing available resources. To illustrate, a goal would be to "maintain a system of health care that will minimize preventable deaths," while an objective would be to reduce infant mortality to a specific rate. The goal of good health would likely remain constant over time, whereas the objective, a specific optimum rate, would vary over time with changes in scientific knowledge and technology and with changes in the social and economic systems. Goals are thus expressed in words, and objectives are expressed in numbers. The numbers employed to measure objectives designate quantifiable impacts upon individuals, the environment (both natural and man-made), and upon other institutions–public, private, and voluntary.

Translating these concepts into the language of program structure resulted in eight goal-oriented major Commonwealth programs which were in turn broken down into program categories consisting of more specific substantive goals. For example, under the Commonwealth program, Health, Physical and

Mental Well Being, a program category was Maintaining a Physical Environment with Minimum Health Hazards.

Under the Commonwealth system, the program subcategory was the critical point of conversion from values, expressed in words, to facts, as represénted by numbers. The program subcategory represents the major substantive element clusters which are directly aimed at accomplishing specific quantifiable impacts upon individuals or the environment. The impacts are the products of the outputs of program elements. It was at the subcategory level of program structure that agencies were required to convert the value-oriented goal statements of the program categories into specific sets of objectives, quantifiable as impacts, by identifying subcategories within each program category. The logic employed required that objectives be expressed in terms of effects upon individuals, institutions, and the environment, not in terms of how much work was being performed. The measure of objective achievement, therefore, was in terms of what the organization accomplished in the world external to it rather than in terms of the level of its own activity.

Program subcategories were in turn broken down into program elements. Program elements are the basic modules of activities, that is the building blocks that, when aggregated, make up the program subcategories. An example of elements under the Air Pollution Control subcategory could include: plant inspections, air monitoring, education for private industry, and so on. Each element consumes resources and has specific outputs such as the number of inspections and the number of trainees. The aggregate effect of the elements should be to accomplish the objective of reducing or slowing the increase, depending upon the target impacts, of the amount of air pollution. The elements, their mix and quantity, are the means selected through budget allocations to accomplish the objectives expressed as impacts at the subcategory level.

Since the program structure logic required that agencies classify all of their activities within a framework in which the work that they performed in terms of outputs was related to the effects of that work as measured in terms of impacts, the agencies, in effect, were being asked to demonstrate the causal relationships between what went on within government and what happened as a result of organized governmental efforts. Although all agencies had some degree of difficulty in applying the logic to prepare program structure, two types of problems are worthy of note.

One problem stemmed from the propensity to define goals in idealized terms and the reluctance to define achievable impacts in realistic terms. Clean air is a laudable goal for a program category, but achievable impacts, given current resources, technology, and attitudes, may at best be to retard or stop the rate at which the atmosphere is getting dirty. Since traditional program rhetoric was usually optimistic in its claims of promised results, there often was resistance to a program-structure logic that insists on stating objectives in terms of effects that

172

can actually be measured. This resistance was greatest in those program areas where the results of governmental effort were likely to be imperceptible, or so mixed with other activities, such as an advertising program to attract new industries to a state, that the impacts of the governmental effort were difficult to identify.

A second problem, particularly related to programs in the human services, was the acceptance of arbitrary measures to establish a relationship between outputs and impacts. For example, doctrine supplies many of the formulas for resource allocations such as teacher-pupil ratios, psychiatrist-patient ratios, and so forth. The inference was made that if professional-staff levels were maintained as prescribed by professional doctrine, objectives would also be obtained. A system with a built-in capacity to examine the relationship between an element output based upon doctrine which uses illusive tests and target objectives measured in terms of impacts has an ongoing capacity for examining the efficacy of that doctrine, not the achievement of objectives. Especially at a time when traditional doctrine in education, social welfare, public health, and other human service programs was being questioned, the relationship between doctrine and impacts was a particularly sensitive one.

A consequence, therefore, of the requirement to develop program structure was conflict both within agencies and between agencies and the central fiscal office concerning the use of outputs based upon doctrine as a substitute for an impact measure. For some programs in mental health and welfare, program personnel insisted that impacts could not be identified and that outputs would have to be treated as if they were impacts. What this resistance demonstrated, was not so much reluctance to change per se within the bureaucracy, but, rather, the primitive state of knowledge concerning what can be accomplished by organized efforts through many of the human-services programs which now receive vast resources while citizens are increasingly dissatisfied with the results. In some agencies and program areas an age differential could be detected; younger professional personnel were more likely than older to be willing to reexamine doctrine in the light of its relationship to providing viable means for accomplishing the desired impacts.

Institutionalizing the New Decision Process

The development of program structure provided a framework for dealing with the state as a total decision system. But in order to provide an ongoing research-oriented, information-sensitive decision process, it was necessary to institutionalize new responsibilities and establish a new decision cycle.

The diagram which follows on page 174 illustrates the decision cycle that was installed. The Commonwealth program plan consisted of the complete file of program and financial information organized in terms of program structure. When first assembled, the program plan was a plan in name only, since it consisted of assembling data for future years, a budget year plus four, based upon current

Robert J. Mowitz

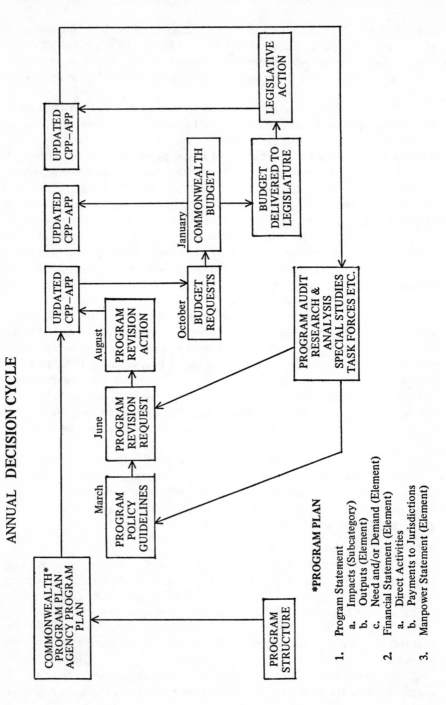

ANNUAL DECISION CYCLE

*PROGRAM PLAN

1. Program Statement
   a. Impacts (Subcategory)
   b. Outputs (Element)
   c. Need and/or Demand (Element)
2. Financial Statement (Element)
   a. Direct Activities
   b. Payments to Jurisdictions
3. Manpower Statement (Element)

commitments. As the new decision cycle began to function, however, the annual program-revision-request process permitted an annual opportunity to revise the allocations within the system, including the elimination of some programs and the adding of others to the extent desired by the governor. Each of the steps in the annual decision cycle required organizational changes and had other implications for changing the focus of decision-making.

Program policy guidelines are issued annually by the governor in the spring of the year and provide guidance to agencies for program-revision requests. The document consists of three parts: Part one deals with major overriding issues affecting programs in most agencies; part two identifies specific issues and problems in each of the substantive Commonwealth programs included in the program structure; and part three provides demographic- and economic-trend data to be employed in anticipating future needs and demands and citations of special studies, messages, and other relevant sources of background material.

The preparation of the guidelines is the point at which planning makes a significant contribution to the program decision process. To provide a planning capability within the Bureau of the Budget, a Division of Planning and Program was established and given responsibility for assembling and drafting the guidelines. About the first of January, formal notice is sent to agency heads notifying them that the guidelines are in the process of preparation and requesting that agencies submit to the Office of Administration issues that should be considered for inclusion within the document, the issues to be identified by program category, subcategory and element. At the same time, a formal request is sent to the state planning board for background papers describing social, economic, and demographic trends, and forecasts which would serve both as background material in preparing the guidelines and as appendix material for the guidelines themselves.

In addition to the Division of Planning and Program, two other newly organized units within the Office of Administration contributed to the guidelines: the Division of Program Audit within the Bureau of the Budget, and the Bureau of Systems Analysis. The Program Audit Division was established within the Bureau of the Budget in order to provide an ongoing scanning of the relationship between element outputs and subcategory impacts. Since the new decision process focused upon the achievement of objectives at the subcategory level, monitoring of the capacity of elements to achieve objectives was necessary in order to provide a basis for future program decisions. As a result of its ongoing program audit, the division was to provide significant inputs into the guidelines, particularly with respect to pointing to the need for new alternatives where existing elements were not producing predicted impacts. The Bureau of Systems Analysis was organized to provide an ongoing analytic capability within the Governor's Office of Administration. A major mission of the new bureau was to conduct in-house studies as well as coordinate contract research to assure that the theoretical perspectives and advance research methodologies of sophisticated analyses would be employed in the examination of program alternatives. The findings of such studies, of course were also to provide essential inputs into the program policy guidelines.

Although the program-policy-guideline process called upon the total research and planning resources of the Commonwealth to identify issues, the document was a policy statement in the strictest sense. The Governor and his political advisors made the final decision on issues for inclusion, as well as the decision concerning what overriding issues, that is major priorities, were to be identified.

The program revision request process is the formal means by which annual changes in the agency program plan and the Commonwealth program plan are introduced. Among the instructions for required back-up information are the following: a justification indicating the relationship to the guidelines, any significant changes in the environment to which the agency is responding, special analytic studies or other relevant research supporting the proposal; indication of alternatives that were considered, including summary information about cost and benefits of alternatives, explanation of which programs, if any, will be phased down or eliminated if the revision is approved, and the relationship of the proposed change to other elements, subcategories, or categories, if relevant.

The Planning and Program Division of the Bureau of the Budget has the responsibility for processing the program-revision requests. But the other two divisions of the bureau, Budget Analysis and Program Audit, also review and comment on the request, as does the Bureau of Systems Analysis and Bureau of Personnel within the Office of Administration. During the summer of 1970, the program-revision hearings were held, for the first time, on the basis of program categories and subcategories. One result, for example, was that several different agencies contributing to a water quality-control program were involved in the same hearing so that the full spectrum of program revisions aimed at dealing with water quality was examined during the hearing.

As this brief description suggests, it was quite clear that the new decision process required new organizational units within the Governor's Office of Administration in order to establish a program planning and a program audit capability within the Bureau of the Budget, and in order to strengthen the in-house capability for program research and analysis. What was of equal importance, was that the institutionalization of the new decision cycle required a different type of input at the agency level in order to obtain resource support for programs. The program policy guidelines focused upon desired results—impacts—in order to achieve gubernatorial goals, and the program-revision request hearings concentrated upon the credibility of the linkage between proposed elements and promised impacts. The focus was thus shifted from the amount of money requested to the probability of results being accomplished as a result of a decision. The shift in focus required a different type of back-up in order for the agency head to support his claims, and it meant that he had to rely more upon program personnel and those engaged in research in order to support his requests. Since the critical resource decisions were made on the basis of the program-revision request process, budget preparation amounted to little more than an up-dating of the agency's program plan for the budget year based upon decisions made through the program revision request process.

Program and Financial Information Systems

The logic employed in the program structure translated itself into requirements for three major types of information: information concerning values, information on what effect governmental programs were having upon human behavior and the environment, and information concerning the outputs of work that resulted from the expenditure of governmental resources.

In a formal sense, information concerning values was introduced through the program-policy guidelines followed by program-revision requests and program revision actions. The values of political executives and professional program personnel come into play throughout this process, reflecting not only their own views but their perceptions of the support available from individuals and groups outside of government. Strictly speaking, the legislature makes its contribution through hearings and legislation. Undoubtedly the political system guarantees that values are heard, but there is no guarantee that decisions are based upon the best possible information concerning what governmental programs can be undertaken to assure that the goals as expressed by the values are likely to be achieved. It is in this latter sense that the design of the information system took on great significance.

The second type of information required by the decision logic, the effect that governmental programs had upon behaviour and the environment—impacts—such information was essential in order to assure that objectives were being accomplished to satisfy goals. Identifying an impact measure for a subcategory established a requirement that the information necessary to account for that impact be collected, and at the same time established a variable against which the performance of elements within that subcategory were to be tested to determine their capacity to affect the subcategory variable.

The third type of information described what goes on within government—the outputs of work and the resources that are expended to produce those outputs. Governmental reporting systems have devoted almost exclusive attention to reporting this third type of information. The problem posed by the program structure in dealing with the third type of information was to provide data at the element level in a degree of detail which would permit the linkage of the units of outputs of elements to an effect upon human behavior or the environment. It should be emphasized that the linkage of the element outputs to

177

subcategory impacts involves the search for a causal relationship—in many instances among plural sets of variables. Without question, this is one of the most difficult methodological challenges to science. On the other hand, to make decisions as if they had the capacity to bring about impacts without having any ability to determine if the impacts have indeed been brought about would seem to breed disenchantment with the relevance of the governmental decision-making process.

Because of the paucity of existing reporting systems which would reveal whether or not impacts were being achieved, it was necessary to have agencies specify desired impact measures. These then served as requirements for the development of information-gathering techniques which would provide the required data. In many cases external data sources had to be consulted, external, that is, to a given organizational unit, in order to determine what effects its programs were having.

Although it is difficult to do justice in a short space to the complexities involved in the design of an information system for an organization as complex as a whole state government, a few generalizations are in order. The design strategy employed was to develop the system from the top down. It was first determined what the governor needed to know for his decision purposes; what the Governor's Office of Administration needed to know for their management purposes; and finally what agencies needed to supply in order to satisfy the element (building block) data requirements. The governor's decision horizon included the dollar allocations for achieving Commonwealth goals at the Commonwealth program and program category levels and the specific levels of objective accomplishment as measured by impacts and the costs for achieving these impacts at the subcategory level. If he needed or wanted more information, details at the element level would be readily available, including element summaries for each subcategory. The Governor's Office of Administration was primarily concerned with the relationship between impacts and outputs and therefore had to be satisfied that the information included at the element level would be sufficient to satisfy subcategory aggregations the governor would need for decision-making. Agencies, therefore, had to meet the requirements specified for information at the element and subcategory levels. It was assumed, rightly, that most agencies would have to adjust their reporting systems in order to provide information concerning impacts, outputs, and need and/or demand estimators. But it was left to agencies to determine what detail was needed below the element level for their own management information purposes.

A second aspect of the design strategy had to do with the linkage of the program-information system built around elements to the accounting system. The solution employed was to establish a four-digit code within the accounting-code structure to identify subcategories and elements and to identify an element subsystem known as an "element component. . . .that portion of an organization which supports a single element and which receives support from a single appropriation." The element component, therefore, "is the highest level of aggregation of an organization which represents no more than one appropriation and one element." By employing this concept, it was possible to aggregate financial data by program, agency, and appropriation. But it would be misleading to suggest that this approach solved all the problems of providing a straightforward linkage into the accounting system which would both satisfy normal accounting requirements and provide current expenditure data for each element. The new codes were introduced at the same time that a new centralized accounting system was being installed, and the latter had a tendency to produce a proliferation of reports for which no one seemed to have any use.

The importance of providing program and financial information support for the total decision system cannot be overstated. Because of the novelty of the information requirements generated by the program-structure decision logic, it was necessary to accept at the beginning estimates and educated guesses for impact data and in some cases even for outputs. It was also necessary to employ estimates for financial data for many of the elements. But as the accounting linkage is refined and new reporting systems designed to satisfy program requirements begin to produce information, the quality of the data improves.

Current Status and Future Prospects

On December 31, 1970, the Commonwealth PPB project formally terminated. At that point of time the status of the system was as follows:

1. All State agencies under the governor's jurisdiction were incorporated within the program structure and had prepared agency program plans including both program and financial data which were incorporated into the Commonwealth program plan.

2. Automated support for the system included: the Commonwealth program-plan file, composed of program and financial information for all agencies and all levels of program structure down to the element component level; an automated updating process whereby the agency program plans and Commonwealth program plan could be updated based upon changes resulting from program revision decisions, budget decisions, and legislative decisions; the capability for printing budget proof documents for use at both the central fiscal office and agency levels, and for printing out detail to be included in the budget document; and the software for a reporting system to be used in budget execution which recorded outputs, impacts, and financial data on an exception reporting basis. The software had been tested but the reporting system had not as yet been installed within the agencies.

3. Two passes had been made through the new budget cycle; the first involved eleven of the major state agencies for the 1970-1971 fiscal year (about

90 percent of the general fund budget) and the second included all state agencies for the 1971-1972 fiscal year. For fiscal year 1970-1971 both the traditional and a program-budget document were prepared and submitted to the Legislature.

4. A four-digit code which identified subcategories and elements had been developed and included within the accounting code structure. This provided a direct linkage into the accounting system. Not all of the bugs were out of this system, since a newly installed central accounting system was forcing the coding of transactions at a level of disaggregation which resulted in an overproliferation of reports. But efforts were underway to identify more appropriate levels of classification in order to retail the identification of element costs without at the same time overburdening the system with minutia.

5. Within the Governor's Office of Administration the responsibilities for maintaining the new system had been institutionalized. No single organizational pattern had been prescribed for agencies, and each had made the necessary internal adjustments for institutionalizing responsibilities. In larger agencies this resulted in new units and/or positions as well as a realignment of roles and responsibilities.

Governor Shafer remained committed to the PPB project throughout his term and provided indispensable personal support during the early installation stages when resistance to change was the greatest. He emphasized that management improvement was not a partisan issue and that the purpose of the PPB project was to enhance the capability of any governor to make policy choices with some assurance that the decisions would lead to results.

In January 1971, Milton J. Shapp was inaugurated as the new governor of Pennsylvania. At this writing, it is fair to say that the basic concepts, structure, and decision cycle will continue to be employed by the new administration. Modifications and refinements will be necessary in order to sharpen the definition of impacts and to identify reliable impact indicators. It will also be necessary to refine the identification of outputs at the element level and to simplify the linkage of outputs to the accounting system so as to make the shift from accounting for activities to accounting for outputs. Probably the system will be relabeled something other than PPB. ("Priority budgeting system" seems to be the current favorite candidate.) The first Shapp budget will be based upon decisions made within the context of the program structure—primarily at the subcategory level. But the budget document is likely to continue to have two parts, one of which expresses decisions in the traditional form by organizational unit and the other in terms of program structure.

CHAPTER 22

State of Vermont,
Program Budgeting, 1970

by R. E. W. Crisman

Director, Budget and Management Division
State of Vermont

Two acts of the 1967 Vermont Legislature authorized (and appropriated funds for) the development and implementation of a program budgeting system within Vermont state government. The $40,000 appropriation by the state was supplemented by grants from the United States Department of Housing and Urban Development ($124,000 over a two and one-half year period), the Economic Development Administration, Department of Commerce ($50,000 over a fifteen-month period), and the State and Local Finances Project, George Washington University ($10,000 over a one-year period).

Design and development efforts were initiated within the Budget and Management Division of the State Department of Administration in June 1967. Initial enthusiasm within both the division and the special project staff for program budgeting was extremely high. In fact, some suggested that PPBS represented the "primrose path to budgetary salvation."

Program budgeting was not entirely new to Vermont state government at the initiation of the PPBS effort. For several years, certain components of the system had been designed and implemented. Specifically, a program (within agency) executive budget was in use, and budgetary practices required the submission of a program and financial plan covering fourteen years. Each agency in its budget requests showed the previous five years' data, current-year figures, and projections for eight years into the future. In addition to financial information, the multiyear program and financial plan (already in operation) required a statement of goals and objectives and data on work units performed, or accomplishments for each program.

Accomplishments to Date

A number of steps were taken to implement program budgeting. The program (within agency) budget was supplemented to show fiscal information by program, independent of organizational responsibility. This was done in a separate document. Obviously, what was required was the development of a comprehensive program structure covering all activities of state government. In addition, all expenditures made by the state and not merely those restricted to state appropriations were included as budgetary information within the revised program budget. All fund expenditures were presented and total spending by function and by major program area was made available.

The multiyear program and financial plan has been modified to include improved measures of accomplishment, and they have been scaled back from an eight-year projection to one of six years.

The initial efforts in PPB in Vermont recognized the implications of program budgeting for organizational revitalization. However, such consequences were not emphasized at first in order to insure against agency concern and rejection of the system. It eventually became apparent that the revitalization of organization, which was long overdue, required a rethinking of the functions and organizational units needed to perform them. The functional or program structure provided an ideal vehicle to reconstitute organizational units and to improve efficiency while providing additional services. Consequently, the functional and program structure adopted by the state was an important influence on the overall reorganization of state government.

The Budget and Management Division and the project staff recognized the necessity to provide training to operate agencies in order to insure maximum utilization and acceptance of PPB. Consequently, a training program was initiated in the summer of 1968 to educate program directors and senior agency staffs in the principles and use of the system. This training session was supplemented by an operational workshop conducted in the early summer of 1970.

The subject areas analyzed during both the training program and more particularly during the operational workshop were directed towards current major problems facing state government. As a result of this, a number of the studies produced issue investigations or program analyses which impacted the decisions necessary in these problem areas.

As a further result of the training and workshop sessions, the state had developed a usable, practical vehicle for multiagency (or multidiscipline) studies and analyses. Particularly within the operational workshop, the task-group approach proved extremely successful in coordinating the various agencies and disciplines related to a particular problem. Task group members representing various fields of competence were assembled and assigned responsibility to investigate, analyze and develop solutions to complex problems. Through the varying disciplines and talents brought to bear, and because of the quality of the participants and their organization as a task group, several significant state government problems were analyzed and workable solutions developed.

Opportunities for Improvement

While some important accomplishments have been realized to date, not all portions of the PPB system proved uniformly feasible or usable. Measurements of accomplishment for each program were elusive and difficult to develop. Particularly in the human service and education areas, qualitatively defined and quantifiable measures of accomplishments must still be identified and tested for feasibility. In some program areas actual accomplishments cannot realistically be measured, and "proxy measures" must be used instead. For example, if the ideal measurement of accomplishment for an alcohol education program is the number of potential alcoholics or problem drinkers deterred through the program, and if this data cannot be realistically developed, some other measure of less ideal, but more practical utility must be discovered.

While good analysts are required for successful implementation of program analysis and PPB, *consumers* of analysis are an absolute necessity. Agency heads, the executive office, the legislature and *the public* must begin to think of governmental programs in terms of their objectives, accomplishments, and costs. Unless programs are questioned, unless alternatives are required, unless costs and benefits are subject to impartial scrutiny, the prospects of usable and valid analyses are slim.

Program analyses cannot be initiated and conducted only by budget and management staff or other centralized planning or administrative groups. Operating and functional agencies must directly participate (and frequently initiate) in-depth analyses of existing or proposed programs. However, the tendency on the part of operating and functional agencies has been to engage in justification of preconceived approaches. An analysis—whether initiated by a central staff or by a task group of functionally oriented personnel—should be objective, documented, and capable of verification.

Perhaps the most important opportunity for improvement in the implementation of a workable PPB system was the integration and coordination of planning and budgeting within the jurisdiction. Frequently, the planning unit at the state level identified relatively vague goals irrespective of their financial and other resource requirements. Vaguely stated goals, overly ambitious programs and unanticipated resource requirements can only lead to program failure and disillusionment.

On the other hand, short term, single year budgetary allocations or appropriations which do not necessarily relate to long-term goals or objectives, shortsightedly produce only false economies. The planning of goals, the

183

programming of the activities needed to accomplish the goals, and realistic and reasonable budgeting of the resources necessary to the accomplishment of the goals, are basic to the PPB system.

The Future of PPBS

The state of Vermont will continue to approach the implementation of a PPB System in a practical, incremental fashion. The system (and particularly program analysis) has clearly demonstrated a significant value to the decision-making process. It is hoped that each step taken towards implementation will be a significant step beyond previous efforts. However, unrealistic or overly ambitious efforts are to be avoided.

Refinement of objectives and measurements of accomplishment for each program will continue. Professionals within the operating agencies will be the ones to initiate or to assist in the development of these measures. Several projects are already under way in several functional areas including education and social welfare.

Future efforts will focus on anticipated as well as already existing alternative solutions to problems. For example, it is unrealistic to consider solid-waste disposal without anticipating the development of feasible, efficient recycling methods of waste management. Similarly, computerized instruction will undoubtedly contribute significantly to educational processes even though current availability is limited.

The single most important benefit to be gained in this effort is a rediscovery of the analysis process. Major government problems can be solved only by judicious use of multiagency task-force studies. If the people who ultimately must manage the programs are included early in the analysis process, a prevailing sense of commitment and understanding results which is not easy to engender at a later date.

The PPB system is not considered to be the final solution to all administrative, budgetary, planning, and decision-making problems. It is a tool among others to enhance the awareness of decision-makers, and hopefully to improve the quality of decisions. The state of Vermont will continue to adopt a practical and realistic appreciation of the potentials of PPBS.

CHAPTER 23

Program Budgeting

in the City of New York

by Frederick O'R. Hayes

Formerly, Director of the Budget of the City of New York
Currently, Chair of Urban Management, The Urban Institute

The basic structure of the budget in the city of New York is established by the city charter. The charter provides for two budgets: one for capital outlays and the other for expenses.

The capital budget is prepared initially by the City Planning Commission. It submits a draft capital budget for the fiscal year beginning the subsequent July 1, to the mayor on or before the first day of January. The draft is a public document. The mayor is required to submit the executive capital budget to the City Council and the Board of Estimates a month later, on February 1. In it he must identify all changes from the City Planning Commission's draft.

The executive expense budget must be submitted to the City Council and Board of Estimates by April 15, after legislative action has been completed upon the capital budget. Like the capital budget, the expense budget provides appropriations for the fiscal year beginning on the next July 1.

The expense budget is a program budget and has been for some time. The appropriation structure is rough and imperfect but, in most areas, it is reasonably adequate for program purposes. Executive direction and administrative support are, in most agencies, provided for in separate appropriations rather than allocated among programs.

The line-item budget was eliminated as an appropriation document by the 1963 charter. However, the charter still requires the submission of supporting schedules—the old line-item budget—which the council and the Board of Estimates have no authority to change. The budget must, however, be administered from the line schedules; that is; any change in the amounts shown for each personnel-service position and each non–personnel-service code must be effected through a formal modification procedure requiring the approval of the mayor. Charter changes have greatly increased the mayor's budgetary authority and flexibility but the tyranny of the "lines" over the entire process is still significant.

Prior to the beginning of the Lindsay administration in 1966, the budget was, in fact, prepared and administered as a line-item budget. The agency budget officers and the Bureau of the Budget examiners repriced the current-year budget on the basis of revised salary and cost levels on a line-by-line basis. Incremental requirements for so-called mandatory or inescapable expenditures were separately examined. Possible economies were reviewed in much the same manner. Discretionary or supplemental requests were dealt with harshly and cavalierly unless federal or state funds were available to finance a significant part of the additional costs. The process suggests, in fact, an almost classic case in incremental budgeting.

The Lindsay Changes

Five years after the beginning of the Lindsay administration, the above process is still extant. But, as a result of the administration's effort to introduce a planning-programming-budget system, activities orientated toward an analytic process have been superimposed upon and integrated with the traditional budget operation. The legal structure remains unchanged; the council has failed to act upon charter amendments to integrate the capital and expense budgets and to permit grouping of lines in the supporting schedules. More ambitious changes have been promised by the mayor but have not yet been submitted to the City Council.

In the first year after his inauguration, Mayor Lindsay gave major emphasis to fiscal and budgetary questions. He came into office convinced of the need to install a modern budgeting system. Discussions with many of the Washington officials associated with budgeting led him to consider a planning-programming-budgeting system modeled after the Federal approach.

The approach followed by the city was unusual in many respects. The first stage was a program-budgeting reconnaissance, an effort to apply program analysis to high opportunity areas in 1967–1968 and the 1968–1969 budgets and to build up during that period the analytic resources necessary to move into a formally comprehensive system beginning with the 1969–1970 budget.

For the second stage, a new governmentwide instruction was issued providing for the preparation of the 1969–1970 budget under PB with provision for a budget-preview process to provide better opportunities for review and handling of basic policy issues. A new and modified instruction was used for 1970–1971 which reduced and simplified requirements based on the lessons of the 1969–1970 budget.

The best illustration of this is the police program, Law Enforcement and

Protection Against Crime. The conceptual structure of the problem was simple. It required the projection of the expected level of criminal activity likely to result without changes in the current level of resources devoted to law enforcement and crime protection. It demanded, secondly, a goal of achieving some lower level of crime. Lastly, it required the ability to identify the level and character of inputs needed to reduce the expected level of crime to the level specified as a goal. In truth, staff was properly chary of our capacity to project crime levels and was still basically ignorant of the relationship between police patrol and other inputs and the level of crime. It was difficult to see the usefulness of a five-year police forces plan compounded on the basis of so thin an understanding of the problem.

On the other hand, in certain selected areas, the multiyear plan and projection was feasible and useful, especially for capital and capital-related programs. And in fact, some limited work has been done on multiyear planning in such areas. Moreover, the feasible area for multiyear planning expands as we learn more and more about our current operations and the alternatives to them. In the next stage of the development of program budgeting in New York, multiyear planning should be a major element.

Analysis

The thrust of program budgeting in New York to date (1971) has been upon program analysis and upon building an analytic capability. Management has tried to instill the habit of analysis, to institutionalize in very tradition-bound organizations the famous entreaty of Oliver Cromwell, "Gentlemen, I beseech ye in the bowels of Christ to search ye selves that ye be not mistaken."

The analytic staff needed to properly carry out this mission in a government of the size and complexity of New York's was large indeed. New staffs totaling nearly forty professionals were added to the Bureau of the Budget for program planning and analysis and for budget and information systems. More than one hundred additional professionals were recruited for parallel staffs in the operating agencies. The city in partnership with the Rand Corporation created a new program research organization, the New York City-Rand Institute, which provided some 60 professional staff members and an additional 50 part-time consultants. The urban-practice division of McKinsey and Company and the Vera Institute of Criminal Justice were also heavily involved. Another 125 professionals were engaged by Kerr Associates, MDC Systems, and Meridian Engineering, and by the city in consultant or direct work on supporting project management systems. Information system development constituted another very sizable supporting area. And yet, the total effort was still far from adequate and, in some agencies, had barely begun.

The staff recruited by the Bureau of the Budget and the city's operating agencies had a sprinkling of systems analysts and operations researchers. It was in the main, however, a generalist staff consisting of the brightest graduates of the better law schools, business schools, and graduate schools in public administration and economics. Despite relatively thin education in quantitative analytic techniques, it was found that they learned fast and performed superbly. Their youth—the average was less than thirty—and inexperience more than likely will prove to be assets as innovation comes easiest from those not already immersed in existing systems.

The consulting support from the New York City—Rand Institute and from the various profit-making consulting organizations was integrated into the city effort as closely as possible. The close partnership has paid high dividends, and the "report and run" consultant has been almost unknown in the city's program-budgeting effort. The use of consultants made possible acceleration of the total program that would not have been possible through direct staff alone.

If this author may be permitted a moment of personal reflection, I would note that most of the cajoling, directing, pressuring, nursemaiding, and persuading of weak, anti-intellectual or hostile administrators is a waste of time. The time might be better used to persuade the mayor to cull the turkeys from his flock, and the mayor's willingness to replace ineffective appointees has been an important factor of success. A caution of the same kind applies to consultants. They can be a valuable addition to in-house capacity, but are valueless unless there is enough in-house capability to manage and direct consultant activity.

Examples of the Use of Analysis

The impact of program issue analysis on decision-making has been substantial, especially in the Police and Fire departments, the Environmental Protection Administration and the Housing and Development Administration.

Some examples follow:

Use of ten single-shift peak-hour fire companies, at one-third the cost of full-time companies.

The substantial expansion of one-man police patrol car sectors after demonstration of 35 percent reduction in response time without increase in injuries or

The substantial expension of one-man patrol car sectors after demonstration of 35 percent reduction in response time without increase in injuries or accidents—discontinued after union opposition.

The consolidation of redundant police precinct stations—proposed withdrawn after community opposition.

Design of the fourth-platoon approach to police patrol, nearly doubling manpower in the affected precincts on the high-crime evening shift.

Substantial substitution of lower-paid civilians for uniformed officers in police and sanitation.

The substitution of summons for arrest in certain police cases, with substantial savings in police time.

A Traffic and Crime Alert program to eliminate unnecessary court appearances for arresting police officers.

Pre-arraignment, extended arraignment hours, and all-purpose court parts to increase productivity and effectiveness of the criminal justice system.

An expanded policy of liberalized bail and release on recognizance to cut down pretrial detention.

A Manhattan alcoholics project which has eliminated most arrests for drunkenness.

A separation of income maintanance and social services in the public assistance program, with savings already around $40 million per year.

The relocation of maintenance shops to borough rather than district level, resulting in 15 percent improvement in vehicle availability.

A new approach to rent control—more responsive to changes in costs and to the acute problem of undermaintanance.

The redesign of housing-code enforcement to provide for automated processing and the differentiation of violations dangerous to tenant health and safety.

Streamlining tax collection procedures at a saving of over $1 million annually.

The development of a service-area-priority scheme for community mental health projects.

A sharp reduction in the number of housing sites acquired and cleared to better accord with the availability of housing financing.

A shift in priorities in the municipal loan program to more modest rehabilitation on better housing, to increase both program impact and loan repayments.

A new approach (1) reducing time requirements by 50 percent in the program for demolition of abandoned buildings and (2) identifying salvageable structures in the pipeline.

The establishment of a computer program for evaluation of the effect of alternative city rehabilitation programs on specific housing in terms of cash flow, rent levels, loan repayment, and discounted present value.

A new policy on city automobiles including two-year replacement, purchase with optional equipment to maximize resale, and special efforts to improve resale. Annual recurring savings exceed $1 million.

Shorter-term replacement of sanitation and fire trucks to reduce maintenance costs and number of equipment breakdowns.

Effort to shift solid-waste collection, where practical, to large detachable containers and front-end loaders.

Authorization, after pilot experiment, of use of large disposable paper and plastic bags in lieu of metal garbage cans.

Solicitation of bids for removal of abandoned cars from city streets by private contractors, saving at current levels about $4 million per year.

Substitution of new, larger compactor sanitation trucks for old escalator model, with resulting 6 percent increase in productivity.

A major aspect of the effort has been the program and administrative design for new ventures. Among these are:

The development of a wholly new management system for the Health and Hospitals Corporation which assumed responsibility for the city's hospitals on July 1, 1970.

The design of a new administrative tribunal, the Parking Violations Bureau, which took over the job of processing 4 million traffic tickets annually beginning on September 1, 1970.

The development of systems for the new Off-Track Betting Corporation, a potential eventual source of additional city revenues of $150 million annually.

The design and scheduling of large-scale new health programs for abortions, for methadone treatment of drug addicts, and for lead-poisoning identification and treatment.

The above are illustrative of the decisions made on the basis of program analysis. Moreover, the capacity to design and choose new options, to create innovation and needed change, is increasing rapidly, and the rate of activity will continue to rise at a very rapid rate.

Results

Program-analysis efforts were initiated, not exclusively but predominantly, through program budgeting—and hence, linked to the budget process. While the various budget reviews provide an apt forum for summing up program status and agreeing on future approaches, program analysis in New York City tends, less and less, to be tied to the budget process. There are several reasons for this.

First, contrary to theory, program analysis contributes little to major resource allocation problems in the city. The New York City budget, in fact, involves only minor marginal resource-allocation issues.

Secondly, the pressure on nearly all city systems is such that, where possible, winnings from program analysis have to be reinvested in improved effectiveness in the same functional area rather than in dollar savings. This is also crucial to the psychology of cooperation from administrators and commissioners.

Third, the ties to the budget were strongest when the Bureau of the Budget still held the lion's share of the city's analytic capacity. With the buildup of staffs in the operating agencies, the bureau tended to play a more modest role on matters that were not inherently budgetary issues.

The net result was that the analysis effort under program budgeting tended

190

to become a wide-ranging management improvement program. The effort was performed under the watchful and concerned eye of the mayor as well as that of the Bureau of the Budget.

It has produced massive changes in mayoral decision-making—a revolution of rising expectations on the part of the chief executive, a feeling that he can now demand and often get rational analyses of recommended program actions and of the alternatives.

CHAPTER 24

Recruiting and Developing PPB Staff

by Chester Wright

Director, Management Sciences Training Center
Bureau of Training, United States Civil Service Commission

One of the most significant provisions in the original Planning-Programming-Budgeting System implementation document, Bureau of the Budget Bulletin 66-3, was the requirement for the development of an analytic staff in each of the agencies directed to estblish a PPB system. In practice this amounted to a need to establish and fill approximately 1,000 new positions for systems analysts at the top level of each one of 19 federal agencies. (Chapter 25 reviews the situation in 16 domestic federal agencies in 1968.)

There are three ways in which an analytic staff can be acquired: (1) It can be recruited; (2) present staff can be trained to perform the new function; or (3) a combination of recruiting and training can be employed. These approaches were tried in the U.S. federal government with widely varying degrees of success. Some of the problems of recruiting and training will be discussed. But first, let us examine the qualifications of an ideal PPB analyst.

Qualifications of a PPB Analyst

What should a PPB analyst know? He should know some economics, specifically microeconomics and its application to problems of the public sector. This clearly presents a problem, since most of the interesting work in economics for a good many years has been in macroeconomics and there is little published material applying the insights of microeconomics to problems in the public sector. Theory, in fact, is deficient in this area and needs considerable development before the "theory of the public firm" can become a useful tool.

We are most specifically not talking about the applications of welfare economics. There was an early temptation of the part of some people to equate welfare economics with the analytic endeavours required by PPB. This is simply not the case. In the first place, PPB is not as normative as most of the theory under welfare economics tends to be. Nor do convoluted mathematical and

193

mechanical computations, which seem so alluring to most of the people writing in the welfare field, have any useful application in the real world of political intrustions and data deficiencies.

The ideal analyst should also possess knowledge in the fields of mathematics and statistics. It need not be extensive but should include some of the more useful tools that lie in the field of vectors and matrices, and some idea of basic notation, sampling techniques, probability, and simulation modeling. He should also be aware of what some of the so-called management sciences derive from the practical application of mathematics. Particularly useful seem to be linear programming, regression analysis and some knowledge of the basic techniques of computer application.

In addition, he must have a practical knowledge of the area in which he is working. He either must have this to start with, or must gain it. It is not true that analysis can be applied in some sort of pure fashion to an area of public endeavor about which the analyst has no real insight or useful experience.

He must also know something about budgeting: the way that budgets are constructed and the whole process of budget analysis, presentation, and approval. He must know something about accounting from the standpoint of information on the handling of accounts and how this information is aggregated and presented to management. He must know something about the management process *in toto*. He should have some insight into how large-scale enterprises are organized and managed. There is no particular advantage in his being a recognized expert in one or more of these fields, but he must have a rock-hard grasp of the fundamentals in each area if he is to avoid making calamitous mistakes.

So much for what he should know. Now let us look at what he should be able to do. One of the results of analysis is the reallocation of resources. The reallocation of resources can mean that programs that are the cherished preserve of certain individuals will be cut back or discontinued entirely. The competent analyst is frequently going to find himself opposing "cherished preserves" at the storm center of bureaucratic intrigue. If his products are to be used or useful, he must be able to handle such a situation. He cannot constantly depend on higher-level sponsors within the organization to protect him.

He must be able to communicate capably with specialists in each of the fields indicated above. He must be able to understand when he is being led down the garden path by an expert who has allowed himself to become a special pleader for his particular discipline in any area.

If a group is involved, the senior analyst must be able to manage his own organization successfully. That means he must be a manager as well as an analyst if he is to successfully carry on the day-to-day work of organizational life, contain the inevitable tensions of a creative staff, assign his people properly to priority work assignments, and maintain a smooth and orderly flow of work through his shop.

It should be clear by now that what we are describing is not only the ideal analyst but one who can be the top man in an analytic organization. It is unreasonable to hope to find two people of this description and to employ them both in a single organization. However, once a man such as the one described has been found, he can head the organization and can attract other people as nearly like himself as possible.

Lastly, there is the question of what the ideal analyst should be like. He will, above all, be a person with a questioning attitude. A person who challenges the answers he receives to his own questions, who questions the data behind the answer. Who says constantly, "How do you know?" A person who questions the problems. Who says, "Is this really the problem we are trying to solve?" Who questions the objective. Who says, "Is this really what we want to do?" Who questions the assumptions, saying "How do you know that this thing that we always believed was true, is in fact true?" A person who questions the alternatives. Who says, "Are these really all the routes that are open to us to a possible solution of this problem?" He should be a person who is innovative. One who thinks of new ways, who thinks of ways of doing things that may at first seem to be completely unrealistic or unthinkable. (This is a time in history when the unthinkable must be thought about quite frequently.)

In short, he is likely to be an annoying, abrasive, hard-to-have-around sort of person. Of course, he should be able to conceal these characteristics at will on those occasions when the bureaucratic in-fighting makes it necessary for him to put on a public face quite different from the one he uses when he is being an analyst.

Recruiting

Owing to a natural inclination of federal careerists to recruit from their own ranks, and possibly because of the necessity to develop analytic staffs almost instantly, at the time of the original PPBS implementation in 1966 a great majority of the 1,000 new PPB analystic positions were filled by reassignment of federal people.

Of the two potential sources of supply, inside and outside of government, the outside sources were very limited indeed. An approach was made to the staffs of such analytic think tanks as The Rand Corporation, the Institute for Defense Analyses, and similar organizations, as well as to university staffs. Recruitment from these sources was limited however, owing to a natural reluctance on the part of the people in these organizations to leave the work they had chosen and because first-rate people in consulting organizations and the universities were well paid.

Looking for analysts inside the government presented a fairly wide range of choices. There already existed many so-called analytic positions. There were management analysts, program analysts, and many other kinds of analysts. There also was the possibility of selecting budget analysts; since the last word in the name PPB is budgeting, there was a natural inclination to look to various budget staffs. Agencies that already employed large numbers of economists, noting that Budget Bulletin 66-3 indicated that there was a certain amount of economics associated with PPB, tended to look among those staffs as a recruiting source. There was also the belief in some cases that people who had actually been working in various programs for a good many years should know enough about those programs to be able to analyze them.

One source that was largely overlooked in the beginning was various engineering staffs, particularly industrial engineers. In retrospect, this seems to have been a fairly serious oversight and is slowly starting to be corrected.

The major problem at the beginning, however, was that there was no clear-cut idea of what kind of background and training was best suited to the task. No one had a very clear idea of just what a PPB analyst was. The result was that selections were made from all potential sources identified above. The selectee was called a PPB analyst, and through the magic of the federal classification system, lo and behold he indeed was one!

A point that cannot be emphasized too much is the fact that PPB analysis is truly interdisciplinary in nature. No single academic discipline has a monopoly on PPB analysis. No one from any presently existing discipline can be a good PPB analyst unless he has acquired insights and skills from related disciplines. While it is true that there is at present no academic regimen that produces completely qualified PPB analysts, some come much closer than others. Engineering economics as it is taught, for example, at Stanford University Engineering School, or business administration as it is taught at the Business School at Harvard, are capable of producing people well on their way toward becoming PPB analysts, although they are not such on graduation. The program in public policy analysis currently being developed at the John F. Kennedy School of Government at Harvard should come the closest yet. The recruit who starts with a background in quantitatively oriented subjects is most desirable.

The difficult problem of recruiting has not been solved by the U.S. federal government with complete success by any means.

Training

The other possibility is to train present staff. Experience with PPB training in the civilian sectors of the federal government commenced with the first Civil Service Commission orientation course in January of 1966. From that time to the present, this experience has ranged from two-day courses to one-year programs and has included thousands of participants— federal, state, local, and foreign. A great deal was learned in that time and much of it has not served to make the Commission happy.

It is difficult for someone not actually associated with the early days of PPB to understand the problems faced at that time. The civil agencies were under orders to install, instantly, a comprehensive new management-decision system. While the elements of this system were not entirely new, combining them into a single decision-making system was a mind-boggling innovation. To compound the problem, the system was completely dependent on a species of analysis not generally practiced in government or many other organizations. The problem then was to install a management system that most managers did not understand, supported by analysis where analysis was practically nonexistent.

It seemed obvious at the first, and still seems true, that there were two quite distinct jobs: (1) to train managers, and (2) to train analysts. The first seemed both more urgent and, given the time constraints, more possible. However, under the conditions that existed, and continue to exist, in the U.S. federal government, such an undertaking was fore-doomed. More about this later.

The Commission believed that the manager, to be a successful user of a PPB system, needed two qualifications: He had to understand the various elements of PPB and how they fitted together into a closely integrated structure; and he had to understand and be able to use the products of analysis in his decision-making processes. In its innocence, the Commission erred to the extent of imagining that federal bureaucrats would demand program-oriented analysis as a preliminary to important resource-distribution decisions, along the model of McNamara.

Analysts, too, needed a dual body of skills. They had to be able to produce systems analyses that were useful and relevant to the decision process at hand. In addition, they had to be able to communicate the reality of these studies to the decision-maker in terms that were meaningful to him.

With neither managers nor analysts was a satisfactory level of results achieved. The essential failure of management training was that it never reached a significant portion of top-level line managers. Training programs specifically designed to reach these people were attended by swarms of assorted staff specialists. The occasional line manager present was a conspicuous exception. Staff people came, of course, because they viewed planning and budgeting as their job. They came to learn the new system. Probably as many came to learn how to thwart it as came to learn how to make it work, but they came.

Managers did not come for the best of reasons; they felt no need to learn a new decision system. The decisions they were then making were fine; they had the best of all possible proof—their high-ranking positions. In the absence of any alternative criteria, position was success's best measurement. The federal bureaucrat's occasional moments of discomfort come not when he is confronted with a negative cost-benefit ratio, but when a lot of angry people occupy his office. If this sort of thing happens often enough, he might be interested in a

197

good program in interpersonal relations, or more likely a new public relations man. He will not even consider that it might help if he did his job better. In the absence of program budgeting, or something like it, he has no way of knowing that he is not doing a good job now. Until he knows, he will not go through the discomfort of learning a new way of thinking

There was, of course, another way that line managers could be provided the incentive to undertake the troublesome or frightening task of learning new skills. They could be directed to do so, powerfully and persistently, from the highest levels.

It is the dream of everyone in government to have his program receive the personal support of the President. Program budgeting received that sort of initial push, but it was subsequently entrusted to the management of an assistant director of the Bureau of the Budget. This was a staff office that was woefully under-staffed, with a tradition of self-imposed niggardliness. It had no line authority whatsoever.

Even so, the system might have survived its early crises of confidence if the corps of budget examiners had understood the system and attempted to apply its rationale in their reviews. But the fact was that there was no systematic attempt to train budget examiners. The result was that many of them considered program budgeting to be an attack on their status and an insult to their profession. If they were not actively hostile, they were certainly actively passive.

After the first budget was submitted under the PPB rubric, the lesson for management was clear. There was no reward for compliance, no punishment for simply ignoring the whole thing.

Analyst-training was a different problem. Analysts wanted to be trained. In their case, there were powerful incentives. It looked as though something wonderful and exciting was going to be happening in government and here was a chance to be a vital part of that change.

For the less idealistically motivated there was another reason for participation. If the agencies were not following the spirit of President Johnson's directive, they were following the letter. They were setting up "analytic staffs" and anyone, it appeared, who could spell PPB was being promoted.

Problems arose chiefly in trying to get people to apply austere and disciplined modes of thought to problems affecting not molecules or protozoa, but the lives of their fellow humans, and in trying to teach an interdisciplinary approach to graduates of schools where academic disciplines were narrowly defined and rigidly segregated. In this educational system theory became mysteriously transmuted into fact and those facts were memorized and sanctified. (Consider the case of the "law" of supply and demand.) It was important for example, to direct an engineer toward analysis of the social consequences of a building program, or to convince an economist of the advisability of including a physician in a team studying a public health program.

A not inconsiderable part of the problem of training analysts lay in the area of communications. Many analyst trainees, particularly those who had taken a one-year academic program, clothed their analysis in a haze of jargon apparently incomprehensible to the uninitiated. The short-term training of analysts was also particularly unproductive because their lack of training in mathematics and economics left them without a background in relevant analytic techniques.

In spite of the problems, there were some heartening successes. Success, not surprisingly, was closely related to length of training, which ranged from three-week to one-year programs. The most successful students generally were those who had been trained in a discipline requiring the application of analytic rigor. It may surprise some to learn that these included philosophy and the law.

Conclusion

The intention in the immediate future is to concentrate on what can be done in very limited amounts of time. Narrowly defined, specific analytic techniques can be taught; for example, correlation and regression problems for computer solution can be taught in three days. Although it is a long way from systems analysis, it is a better beginning.

As for the longer-range future, there are hopeful stirrings in the schools. There are still one-year programs going on in five universities. State and foreign governments are also starting to show an interest which should serve to strengthen these programs. The schools themselves are getting better and some show promise of becoming very good indeed. The increase in cross-disciplinary programs at the graduate level is a most hopeful sign. In the meantime, the programs to upgrade and retool mid-career people must be strengthened and expanded.

Up to this point, a question basic to the entire discussion has not been asked. Can we realistically expect to develop through training the kind of superior analyst described earlier; The answer must be a qualified *no.* Too much hinges on characteristics formed long before the individual enters graduate school; qualities such as curiosity, flexibility, courage and integrity and the rarest and most precious quality of all, the ability to think the unthinkable.

The whole conservative force of society works to screen this last quality out of the population. And don't be deceived, the universities are right in there screening with the best of them. It is a tribute to perseverance, cunning and general cussedness that some few still slip through. They are more likely to be found in areas like theoretical physics or low-temperature chemistry than in economics or public administration, where unorthodox thinking is more likely to attract unfavorable attention from the professors.

It is unlikely indeed that there are enough of these people in our world to man the analytic staffs of the larger corporations and governmental units. But you don't need or even want an entire staff of this sort. You need one as a catalyst and integrative factor to first stimulate and then integrate the important and necessary contributions of the other staff specialists.

These latter can be trained. They can even be broadened through the cross-disciplinary training of the kind recommended to the point where they will support and reinforce the resident genius rather than fight him.

If you can combine this kind of staff with an involved and receptive management, you will have something very fine indeed.

Instant results should not be expected even from an ideal staff. Skills in what is essentially a new and complex form of analysis must be developed and sharpened through experience. Individual deficiencies have to be corrected through short-term training. Communication channels to management have to be opened. A data base has to be developed. (It is almost axiomatic in the PPBS business that no organization is producing the kind of data that is really useful for systems studies.) Methods to exploit faculty experience must be found. While it has been suggested that the campus is not the place to look for analysts, there are people on the campus with specific analytic skills in economics, sociology, urban affairs, and the like, that can be highly useful if they are fed through the filter of a broadly gauged analytic staff that is able to spot deficiencies in reasoning that arise from too narrow a viewpoint.

Most important of all, and perhaps hardest of all, top management itself must learn to understand and to use the products of the analytic staff.

CHAPTER 25

Personnel Limitations
of "Instant Analysis"

by Edwin L. Harper

Special Assistant to the President

Fred A. Kramer

University of Massachusetts

Andrew M. Rouse

Executive Director
President's Advisory Council on Executive Organization[1]

The unprecedented personnel problem for the federal establishment created by President Lyndon B. Johnson's 1965 decision to implement in all major domestic agencies planning-programming-budgeting systems modeled on the one that appeared to be operating successfully in the Pentagon was discussed in terms of recruiting and developing staff in the preceding chapter. This paper addresses the problem of quantity and quality of analysts in the federal government three years after President Johnson's order for "instant analysis."

In late 1968 the authors under the auspices of the Bureau of the Budget undertook a study of the efforts of 16 domestic agencies[2] to build an analytic capability. It involved over 300 interviews with PPB analysts, their supervisors, budget officers, and program managers, including several at the assistant

---

[1] This paper represents only the personal and unofficial opinion of the authors. It does not necessarily represent the views of the Office of Management and Budget or the administration.

[2] The agencies studies were as follows: Agriculture, Atomic Energy Commission, Commerce, Army Corps of Engineers-Civil Works, General Development, Interior, Justice, Labor, National Aeronautics and Space Administration, Office of Economic Opportunity, Post Office, Transportation, Treasury, and Veterans Administration.

secretary level, as well as personnel data on more than 700 analysts and supervisors. (Some of the results of this study were reported elsewhere.)[2]

Quality

The study was based on the assumption that the analysis which decision-makers find useful is produced only by able analysts. Interviews with decision-makers revealed that several analytic staffs were turning out a product that was considered useful. A review of the personnel data of the professionals on these staffs showed that they had similar backgrounds and that these backgrounds were consistent with the profile generally thought to be that of a good analyst.

These data for staffs producing useful analysis showed that they:

1. were younger than the average analyst (average: 41.2 years)

2. had more years of formal education than the average analyst (average: 17.0 years)

3. More often had quantitatively oriented majors (engineering, maths, economics) than the average analyst (average: 47.0percent of the total with quantitative majors)

4. Had more quantitative work experience than average (average: 28.3 percent of the total with quantitative work experience)

The qualifications of members of all analytic staffs ranged widely. For example, in one agency 91.7 percent of the central-analytic staff had quantitative college majors and in another only 14.3 percent of the central group had such preparation. Similarly, wide ranges were found in the other aspects of education, training, and work experience that were used as criteria.

The scarcity of analytic skill in most agencies was evidenced by the fact that only 37.8 percent of the central-analysis staff members and 23.9 percent of the bureau staff members had had quantitative experience. One possible explanation for this scarcity of analytic skills among persons selected for the analysis staffs was that many of them were transferred into PPB work from related-agency occupational categories such as budget analyst and procedure or management analyst without specific reference to prior analytic or quantitative work.

Most administrative skills such as management analysis, public information, accounting, and the like, were not directly transferable to the kinds of analytic activities necessary for program or systems analysis, and almost 50 percent of the agency staffs came from these occupational classifications. Agency detail on personal background for what was identified as "analyst" positions in the agencies, showed that only 11 percent were either professional economists,

---

[1] Edwin L. Harper, Fred A. Kramer, and Andrew M. Rouse, "Implementation and Use of PPB in Sixteen Federal Agencies," *Public Administration Review*, Vol. 29, No. 6 (November–December, 1969), pp. 623–632.

system analysts, or younger persons whose first jobs beyond college were as PPB analysts.

When the definition of analyst was expanded to add "near-analysts"— engineers, operations analysts, program analysts, and mathematicians—the group qualifying as "analyst" increased to over 30 percent of the total in all agencies. Broadening the qualifications to include persons affiliated with universities, lawyers, or government advisors increased the qualified portion of agency staffs to almost 50 percent. However, no matter how the definition was stretched, there just were not enough qualified individuals in the agencies to meet the requirement.[1]

Quantity

The problems involved in determining the sufficient quantity of analysts began with enumeration: When should an individual be counted as a PPB analyst? For the purposes of the study, an operational definition of a PPB analyst was developed. Any person spending 25 percent or more of his time on PPB work—preparing program and financial plans (PEPs), program memoranda (PMs), special analytic studies (SASs), or developing procedures for these activities—was defined as a PPB analyst.[2]

The study identified 793 individual analysts and another 273 analyst positions which were authorized. According to two tests of sufficiency there seemed to be a sufficient number of analyst positions authorized to make the PPB system work by 1968 even though the positions might not be optimally placed.

One test was to assume that enough analysts should be employed to prepare a PM and a SAS for every subcategory in the program structure of the 16 agencies. From these assumptions it was estimated that 960 full-time analyst equivalents would be required.

A second test to determine the number of analysts needed to implement a workable PPB system was to compare each of the sixteen domestic agencies with the Department of Defense. (DOD) By that standard, five domestic agencies— Health, Education and Welfare (HEW), Housing and Urban Development (HUD), Justice, Labor, and Post Office—were slightly understaffed. Three agencies— National Aeronautics and Space Administration, Transportation, and Treasury —appeared to be somewhat overstaffed.

The study regarded the manning of the PPB system by DOD as the standard of a desirable distribution of analytic staff between the central and bureau staffs.

---

[1] Mounting large recruitment programs was not an available alternative because of a governmentwide job freeze at the time.
[2] The time standard was lowered to 10 percent in the case of HUD since there were so few people spending 25 percent of their time on PPB activities.

Edwin L. Harper, Fred A. Kramer and Andrew M. Rouse

Taking the relationship of DOD's central analytic staff to the amount of budget authority exercised as a criterion, the civilian agencies' central staffs were seen to be undermanned by about 100 analyst positions.[1] This Figure may not seem large in absolute numbers, but the addition of 100 analysts represented an increase of almost 50 percent in the size of central staffs doing analytic work.

Using the DOD standard also involved assumptions (1) that DOD was successfully implementing a PPB system, and (2) that the analytic problems faced by the domestic agencies were similar in their degree of complexity to those handled by DOD. It is generally accepted that the problems faced by the domestic agencies in trying to develop adequate benefit criteria and output measures were at least as difficult as, and often more difficult than, those faced by DOD analysts. The first of these assertions indicated the worth of accepting the analytical operation of DOD as a model to be emulated. The second assertion indicated that the domestic agencies might be in need of an even greater number of qualified people than this study would indicate.

Problem and Suggestion

The personnel problems created by President Johnson's demand for instant PPBS operation in the domestic agencies were only partially solved. Agencies were able to produce the "warm bodies" to fill the analyst slots, but the agencies were not able to fill all of the posts with clearly qualified analysts. There were simply not enough professionals in government (or outside of it) with the skills deemed necessary for successful PPB analysts—at least not enough professionals with such skills were placed on the formal PPB staffs.

Some observers have claimed that the demand for implementation of PPB in all the domestic agencies represented the highest degree of commitment to organizational change from the leaders in the Administration.[2] The present authors view the instant across-the-board implementation strategy to be a set-back for meaningful systematic planning and analysis in the federal government. It amounted to spreading the forms of PPB around to all agencies while skimping on the substance.

An alternative strategy would have been to develop cadres of highly skilled analysts in a few agencies. Hopefully, they would have produced studies useful to decision-makers, and thereby stimulated a demand among other program managers and department heads for the benefits of good analysis. This demand would not have been expressed in all agencies overnight. There would have been a gradual demand for professionals with good analytic skills as management gained an idea of what analytic skills were needed to do a job. Some, but not all,

[1] A particularly acute problem in HEW.
[2] Reported in Stanley B. Botner, "Four Years of PPBS: An Appraisal," *Public Administration Review*, Vol. 30, No. 4 (July–August 1970), p. 424.

agency heads would seek to develop an analytic staff so they would be better able to compete for resources with the agencies that had a developed analytic capability. If small numbers of skilled personnel were required, they could be recruited—even during a job freeze—or adequately trained.

True commitment to improving resource-allocation procedures could occur only if the analysis produced were of high quality. Dispersing the available number of analytic professions who had the required skills among all agencies to meet the demand for instant analysis effectively guaranteed that the quality of analysis would suffer. That it did suffer and generally was not used by either the agencies or the Bureau of the Budget suggested that the effective integration of analysis with government decision-making could better be accomplished by some strategy other than to artificially create a demand by administrative fiat.

CHAPTER 26

Recent U. S. Federal Government Experience with Program Budgeting

by Jack W. Carlson
Office of Management and Budget

There is a long history of periodic attempts at improving features of U.S. federal government budgeting and management. President Taft in 1912 submitted to the Congress a model budget based on expenditures by function, by organization, by type of activity, by capital and current expenditures, and by cross-classification among each category. The Rivers and Harbors Act of 1902 and the Flood Control Act of 1936 required estimates of benefits and costs of proposed water-resource investments so as to assure that "the benefits to whomsoever they may accure are in excess of the estimated costs."

Until 1921, each bureau since the early part of the nineteenth century prepared its own budget and usually submitted it directly to the Congress. In that year, the Bureau of the Budget was created to develop an executive budget. During the next three decades, its major function was concentrated on controlling expenditures to assure conformity with appropriation acts. During the 1940s and 1950s, especially after the reports of the Hoover Commissions, the bureau slowly expanded its activities in the directtion of seeing that the agencies gained in managerial efficiency. During the 1960s a third function was added, strategic planning. Strategic planning was used to assist in setting long-term priorities.

Until the 1960s, changes came about slowly and their acceptance was gradual. In contrast, in the 1960s the untried or embryonic features of program budgeting, or the planning-programming-budgeting system, as it was called by the bureau, were introduced with unusual vigor. fanfare, and, in retrospect, exaggerated expectations.

In evaluating or describing this effort, it is important to keep it in the context of decision-making in a highly complex governmental apparatus that oversaw the spending of more than $300 billion annually—more than 20 percent of Gross National Product. This occured in an environment of several layers of decision-makers and a fragmented and intensely political legislative process.

The following conditions provided motivation for change:

1. Bureaus within departments and the authorization committees and appropriations subcommittees of the Congress were the most significant participants in decision-making. Department heads and the President tended to be eclipsed by the process.

2. There was no overall planning. Only a few program managers planned their resource allocations for several future years. Even in the few areas they did plan, they did not do it on the basis of benefits expected and anticipated costs or some kind of priority schedule or resource constraint. Resources were committed largely by accretion over time, without specific attention to the relationship between the universe of needs and the effectiveness of particular programs.

3. In any year, only a small portion of the budget was subject to the effective control of the bureaus, departments, the President, or the Congress. Legal and moral commitments made by past decisions were overriding.

4. There were few attempts to hold program managers to any predetermined plan or to use appropriate funds on a time-phased basis with performance tied to resource use. Very little was known about the results of expenditures, even in terms of the most simplistic output measures.

Developments Since 1961

Starting in 1961 in the Department of Defense, in 1965 in twenty other agencies, and subsequently in five other agencies (for a total of twenty-six), a deliberate and major effort to effect reforms more rapidly was undertaken. There were two forces behind this change: First, the belief that the expansion of *knowledge* in the social and physical sciences, together with increased data, held great promise for improving both the broad and narrow decisions of government. It was recognized that this knowledge and information had to be brought to bear on problems at the right time and in the right place.

Second, that a system to bring this information to the decision-maker at the right time and in the right place was required to reap the rewards of the new knowledge. Upgrading available knowledge and improving the decision process are very much intertwined activities.

The formal system developed, or PPB, was based on two premises: First, it would be tied into the *budget cycle*, which is the only recurring administrative process through which most major decisions must pass and also is the government's formal resource allocation process and decision-forcing mechanism. Second, although major responsibility for developing the system would belong to the agencies, emphasis was placed at the highest agency level instead of at the intermediate level of bureaus and divisions.

On this basis, the 26 federal agencies (1) established analytic staffs reporting to the agency head or his deputy[1] and (2) developed some or all of the component parts of the PPB system and incorporated them into the budget process. The component parts were program structures, issue analyses, program memoranda, and multi-year program and financial plans.

Implementing the System

Each agency was required to identify the major objectives it was pursuing and display its financial data in these terms. This became the third way to display federal-agency budgets:

1. Appropriations for control of expenditures
2. Activity for management efficiency
3. Program for planning

Policy Issue Analysis

Major issues were identified, analyzed, and incorporated in the budget and other decision-making vehicles. When issue analysis extended over a long period of time and became somewhat self-contained, the effort was described as a special analytic study.

Program Memoranda

The Program Memorandum was intended to be a brief written document showing alternative ways to resolve budgetary and related work problems. It was to be prepared either for selected or for all program categories of an agency and to include the results of the issue-analysis effort. It was to be the vehicle for both policy debate among policy-makers in the executive branch and for communicating the final policy guidance.

Program and Financial Plan

This document was designed to show program expenditures and associated outputs for the past two years, the budget year, and four future years based on specified ground rules. Since the President must recommend his budget to the Congress in terms of the congressionally established appropriations structure, the plan also provided a crosswalk which translated program outlays and costs into individual appropriation accounts.

The Program and Financial Plan was intended as a bridge between annual budget allocations and setting longer-range priority. It also was a tool for department heads to gain more discretion over future budgets.

---

[1] See Chapters 24 and 25 for a discussion of recruiting and training problems in developing analytical staffs.

Jack W. Carlson

Evaluating the Experience

Based on this summary of the accelerated approach used to implement program budgeting, an evaluation can now be made on two bases: (1) Did it accomplish the ideal sought? (2) Even if the ideal was not achieved, were the changes significant in improving the decision-making process and the substance of the decisions made?

Extent of Change

The U.S. experience was clearly short of the ideal. Initially, PPBS became a different, somewhat competitive channel for decision-making, appended to the traditional channels of budgeting in support of appropriation requests and legislation handled through legislative liaison and general counsel offices. The intent was to provide more useful information for the development both of budgets and legislation, but that was not the initial result.

Three channels for decision-making existed in varying forms at the bureau level, the agency level, and in the central part of the government. Each had data requirements, time schedules, and semi-independent players with only partial overlap and communication. Since 1968, there has been an effort to merge these parallel but separate channels and provide adequate analysis at the key decision points of each one. Some progress has been made but it has been a slow and gradual process.

Program Structure

The program structures developed by the twenty-six agencies differed widely in quality and utility. Some represented helpful new ways of looking at agency activities for analytic purposes. Preparing them was an educational process for some of those involved and they highlighted programs which should have been considered together. In some cases, they provided officials with their first appreciation of agency efforts in pursuit of particular objectives and the triviality of some of the activities. In many cases when they were not used for most decision-making purposes they became an unnecessary burden.

Program structures were initially prepared by individual agencies and were not tied into a governmentwide structure. This was a shortcoming which did not assist higher-echelon decision-makers in comparing programs that were close substitutes or complements in several different agencies. For example, federal programs aimed at providing manpower training and job-related information are found in seven agencies. Nearly half of them are outside the Labor Department. In 1969, the Program Overview Project attempted to display federal programs by governmentwide program areas with common input and output measures and estimates of the characteristics of the initial beneficiaries. Both the effort to develop agency program structures and the Program Overview Project demonstrated the usefulness of having a capability to display federal program information across the entire government and in a number of ways, not just one or two.

Policy Issue Analysis

The issue definition process, subsequent analysis, and final reporting have changed both in process and quality. Initially, issues were identified haphazardly, in large quantity and without participation by the relevant decision-makers. This applied equally to issues raised by the central part of the federal government, by each department (including Defense), and by some bureaus. Moreover, too many issues were raised in relationship to the scarce analytic capability available to work on them. In the case of the central government in 1968, about 380 were posed to 17 agencies by the Bureau of the Budget[1] at the end of April and completion dates were set for May through September. The results were disappointing. Less than one-fourth of the responses provided useful information and many of these were on very minor issues.

Since 1968, the number of issues has decreased, they were being identified earlier in the year, key decision-makers were involved in the selection process, a greater proportion was completed, and most of the work done was useful for decision-making. Public-policy bargaining has been sharpened and needless friction avoided by the use of the additional analysis. Decision-makers' judgment has been applied more knowingly in making choices than previously would have been the case.

There were many difficulties involved, however, in doing usable public policy analysis. First, analyses aimed at identifying ways to achieve national objectives were greatly constrained by the fact that several tiers of decision-makers were involved (often with many agencies in each tier). In addition, federal programs were frequently delivered through state and local governments. This could mean that seemingly obvious improvements were thwarted by the multiplicity of agencies and program managers, each with a *de facto* veto over change. Since policy analysis included evaluation of institutions as well as measurement of returns from public investment, it necessarily stepped on managerial toes.[2]

Second, some agencies concentrated their limited analytical resources on fairly minor issues. Sometimes major issues involving hundreds of millions or billions of dollars were given only superficial analysis. This occured because

[1] Changed to Office of Management and Budget in 1970.
[2] In 1969, program budgeting was directed towards the institution problem of multilevels of government. This was accomplished by evaluating improvement in federal management and coordination from the perspective of federal management and importantly by launching an effort to improve program budgeting at the state and local government levels from the perspective of these governments. The latter effort was christened the Federal Technical Assistance Program or the "Flying Feds."

there was inadequate incentive for program managers or agency heads to analyze their programs, since one result of analysis could be the phasing down of the programs under their direction. The additional information also may have meant less discretion for the program manager. This lead many executives and legislative leaders to prefer little or no analysis rather than more analysis.

Third, individual agency studies usually did not encompass the full breadth of the program since activities in several other and different agencies were involved. In the federal manpower programs, for illustration, it was evident that training objectives can be partly or completely satisfied by programs in the Labor Department, the Office of Economic Opportunity, the Department of Health, Education and Welfare, the Veterans' Administration, and the Department of Defense. Lack of an adequate cross-agency capacity or sufficient incentives for analyzing policy issues that impact on several agencies was and is a major shortcoming. Some steps have been taken to overcome this, but these efforts have been inadequate so far.

In spite of the current inadequacies discussed here, a considerable improvement in the basis for decisions had been made from 1965 to 1971. The quantity of adequate-to-excellent and useful analysis increased severalfold. Since the managers of the federal system shifted their emphasis from structure to substance in 1968, there has been something like a fourfold rise in relevant analysis. In relationship to an ideal level of policy analysis, this may mean a rise from 5 to 20 on a scale of 100.

Program Memoranda

The Program Memoranda (PMs) or comparable documents also have been of uneven quality. Most contained useful information, especially when results of issue analysis were included. In the early years, about 25 percent and since 1968, about 50 percent, could be judged as adequate to excellent. Most of the others did not identify major alternatives, concentrate on policy decisions, or present a multiyear strategy directed toward specific objectives and outputs. Many of the PMs were descriptive, verbose, nonanalytic accounts of existing and proposed programs, usually coupled with an impassioned plea for funding at the full request. Since it is difficult to know if an "urgent necessity" is more important than a "dire national need," a "must expenditure," or a "vital responsibility," such statements were not very useful in making national resource-allocation decisions.

However, PMs and related documents did become important, since they created something that had not existed before. They provided available information to all levels in the executive branch and frequently provided a summary related to specific issues embedded in a broader program. In those agencies where a substantial part of the staff was active in preparing the program memorandum, the educational gains to executives and subordinates involved in the exercise made it worthwhile for this reason alone. *Documents of the PM type proved their greatest usefulness in areas requiring major policy change.*

Program and Financial Plans

There were significant difficulties with the program and financial plans (PFPs) from the very start. In the beginning, the agencies were asked for planning figures on how much and in what way they would spend money in the future. The result was a series of wish-lists of what the agencies would like to spend on their programs if no fiscal constraints were imposed. Some agencies showed program increases in all areas of more than 100 percent per year, while other agencies showed the small increases they thought politically feasible. Failure to provide consistent future resources constraints made this exercise meaningless.

In 1968, the definition was changed to include only future appropriations to which the government is committed by legal or moral obligations from past decisions or requirements resulting from current decision. "Commitment" was not well defined, and this restricted the utility of the modified PFPs. Each agency imposed its own standard of resource limitations and definition of commitment. In the last year or two, more precise definitions were applied, especially in the central part of the government. Requirements for the agency PFPs were modified again in mid-1971, in part, to respond to the Legislative Reorganization Act of 1970 and in part to reduce the burden of poor PFPs. Agencies are now required to submit future-year projections of expenditure estimates for proposed legislation which authorizes the continuation of existing programs or new programs.

The PFP has been helpful to some agencies. In the Office of Management and Budget it has helped to identify unforeseen growth in aggregate terms of the seemingly uncontrollable expenditures and to anticipate where expenditures may go within five years. However, in its original form, for the most part, it was not used, or useful.

Staffing and Growth

The directions on PPB issued in 1965 instructed the agencies to provide an analytic staff reporting to the department head or his immediate subordinate. In addition, they encouraged the creation of analytic staffs located in key bureaus. These newly designated staffs grew quickly in 1966 and 1967, and at a slower rate since, until the total of new professional positions has exceeded 1,000. [1]

[1] See Chapters 24 and 25. Other efforts included the Educational Program in Systems Analysis, a nine-month program at five universities for developing resources-analysis skills. Also, attempts to reform university curricula so as to develop skill in public policy analysis; e.g., the Policy Analysis program at Harvard.

213

The professional competence of these staffs fluctuated widely. Agencies which initially developed strong analytic staffs such as Defense and HEW, experienced a loss of capability at the turn of the decade. Departments which developed and maintained strong analytic capability were Agriculture, Office of Economic Opportunity and the Atomic Energy Commission. A few agencies merely went through the motions and never developed an effective analytic staff, for example, the Department of Justice. The remaining agencies were found in the middle of this range of experience.

Besides the specially designated PPB positions, other personnel were and are involved. The total federal cost of these people and supporting personnel has been estimated to be $40 million annually or about two ten-thousands of one percent of total federal expenditure.

Some funds have also been designated for program impact studies by outside contractors. Congress has enacted legislation that requires one-half to one percent of the program funds to be used for program evaluation. Other funds have been specially earmarked for experimentation and distantly related social research and development. The total of all of these in FY 1970 was $345.7 million and was estimated to grow to about $500 million in FY 1973.

The growth in analytic resources not only added to useful information for decision-making but importantly enhanced the role of the department heads and increased the capacity of the Office of Management and Budget. Although it could have been used neutrally, it was used to change power relationships.

Significance of Changes

The second basis for evaluating PPBS is to measure the achievement in process and substance. On this basis, the improvement has been substantial.

Program budgeting has led federal agencies to reappraise their functions and missions. The result has been an increase in understanding of their programs and an awareness of possible alternatives. This broad reassessment would not have occurred without program budgeting or something like it. These efforts provided useful information for reorganizing federal departments and clarifying the relationship of federal programs with state and local governments. The President's 1971 proposal to reorganize seven major departments into four with more closely related programs benefitted from this effort.

During the last six years, the quality, relevance, and structure of information developed by federal agencies has improved substantially. There is more solid information on program inputs and outputs than was available a few years earlier. The public debate on national priorities has been sharpened and enlightened. For specific examples one need only observe the benefit that additional information had on the public discussion of the Liquid Metal Fast Breeder Reactor, Job Corps, Supersonic Transport, Family Assistance, Revenue Sharing, Family Health, Oil Shale Development, and other programs. This came from processes, data, and staffs created through the implementation of PPBS.

The federal government has not and does not now obtain sufficient feedback on the results of its programs. There is general agreement that it is important to measure the accomplishments of programs and to obtain information on whether the concepts behind each program are appropriate. PPBS has emphasized this, and in the last six years the amount and caliber of program evaluation has increased. Summaries of what we know and do not know about each program in relationship to related programs can now be developed.

These efforts have been helpful in directing the use of the federal government's scarce analytic resources. PPB efforts showed the need to experiment with programs and concepts and carefully evaluate them for possible wider use. R & D funds in social areas have doubled in the past three years. The growth has been coupled with increasing concern on the use of these resources which is answered, in part, by material now developed through PPBS. This is part of increasing recognition by program managers and other key decision-makers of the value of quantitative and qualitative analysis. The educational impact of PPBS has been significant.

A number of things detracted from the initial efforts to implement PPBS. One was directing it immediately to the entire government instead of pacing implementation to match the capacity of agencies to absorb it. There was too heavy an emphasis on examples drawn from defense, on the importance of economic skills. There was no effort to allay the fear of replacing a generalist's judgment with the narrower view of an "expert" and inadequate recognition of the counterattack by parts of the bureaucracy that might be overshadowed by the innovation.

Because of PPBS, it is generally recognized now that knowledge of the costs and benefits of existing programs and identification of alternative programs helps sharpen political bargaining and reduces the possibility of continuing or initiating policies that are less desirable. By 1970 there was a realization that PPBS was not a substitute for the bargaining process but instead was an important part of it. There also has been recognition that quantitative data serves to help the decision-maker. The final decision reflects the decision-maker's substantive determination on the important objectives to pursue, not just data. However, for analysts, decision-makers, and the public, there has been a growing recognition of the fact that good judgment is made better when it can operate on the basis of good analysis.

Conclusion

One of the most difficult questions to answer is whether PPBS should have concentrated completely on analysis of individual issues and ignored the concept of a decision-making system. The argument in favor of this is that requirements by the decision-making system effort drained off valuable resources that could

Jack W. Carlson

have been devoted to analysis and evaluation. This is especially important in the light of the value of the documents produced in the system.

To increase the use of analysis in government decision-making, however, one needs not only a supply of relevant analytic work but a demand for it. One of the objectives of PPBS as a decision-making system is to create this demand. If one were to rely totally upon supply for the creation of demand, several issues would arise:

Good analysis might lie fallow if its relevance at a specific decision point was not clear—as under traditional government decision methods.

Analyses designed without participation by those who must use the results are much less likely to be relevant to actual decisions.

The government, not to mention the private sector, already turns out thousands of analyses, evaluations, and studies every year. Their influence on policy is usually negligible. This indicates that more than an increase in supply is needed.

There is no reason to think that the early efforts that produced poor analysis and Program Memoranda would otherwise have produced good studies. The major-policy-issue process and the writing of PMs is largely an exercise in asking the right questions and developing answers. This is necessary for doing good policy analysis.

For all these reasons, work to increase demand is as important as efforts to increase the quantity and quality of the supply. Both need a process and structure to assure adequate supply and demand of relevant data.

Appendix A

Example of Program Summary Relationship Through Sublevels
to Program Element

The city of Philadelphia uses a three-step program-classification system. The relationship between the program summary, the subprogram summary, and the program element in this system is illustrated by pages drawn from the 1968-69 budget. Other organizations may use a 4-, 5-, or even 6-level breakdown but the relationship between the program summary and the cost element remains the same as that shown herein.

THE CITY OF PHILADELPHIA

Samples Drawn from the 1968-69 Budget

PROGRAM SUMMARY

CITY OF PHILADELPHIA
1968 OPERATING BUDGET

	NO. A
PROGRAM	Community Development

GOAL

To improve the physical and economic condition of the City.

DESCRIPTION

This program involves a wide range of activities carried on by many City and quasi-public agencies directed toward eliminating blight, increasing the number of suitable housing units, improving the economic well-being of the City, developing major city institutions, preventing decline of selected neighborhoods, and improving the general physical attractiveness of the City.

Contained in this program are the City's efforts to solve many of its major problems with the assistance of the Federal and State Governments. Broad-gauge, comprehensive urban development projects of residential, commercial and institutional nature are undertaken by the Redevelopment Authority with the assistance of various City agencies. The City's Department of Commerce operates major port and airport facilities important to the City's economic health. Job development and job training activities are carried on by several City and quasi-public agencies, and various programs for the general improvement of physical conditions are carried on by several City agencies.

COST SUMMARY BY SUB-PROGRAM

SUB-PROGRAM (1)	1966 Obligation (2)	1967 Appropriation (3)	1968 Request (4)	Increase (Decrease) (5)
Housing	26,172,600	28,050,133	30,955,075	2,904,942
Economic Development	36,672,652	60,999,848	63,191,163	2,191,315
Institutional Development	4,330,000	8,025,000	7,824,000	(201,000)
Federally-Assisted Neighborhood Renewal	119,950	3,020,954	4,406,155	1,385,201
Urband Beautification	449,412	394,075	507,854	113,779
General Support	6,257,463	6,506,180	8,184,374	1,678,194
PROGRAM TOTAL	74,002,077	106,996,190	115,068,621	8,072,432

CITY OF PHILADELPHIA 1968 OPERATING BUDGET			SUB-PROGRAM SUMMARY	
PROGRAM	NO.	SUB-PROGRAM		NO.
Community Development	A	Economic Development		2

GOAL

To strengthen and increase the economic growth of the City of Philadelphia; to increase the number of jobs and to train people to fill available jobs.

DESCRIPTION

Seven City agencies and four quasi-public agencies are involved in carrying on this subprogram. The Commerce Department supervises the operation and development of the Marine Port of Philadelphia, and operates the Philadelphia International Airport and North Philadelphia Airport. Under the direction of the City Representative, business services are provided to commerce and industry. Conventions and trade shows are attracted to the Philadelphia Civic Center's new Exhibition Hall. The Economic Development Unit conducts research into the City's needs for economic development. The Manpower Utilization Commission coordinates vocational training programs carried on by other agencies and supervises an On-the-Job Training Program, as well as advising the Mayor on the City's manpower needs. Job training for the City's youth is carried on by the Department of Public Welfare through its Neighborhood Youth Corps. The Philadelphia Anti-Poverty Action Committee administers the use of Federal Anti-Poverty Funds in providing adult job training by private agencies in the City, especially by the Opportunities Industrialization Center.

The Redevelopment Authority makes available for commercial and industrial construction, blighted areas acquired and cleared. The Philadelphia Industrial Development Corporation acquires, develops, and makes available for industrial use land and existing facilities, as well as assisting industry desiring to remain in Philadelphia and attracting new industry to the City. The Philadelphia Port Corporation operates and maintains existing port facilities and plans the construction of new facilities ot modernize the port. The Philadelphia Employment Development Corporation seeks to assist the long-term unemployed by increasing the number of jobs available to them, matching individuals to the jobs available, and stimulating the development of on-the-job training of those individuals by private industry.

Duplication in the amount of $675,000 has been subtracted from the Subprogram total, representing annual contributions of $600,000 from the Commerce Department to the Philadelphia Port Corporation, and $75,000 from the Commerce Department to P.I.D.C.

COST BY PROGRAM ELEMENT

Agency (1)	Program Element (2)	1966 Obligation (3)	1967 Appropriation (4)	1968 Request (5)	Increase (Decrease) (6)
Commerce	Port Development	14,326,630	701,502	703,143	1,641
Commerce	Aviation Operations	5,300,465	24,956,743	99,455,476	(15,501,267)
Commerce	Business Services	93,622	110,020	108,516	(1,504)
Bd.–Phila. Civic Ctr.	Convention & Trade Shows	2,740,295	3,214,140	1,964,624	(1,249,516)
City Rep. & Dir. Com.	Direction of Commerce Dept.	82,521	84,906	79,343	(5,563)
Econ. Develop. Unit	Econ. Research and Development	11,359	100,320.	103,863	3,543
Mayor	Manpower Utilization	27,224	36,617	36,786	169
Mayor	Manpower Research & Investigation	23,786	18,138	–	(18,138)
Pub. Welfare–N.Y.C.	Youth Job Training	1,452,550	2,264,160	3,000,000	735,840
P.A.A.C.	Adult Job Training	3,452,174	2,909,412	2,909,412	–
Redevelop. Auth.	Blight Removal for Commercial & Industrial Re-use	6,315,000	8,900,000	9,405,000	505,000
P.I.D.C.	Expanding and Retaining Industry	300,000	300,000	300,000	–
Phila. Port Corp.	Port Development	3,222,026	15,678,890	30,900,000	15,221,110
P.E.D.C.	Expanding Job Opportunities	–	2,400,000	4,900,000	2,500,000
	SUB-PROGRAM TOTAL	36,672,652	60,999,848	63,191,163	2,191,315

CITY OF PHILADEPHIA
1968 OPERATING BUDGET

PROGRAM ELEMENT

PROGRAM	Community Development	NO.	A
SUB-PROGRAM	Economic Development	NO.	2

PROGRAM ELEMENT	Business Services	NO.	03
DEPARTMENT	Commerce	NO.	42
FUND	General	NO.	0168

OBJECTIVES

To encourage industrial expansion, assist in the creation of additional job opportunities, and prevent industrial relocation outside Philadelphia by coordinating aid—financial and informational—to local businesses and by assisting business in dealing with the City and other agencies.

DESCRIPTION

Provides liaison with the Philadelphia Industrial Development Corporation (PIDC) and processes payments from the Industrial Development Fund for engineering and land development costs. The City contributes $75,000 per year to PIDC. Serves as the principal City contact for Individual business problems. Represents the Director of Commerce at trade association meetings and with local business groups. Publishes a newsletter for all businessmen with information on financial and other assistance available to the business community from the Small Business Administration, the Small Business Opportunities Corporation, the Philadelphia Industrial Development Corporation, the Southeastern Pennsylvania Economic Development Corporation, the United States Department of Commerce and any other organization which provides business services. Cooperation with the Economic Development Unit of the Department of Finance in carrying out action programs which will assist in the expansion of local business and the creation of additional job opportunities in a major function. The eventual establishment of a one-stop business service agency is contemplated.

COST SUMMARY BY CLASS

Class (1)	DESCRIPTION (2)	1966 Obligation (3)	1967 Appropriation (4)	1968 Request (5)	Increase (Decrease) (6)
100	Personal Services	6622	18020	16552	(1468)
200	Purchase of Services	12000	14232	14232	
300	Materials and Supplies		2200	2200	
400	Equipment		568	532	(36)
500	Contributions, Indemnities, Refunds and Taxes	75000	75000	75000	
	Other				
	OPERATING BUDGET	93622	110020	108516	(1504)
	CAPITAL BUDGET				
	PROGRAM ELEMENT TOOL	93622	110020	108516	(1504)

Appendix B

Subjects Analyzed by Program Budgeting

The material referred to in Professor Mosher's report for the United States is found in "New Aggregated Systems for Planning Programming Budgeting," Fifteenth International Congress of Administrative Sciences, 1971, U.S. reporteur, Frederick C. Mosher. His Appendix II is reproduced here.

Appendix II

Examples of Program Analysis

Selected Topics about Which Decisions Have Been Influenced by Analyses

Electricity for gaseous diffusion plants
Enforcement of civil rights laws
Allocation of legal resources for anti-trust purposes
Structure and program of the Institute of Criminal Justice
Internal Revenue Service audit program
Oil Shale development
Post Office organization and efficiency
Atomic Energy Commission cascade improvement program
Single class priority mail
Highway safety programs
Supersonic transport
USIA media use
Peace Corps volunteer priorities
Collection of customs duties
Fast breeder reactor program
Coast Guard aviation program
GSA motor pools
FAS air traffic control facilities
Infant mortality
Nursing manpower
Disease Control
Medical care prices
Vocational rehabilitation
Nuclear rocket R & D
Demand for park recreation facilities
Manpower Development Training Act program
Helium supply
Heavy metals supply
Timber management
Forest roads

Topographic mapping
Work experience program
Saturn V rocket production
High energy physics
Water resources
Air pollution abatement strategies
Water pollution abatement strategies
Earth resources technology satellite
Job Corps program
Distribution of National Archives materials
Distribution of Federal visual aid materials
Coast Guard merchant marine safety program
Optimum modes for supplying Federal agencies with equipment, services and supplies
Building space acquisition
Off-shore mineral leasing policies
Veterans' pension rates
Area economic development

B. Descriptions of Individual Analyses

1. Housing Program Analysis

The Secretary, Department of Housing and Urban Development, at the request of the Chairman of the Senate Subcommittee on Housing and Urban Affairs submitted a report entitled "Economic Analysis of Ten-Year Housing Program and Estimated Federal Government Cost of Assisted Programs.[1] One objective of the analysis was to compare the economic impact of building six million federally assisted housing units in five years, as recommended by the National Commission on Civil Disorders; with the economic impact of building them over 10 years as proposed by the executive branch.

The approach of the analysis was to examine past experience in the homebuilding industry and to compare past performace with estimated future needs. Future needs were estimated by giving consideration to:

1. Estimated number of additional households forecast to be formed. This figure, 13 million, was taken from a publication of the U.S. Bureau of the Census.

2. Increase in vacant units. This figure was based on the assumption that

[1] Housing and Urban Development Legislation of 1968, part 2, Hearings before the Senate Subcommittee on Housing and Urban Affairs of the Committee on Banking and Currency, Ninetieth Congress, Second Session.

vacant units including seasonal units will increase as a percentage of total housing. This was assumed to result from increased ownership of vacation homes and expansion of the housing market.

3. Population shifts. As rural units are abandoned, new urban units must be built to substitute for them.

4. Demolition, casualty, and other losses

5. Replacement of existing dilapidated units

6. Replacement of units becoming dilapidated over the next ten years.

7. Rehabilitation of substandard units.

With future housing needs estimated the study then compared those needs with past performance in the home-building industry. The comparison was made in terms of the number of houses built and in terms of housing as a percentage of gross national product.

Various tables showed whether the home-building industry had ever produced as many houses in a past year as would be required in future years and whether housing has ever in the past been as large a percent of GNP as it would have to be in the future. The analysis showed, for example,that under the 10-year plan new housing starts in fiscal year 1969 would have to be 62,000 units higher than the number of starts in 1964, a previous high; and that under the 5-year plan they would have to be 262,000 units higher than in 1964. It showed also however, that neither the 10-year plan nor the 5-year plan would result in housing being as large a percentage of GNP as it had been in 1950, a previous high. Other tables correlated past performance to price level changes and projected manpower and financing requirements.

The conclusion of the analysis was that the 5-year plan was not feasible because it would cause quite large dislocations and price level increases in the homebuilding industry, and because of manpower and financial constraints. The 10-year plan of the executive branch was, however, considered feasible despite its similar but less serious effects on the economy. The effects of discounting of costs and benefits were not explicitly stated in comparing the outlay of funds over 5 years and over 10 years.

A number of assumptions were basic to the analysis. They included a set of what can be called macroeconomic assumptions concerning general economic conditions that are expected to prevail during the 10-year period under discussion. These were:

1. A 5.5 percent annual growth of GNP, including 4 percent real product growth and 1.5 percent annual allowance for price increase

2. A 4 percent unemployment rate

3. A 2 percent annual increase in the labor force.

4. Credit, monetary, and fiscal policies commensurate with such economic growth.

2. Income and Benefit Programs

A study published by the Department of Health, Education, and Welfare, analyzed the benefits and costs of a number of alternative methods of increasing the income of persons defined as poor (for example, a non-farm family of four with an annual income below $3,130). Each method of income maintenance was described in some detail, its costs estimated, and the groups of poor persons benefited by the method identified. It was shown for instance that alternative increases in social security payments will decrease the number of persons in poverty by differing amounts and at differing costs. One increase in benefits would raise .6 million persons from poverty at a cost of about $.6 million; another, 1.2 million persons at a cost of $6 million; a third, 1.7 million persons at $9.4 million; and so on.

A number of public assistance alternatives were similarly analyzed. These included proposals to:

1. Close the entire poverty gap for all.

2. Close one-half the poverty gap for all.

3. Close the entire poverty gap for those persons now eligible for public assistance (for example, families with dependent children, the blind, and the disabled).

4. Close one-half the poverty gap for persons now eligible for public assistance.

5. Increase payments under existing assistance programs by a small percentage.

Two negative income tax proposals were examined. One gave a credit of 14 percent against the unused portion of exemptions and deductions. The other paid 50 percent of the difference between actual income and the poverty income level.[1]

In the final section of the study all alternatives were summarized. Their costs were shown, the amount and percent of the income deficit they receive were shown, and the ratio of that reduction to their cost was computed. A single table showed that increases in social security payments were less efficient than public assistance alternatives or negative income tax alternatives, insofar as the single objective of reducing poverty was concerned. Alternative increases in social security payments produced a ratio of income deficit reduction to cost of only 14 percent to 19 percent. Public assistance and negative income tax alternatives produced much higher ratios, ranging from 54 percent to 100 percent.

The HEW study cautioned that the figures presented rested on certain assumptions and that these assumptions need not necessarily be accepted. For

---

[1] For a full discussion of negative income taxes, see Christopher Green, *Negative Taxes and the Poverty Problem,* Washington, Brookings Institution, 1967.

example, the study pointed out that because of a lack of reliable statistics, certain program costs were presented on the assumption that the hidden and institutionalized poor would not be eligible. Obviously if they were eligible costs would be much higher. Similarly, when the burden distribution of various methods of financing increases in social security payments were discussed, the reader was cautioned that conclusion as to where the burden falls depends upon a number of assumptions. For example, if a corporate income tax increase were used to finance increased payments, and if it were assumed that corporations shift the taxes forward to consumers, the burden would fall heavily on the poor.[1] If on the other hand, corporations shift the tax backward to stockholders, the burden falls heavily on the affluent.[2] A table showing the burden distribution under various assumptions was included in the study. Another table showed the burden distribution under various shifting assumptions of increases in payroll taxes as a means of financing increased social security payments.

3. Airport and Airways User Charges

The purpose of this study was to determine the effects of a number of alternative policy decisions on certain groups of taxpayers. Specifically it sought to determine how high the taxes would be on general aviation fuel and on air carrier fares (or tickets and waybills) under various methods of assessing user charges to cover the Government's cost of airports and airways. The basic policy involved was that those who use the nation's airports and airways should pay their fair share of construction and maintenance costs. The policy alternatives considered centered around the definition of "fair share."

The first effort of the study was to estimate what the costs of airports and airways will be over the next ten years. This was done with the aid of a computer in the following way.

1. Appropriations for facilities and equipment (F & E) were estimated, based upon Federal Aviation Agency recommendations. Since appropriations do not coincide with expenditures, the estimated appropriations were lagged in accordance with past experience. That is, if experience showed that certain appropriations were usually expended over a three-year period, the estimated appropriation for year 1 would be spread over years 1, 2, and 3; the estimated appropriation for year 2, over years 2, 3, and 4; and so on. After appropriations had been lagged to fit the years when facilities would actually be purchased, these facilities were expensed over their economic life of 15 years.

---

[1] See Marian Krzyzaniah and Richard A. Musgrave, *The Shifting of the Corporation Income Tax. An Empirical Study,* Baltimore, Md. Johns Hopkins Press, 1963.
[2] See R. J. Gordon, "Incidence of Corporation Income Tax," *American Economic Review,* September 1967.

2. Operation and Maintenance expenses were estimated for the next ten years and added in. Estimates were made considering such things as increasing population, increasing gross national product, projected airline use, and projected general aviation use.

3. Estimated appropriations for airports investment were lagged and expensed in a manner similar to F & E. Economic life was taken as thirty years.

4. Estimated Research and Development appropriations were also lagged and expensed. The expensing period used was 15 years.

5. The unamortized book value of existing assets as expensed over ten years.

With expenses for the next ten years estimated, the study then proceeded to its main concern: allocating those expenses between military aviation and civilian aviation; and within civilian, between air carriers and general aviation. The allocation between military and civilian was made on the basis of percentage of use. That is, if there were six military flights to every four civilian, 60 percent of the costs would be allocated to military aviation, and 40 percent would be allocated to civilian aviation.

A number of alternative methods were used to allocate the civilian portion between air carriers and general aviation. Each method represented a different interpretation of what constituted a fair share of costs to be borne by users of airports and airways. Among the alternatives were:

1. Full cost. All civilian costs were allocated to the user groups on the same basis as the civilian/military allocation: the percentage of use.

2. Full cost of airways only. Airport construction costs were separated from other and treated as a separate policy matter. The remaining costs were allocated on the percentage of use basis.

3. Operating costs only to general aviation. All capital costs were assigned to air carriers, general aviation bearing only its share of operating costs.

4. Incremental costs only to general aviation. No capital costs and no joint costs were allocated to general aviation. All these costs were borne by air carriers. Only those costs specifically associated with general aviation were assigned to it.

5. Numerous variations and combinations of the above methods.

In each of the cases listed, the allocated costs were divided by the appropriate units to arrive at the unit taxes that would have to be imposed on air carriers and general aviation. Air carrier costs were divided by the estimated revenue from tickets and waybills over the next ten years, and a tax percentage obtained. General aviation costs were divided by the estimated amount of aviation fuel to be used and a per gallon tax obtained.

The alternatives selected covered the likely range of possible allocations so that costs for each user group could be determined for different policies. To a large degree, the analysis was based on historical data as to appropriations, operations and maintenance costs, the split in military and civilian use, lagging factors, and so on. Some sensitivity analyses of the effect of changes in such factors appear to have been made.

Appendix C

The New PPBS: A Framework for Decision[1]

In this portion of a 1971 article Colonel Stellini provides a good description of the operations of PPBS for the Air Force in the Department of Defense (DOD) for 1972. Although the illustrations are for the development of military forces, they are representative of what is involved in program budgeting for any organization.)

One of the first tasks that Secretary of Defense Melvin R. Laird undertook after assuming office was to revamp the planning-programming-budgeting system, initiated by Secretary McNamara, to conform to the new strategy and budgeting guidance. By definition the PPBS is an integrated system for establishing, maintaining, and revising the Five-Year Defense Program (FYDP) and the DOD budget. It is a continuous sequence of activities and decisions which integrates strategy, forces, and defense dollars into the President's budget.

The cycle starts in October, about the time the previous year's defense budget estimates have gone to the Budget Bureau. In the form of the Joint Strategic Objectives Plan (JSOP), the Joint Chiefs of Staff provide the Office of the Secretary of Defense with their statement on nations security and military objectives based on their appraisal of the world situation eight years ahead. On the basis of decisions by the National Security Council and the JSOP, the secretary of defense establishes strategic guidance on what he feels are the world military threats, the forces required, and the fiscal limitations on the amount of money that would be available for buying these forces.

The Joint Chiefs, given the budget ceiling and the strategic plan, tell the secretary what they can and cannot buy and the associated risks. This estimate is given in the form of the Joint Forces Memorandum (JFM), which includes the five-year program costs and associated manpower requirements furnished by the services.

In June the services provide OSD with their recommendations for the forces, manpower, and costs developed on a cost-effectiveness basis, within the fiscal constraints established, in the form of a Program Objective Memorandum (POM). After some dialogue between the services and the OSD staff, a "major force issues" meeting is held with the secretary of defense, the Chiefs, and the service secretaires. Dollars, forces, threats, and risks are "balanced."

By midsummer the secretary of defense issues Program Decision Memoranda (PDMs). In October, the services submit their initial budget proposals to OSD. Final service issues are resolved, Program Budget Decisions (PBDs) are issued,

---

[1] From "Force-Structure Planning: Considerations, Problems, and Issues," by Lt. Colonel Edward Stellini, *Air University Review*, May 1971, pp. 1–15.

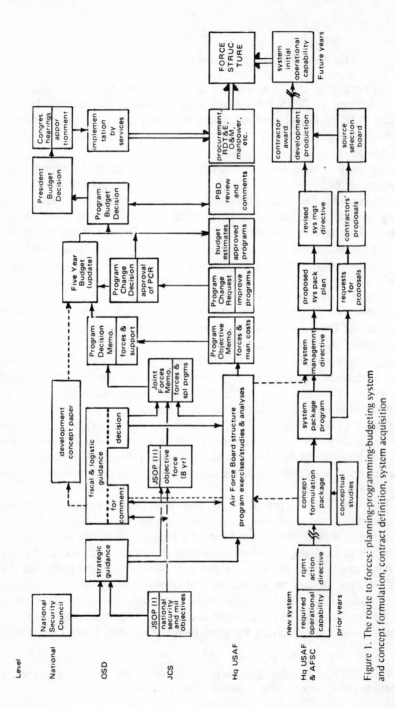

Figure 1. The route to forces: planning-programming-budgeting system and concept formulation, contract definition, system acquisition

and the FYDP is updated. In December, the Office of Management and Budget (OMB) wraps up the defense budget and sends it to the President, who then makes decisions resolving final issues raised by JCS and the OMB.

Allocation to Services and Fiscal-Guidance Categories ·

The organizational and functional framework within which forces will be structured is shown in Figure 1. Within this framework the OSD planner is faced with the following questions:

What portion of the defense budget should be allocated to:
— each service and to each defense agency?
— each of the fiscal-guidance categories, strategic forces, general purpose forces, research and development, intelligence and security, other nations' support, and others?

An OSD planner might ask: What is the best way to allocate the defense dollars available among the fiscal-guidance categories? Theoretically, the solution is simple. What we want to do is to allocate dollars to each category so that any reallocation of these dollars does not increase the total military worth achievable. Our measure of merit, military worth, is a nebulous thing and cannot easily be defined. It probably can best be described as "total national defense."

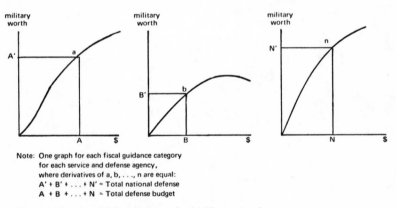

Note: One graph for each fiscal guidance category
for each service and defense agency,
where derivatives of a, b, . . ., n are equal:
A' + B' + . . . + N' = Total national defense
A + B + . . . + N = Total defense budget

Figure 2. Allocation of defense budget to fiscal-guidance categories

The military worth functions are shown in Figure 2 as curves that begin at zero dollars and increase as dollars are added. These functions curve downward, implying decreasing marginal returns, that is, the more we buy of some capability, the less the incremental amount purchased is worth. Interpreting these curves, we have an optimum allocation of dollars when the derivatives at a, b, ... , n are all equal; and when the total dollars expended equal the sum of A, B, . . . , N we have maximized military worth.

This discussion, of course, is theoretical, since the shape of the military worth functions were arbitrarily drawn. In practice these curves are not well defined. It is likely that in actuality they would not be smooth, continuous curves, nor is the formulation of each curve independent of the remaining curves. In fact, the curves cannot be explicitly defined by mathematical analysis. The equations of the curves must be modified to take into account the insight gained through analysis, military judgment, political considerations, and other intangibles.

What happens in the real world is that the precedents of previous years' allocations strongly influence subsequent years' allocations. The trade-offs in dollars are made at the margin; that is, new systems replace the old when it is concluded that the trade-off will result in a net increase in military effectiveness. The trade-offs may or may not cross fiscal guidance categories or service lines. In either case, trade-offs are made within the framework of the PPBS.

INDEX

SELECTED RAND BOOKS

Bagdikian, Ben H. *The Information Machines: Their Impact on Men and the Media.* New York: Harper and Row, 1971.

Bretz, Rudy. *A Taxonomy of Communication Media.* Englewood Cliffs, N.J.: Educational Technology Publications, 1971.

Coleman, James S., and Nancy L. Karweit. *Information Systems and Performance Measures In Schools.* Englewood Cliffs, N.J.: Educational Technology Publications, 1972.

Dalkey, Norman C. (ed.). *Studies in the Quality of Life: Delphi and Decision-Making.* Lexington, Mass.: D.C. Heath and Company, 1972.

Downs, Anthony. *Inside Bureaucracy.* Boston, Mass.: Little, Brown and Company, 1967.

Fisher, Gene H. *Cost Considerations In Systems Analysis.* New York: American Elsevier Publishing Company, 1971.

Haggart, Sue A. (ed.). *Program Budgeting for School District Planning.* Englewood Cliffs, N. J.: Educational Technology Publications, 1972.

Hirshleifer, Jack, James C. DeHaven, and Jerome W. Milliman. *Water Supply: Economics, Technology, and Policy.* Chicago, Ill.: The University of Chicago Press, 1960.

Meyer, John R., Martin Wohl, and John F. Kain. *The Urban Transportation Problem.* Cambridge, Mass.: Harvard University Press, 1965.

McKean, Roland N., *Efficiency in Government Through Systems Analysis: With Emphasis On Water Resource Development.* New York: John Wiley & Sons, Inc., 1958.

Nelson, Richard R., Merton J. Peck and Edward D. Kalachek. *Technology Economic Growth and Public Policy.* Washington D.C.: The Brookings Institution, 1967.

Novick, David (ed.). *Program Budgeting: Program Analysis and the Federal Budget.* Cambridge, Mass.: Harvard University Press, 1965.

Pascal, Anthony. *Thinking About Cities: New Perspectives On Urban Problems.* Belmont, California: Dickenson Publishing Company, 1970.

Pascal, Anthony H. (ed.). *Racial Discrimination In Economic Life,* Lexington, Mass.: D.C. Heath and Company, 1972.

Quade, Edward S., and Wayne I. Boucher. *Systems Analysis and Policy Planning: Applications In Defense.* New York: American Elsevier Publishing Company, 1968.

Sharpe, William F. *The Economics of Computers.* New York: Columbia University Press, 1969.

The Rand Corporation. *A Million Random Digits With 100,000 Normal Deviates.* Glencoe, Ill.: The Free Press, 1955.

Williams, John D. *The Compleat Strategyst: Being a Primer On The Theory Of Games Of Strategy.* New York: McGraw-Hill Book Company, 1954.